POLICING IN AMERICA

Selected Titles in ABC-CLIO's
CONTEMPORARY
WORLD ISSUES
Series

For a complete list of titles in this series, please visit
www.abc-clio.com.

Books in the Contemporary World Issues series address vital issues in today's society such as genetic engineering, pollution, and biodiversity. Written by professional writers, scholars, and nonacademic experts, these books are authoritative, clearly written, up-to-date, and objective. They provide a good starting point for research by high school and college students, scholars, and general readers as well as by legislators, businesspeople, activists, and others.

Each book, carefully organized and easy to use, contains an overview of the subject, a detailed chronology, biographical sketches, facts and data and / or documents and other primary-source material, a directory of organizations and agencies, annotated lists of print and nonprint resources, and an index.

Readers of books in the Contemporary World Issues series will find the information they need in order to have a better understanding of the social, political, environmental, and economic issues facing the world today.

POLICING IN AMERICA

A Reference Handbook

Leonard A. Steverson

CONTEMPORARY WORLD ISSUES

A B C CLIO

Santa Barbara, California
Denver, Colorado
Oxford, England

Library of Congress Cataloging-in-Publication Data
Steverson, Leonard A.
    Policing in America : a reference handbook / Leonard A. Steverson.
        p. cm.
    Includes bibliographical references and index.
    ISBN 978-1-59884-043-8 (hard copy : alk. paper) — ISBN 978-1-59884-044-5 (ebook)   1. Police—United States.   2. Law enforcement—United States.   3. Police—United States—History.   4. Police—United States—Biography.   5. Police—Cross-cultural studies.   I. Title.

    HV8133.S84 2008
    363.20973—dc22

                                    2007013807

12   11   10   09   08   10   9   8   7   6   5   4   3   2   1

ABC-CLIO, Inc.
130 Cremona Drive, P.O. Box 1911
Santa Barbara, California 93116–1911

This book is also available on the World Wide Web as an ebook. Visit www.abc-clio.com for details.

This book is printed on acid-free paper ∞

Manufactured in the United States of America.

*I dedicate this book to my lovely wife Betty,
our daughters Nikki and Misty and their families,
including our grandsons Ashton, Trent, Colin, and Alden.
I also dedicate this work to the memory of my parents,
Amos and Jane Steverson.*

Contents

Preface

The profession of policing has captured the hearts and minds of many Americans, even those who are violators of the law. As citizens, we notice uniformed officers when they enter a building we are in. We certainly notice them, often nervously, when they appear in our cars' rearview mirrors. We observe them racing to emergencies and wonder what happened. We become fearful of criminal activity in our neighborhoods and hope the police can come quickly if needed. We also watch news reports of the abuse of police authority, and sometimes we forget that the police are people, too, and capable of indiscretions—indiscretions that are often publicly displayed.

Policing is a profession that conjures up visions of old-fashioned, hard-bitten police work and officers walking the beat, G-men chasing gangsters, and, more recently, forensic investigators and criminal profilers tracking down criminals using scientific innovations. Our ideas about police officers can be found in popular culture archetypes as polarized as Sheriff Andy Taylor (the calm, rural sheriff without a gun of the *Andy Griffith Show*) and the deadly Inspector Harry Callahan (the aggressive, urban cop of the *Dirty Harry* movies). Many children in various stages of development imitate the police in games of cops and robbers, and gifts of toy police badges and service revolvers are often the treasured keepsakes of childhood.

The police in America have not always appeared as they do today. In fact, the police as we know them are a relatively recent development. The earliest police systems were actually family policing structures in which community members were accountable for controlling the behavior of their own group as well as for their own protection. When the watch system became ineffective and some people became paid police officers, their duties primarily involved service functions. Later they accepted more law enforcement duties but became corrupted by a system that dictated their actions and allowed for little moral or professional decision making. When the police became professionalized, they incorporated modern advancements in the field and were removed from many of the corrupting influences of government; however, they tended to lose touch with the communities they served. As a result, a chasm formed between the communities and the police; citizens in many areas began to see the police as an invading army rather than as an institution whose very purpose is to serve and to protect the public. This division became painfully obvious in the riots of the 1960s when police and citizens clashed in often violent outbreaks. The chasm also became painfully visible later in the Rodney King beating and its aftermath.

Clearly a new philosophy was needed to return the police to their original purpose of serving the public. The change came in the form of community-oriented models such as community policing, problem-oriented policing, and broken windows policing, as developed in the 1970s and 1980s. In these models, the police became more integrated with citizens and used them as allies in their attempts to control and prevent crime. Working in a collaborative fashion with the citizens and being a force in helping solve the unique community problems they faced was not a new idea but rather one that needed to be revisited in the wake of the social upheaval of the 1960s.

The terrorist attacks of September 11, 2001 changed American society in many ways, including how policing was administrated. At the highest levels of government, a new focus on intelligence developed to keep the country free of future terrorist activity. This idea spilled over into the institution of policing because it was posited that, by using carefully analyzed information (intelligence) in a proactive way, street-level crime, as well as terrorism, could be prevented. An evolving system of intelligence-led policing, which can easily be seen as an adjunct to community policing models, has developed and could possibly turn out to be the newest trend in policing.

The police are considered the thin blue line that separates order from chaos. It is often assumed that the police mostly function to maintain control in society through the vigorous enforcement of laws; however, much of the work police officers perform is service oriented. This is why the community models tend to work better in most circumstances than the old professional model. Note that the term "policing" is used rather than "law enforcement," as is standard in many books and texts on police work. This is because law enforcement is part of the order maintenance function and simply one aspect of what the police do; therefore the term "policing," which incorporates aspects of both order maintenance and service functions, is preferred.

This book is an easily accessible source of information about the field of policing and should provide readers with a glimpse into the sociohistorical factors involved in social control measures taken not only in the United States but in other countries as well. The book is intended for not only those who have or are pursuing occupational goals in policing or the criminal justice system in general but to those who want to better understand ways in which societies deal with deviant behavior.

It is hoped that readers will learn more about the field of police work in this volume. The combination of years in academic study and practical application in the criminal justice field have made the author an observer of the field of policing; perhaps readers with an interest in the field will find what they seek or will be able to delve into more depth with the resources provided.

The author would like to thank all of the people involved in the production of this work including the editors at ABC-CLIO: Mim Vasan, Dayle Dermatis, and Kristine Swift, whose patient understanding helped keep me focused on the task at hand. I also would like to thank my family for their continued support through the project—to Betty and the girls and to Millie for offering comfort in the difficult times that occurred during the preparation of the book. My colleagues at South Georgia College were also helpful and their encouragement was sorely needed. I also want to pay tribute to the thin blue line that protects our nation and especially to those who paid the ultimate price when duty called.

List of Tables

List of Figures

1

Background and History

Policing is and has been an extremely important part of American society. Along with the court and correctional systems, it is part of the triad that constitutes the criminal justice system in the United States. Since it is the "front-end" component of the system, it involves much interaction between the police and the members of the communities they serve. The police are therefore said to make up the "thin blue line" that exists in part to hold the line between chaos and order in society. Police systems exist all over the world in different forms to accomplish this and other missions.

The institution of the police, as it is currently known, is relatively recent. Prior to the establishment of the first modern police agency in London in 1829 and its urban American counterparts in the 1840s, policing was an ambiguous and diverse undertaking that morphed after World War I into the entity recognizable today as the police (Monkkonen 1981, 24).

The study of policing is important for a number of reasons. Not only does it aid in understanding the measures instituted by governments to control socially harmful behavior, but it also provides insight into those measures. For example, the "noble experiment" of prohibition in America in the 1920s and early 1930s relied on the police to control behavior. When the ban on alcoholic beverages became clearly unenforceable, the duties of the police shifted to other, more enforceable, behaviors.

Understanding the history of the police also provides a better understanding of democracy. The police not only control the behavior of citizens; they are citizens themselves. The amount and degree of enforcement allowed provide a better understanding not only of government on a broad scale, but also of the relationship between police and community on a personal or community level.

Another benefit is a fuller understanding of bureaucratic structures. It has long been assumed that, as societies develop and become more complex and nuanced, a move to bureaucratization is necessary to maintain efficiency (in other words, to preserve order). Interestingly, in the last few decades, policing in America has moved away from its traditional emphasis on a highly bureaucratized system to one that is community based. Time will tell whether this model, only several decades in place, will give way to a return to the traditional, professional model or to some other approach to policing.

Before exploring the distinctly American version of policing, it is beneficial to look at some of the earliest known forms of social control.

The Early Stages of Social Control

The earliest societies did not have an organized police force but depended on their own citizens to police themselves. It is likely that the heads of families were responsible for maintaining order and settling disputes. As people moved away from their original villages, they encountered others with whom they were unfamiliar and whose traditions were alien. As new communities were formed, defenses were erected to stop invaders from causing potential harm to the residents. These ensconced communities grew into towns and cities whose citizens devised methods to maintain their ways of life (Cramer 1964, 3).

As societies became increasingly complex, the traditional control agents of family and church were not sufficient to control the behavior of the growing populations. Therefore, strategies were promulgated and enforced through the centuries to accomplish this task. The earliest enforcement measures were very different from those of today, and they were subject to continual revision as social conditions changed.

Throughout history, social control can be seen as having passed through three distinct stages: citizen and family responsibility, a volunteer system of "watchmen" with obligations to a larger governmental structure, and a paid police force (Rawlings 2002, 231–233). In the first stage, communities policed themselves.

This system of "kin policing" often controlled deviance through the use of the blood-feud, where the victim of a certain crime, along with his or her family or clan, retaliated against the offender, normally of another clan. To keep the retaliatory actions from turning into full-blown conflicts that threatened to disrupt or even destroy the community, it became necessary to put into place a more formalized means of dealing with actions deemed by the community as deviant.

In the second stage, a governmental force acted as an arbiter between the accused and accuser. This was a more formalized system whereby the governing body, usually the crown, agreed to provide a system of justice, order, and protection from invading forces, in return for loyalty. However, the community also had to provide something to the government: a "watchmen" system of citizens to monitor community activity and to bring offenders to justice. If the community failed to abide by this condition, they would be subject to fines by the crown.

Because this type of policing was unstable and basically ineffective in dealing with a rapidly changing society and with the crises of the day, a move was made to promote a more solid framework for enforcing laws and maintaining order. In the eighteenth century, many citizens hired substitutes for watch or constable duty, turning their responsibilities over to others. In time, a police force emerged, whom the citizens paid to protect them. This last stage was a move that would usher in the new era of policing (Rawlings 2002, 232).

Policing in Early Societies

The word "police" can be traced to early Greek and Roman law. The concept encompassed the ideals of providing safety and welfare to people living in municipalities and promoted city government responsibility for many areas of public life, including the control of crime, the management of unruly crowds, the fighting of fires, and the maintenance of health and sanitation. Much power was vested in the people. who comprised the early forms of police (Becker and Whitehouse 1979, 8).

Many of the early societies created a code of formalized norms that the citizens were made to follow and that were sanctioned to encourage conformity. Possibly the first uniform code was handed down by King Hammurabi (1792–1750 BCE) of

Mesopotamia. The Code of Hammurabi is a system of laws that carried very severe punishments, including death, for a number of offenses.

Other sets of laws have been uncovered, such as those regulating the affairs of the early Assyrians, Hittites, and Egyptians. The group with what could be considered the first formalized police force was formed around 1340 BCE under the reign of the Egyptian King Hur Moheb, who began a force of river patrols to watch over the Nile. Later, in the twelfth century BCE, ruler Rameses III put heavy emphasis on his police force in the maintenance of order. Other early civilizations, such as those in India and China, also created codes for conduct, which people were charged with enforcing. The Old and New Testaments of the Bible also describe criminal codes, most notably the Ten Commandments of the Old Testament (Cramer 1964, 4–8).

The Romans had a system of law based on the Law of the Twelve Tables, partially derived from the Greek system. In this system, as in other ancient legal systems, the government was not charged with the punishment of offenders; this was the obligation of the citizens who were wronged. However, shortly after the Twelve Tables came into being, a group of governmental officials were given the responsibility of investigating crimes involving murder, indicating that the state was now responsible for criminal prosecution (Cramer 1964, 8–9). Later, others groups of Roman officers under Augustus were used as police: the military unit called the Praetorian Guard, a group of people called vigils who worked for the magistrate and who possessed arrest powers, and a night watch service that fought fires as well as crime (Langworthy and Travis 2003, 42)

The British Roots of American Policing

A history of policing in England helps us understand policing practices in America, since the colonists adopted primarily English law enforcement strategies. The modern police structure that emerged in London in the early nineteenth century was copied in American cities; however, only the components that were believed to accentuate the national conceptualization of democracy were utilized (Miller 1977, x). However, there is a very rich history of measures taken throughout the world to maintain citizens' conformity to contemporary notions of right and wrong.

Prior to 1066 in England, there was little need for an elaborate system of law enforcement. The local citizens policed the behavior of their communities' members at this time, and the Saxon kings exerted little control over the communities. From at least the time of King Alfred's reign (871–899), the type of social control involved an unspoken social obligation of the community's citizens to protect themselves.

In what was known as the frankpledge system, the communities divided themselves into groups of ten families or so, called tythings (or tithings), who were responsible for the basic protection of the community. In each of the tythings, the responsibility for protection primarily fell to the males in the family over age twelve; this group of males was headed by the tythingman. Ten of the tythings formed a larger grouping, referred to as a hundred, or shire, and one person was selected as the head of the group, called a hundred-man or royal reeve. The shire reeve was responsible for promoting peace in the shire (similar to a county) and reported to the king. The title "shire reeve" later morphed to sheriff. The shire reeve was able to call on all available able citizens to protect the shire in case of emergencies; this was known as the posse comitatus (Critchey 1967, 2–3).

When the Normans invaded England in 1066 (the Norman Conquest), they modified the frankpledge system to ensure greater control of the citizenry. Manorial courts that governed several communities replaced the tithing system (Critchey 1967, 3). As time passed, the celebrated title of constable, from the Latin term *comes stabuli* (master of the horse, master of the stables, or count of the stables) (Hatley 1999, 1), was conferred upon a citizen who would perform as a major officer of the court. In 1252, a statute raised the social stature of this position. The duties of the constable included pursuing, apprehending, and bringing to court perpetrators of a number of offenses, ranging from serious to minor (Johnson 1981, 2–3; Langworthy and Travis 2003, 55). The constable kept the peace in his region by a number of means, including the "hue and cry," in which citizens were required to cry out when they witnessed crimes so that the offender could be apprehended and brought to justice. Several other terms were given to people possessing this title over the years, including tythingman, borsholder, and headborough (Critchey 1967, 5).

The Statute of Winchester of 1285 returned law enforcement duties to the local communities, promulgated an effective system of policing, and differentiated urban and rural law enforcement practices. From this legislation came the "watch and ward" system, in which constables were able to select up to sixteen male citizens, depending on the town's population, to serve as night watchmen who guarded gates and who turned over law violators to the constables the following morning. The statute brought back an earlier form of control—the hue and cry. The statute also required the arming of all of the king's subjects with weapons in case a hue and cry alarm was raised (Critchey 1967, 7).

The provisions of the statute remained in place for five hundred years but became woefully inadequate. The once elevated status of constable turned to one of derision and mocking. Fewer and fewer of the citizens desired the job, and the more affluent merchants, farmers, and tradespeople were able to hire substitutes to perform this unpaid labor, which came down to maintaining the night watch, taking prisoners, placing them in custody or keeping them in their own homes until delivering them to a magistrate, and initiating the hue and cry. As time passed, the activities of another law enforcement official, called the high constable, supervised this agent (Critchey 1967, 10–15). Eventually the constables were those who were unable to pay someone else to do the work, and so the position often fell into the hands of the community's poor, elderly, disabled, illiterate, and incompetent males (Johnson 1981, 3).

During this period a group of citizens called "informers" would seek out criminal behavior to receive rewards. The informers would often obtain specialized knowledge of a certain crime or of a certain geographic area to receive greater rewards. The common informers, however, were often corrupt and generally despised by other community members. While the informers dealt primarily with minor theft offenses, another group, called the thief-takers, emerged who actively sought out professional criminals. The thief-takers were also despised by much of the population and often were involved in criminal behavior as much as the ones they pursued. The most infamous of all thief-takers was Jonathan Wild, a vicious man who bragged about the number of felons he sent to the gallows and who received much media coverage about his conquests. He himself went to the gallows in 1725, but the position of thief-taker continued to flourish (Hibbert 2003, 92–94). Other unscrupulous people, called trading justices, followed one of Wild's simple schemes: These justices hired people to steal from others, then returned the recovered items to the rightful owners—for a commission (Critchey 1967, 19–20).

By the mid-eighteenth century, crime in London had increased significantly and was a major concern for the city's citizens. The capital was recognized as one of the most dangerous in Europe. A professional police force was strongly resisted, and, in its attempts to control the burgeoning crime problem, the city continued its practice of using a hodgepodge of nonprofessional officials with such names as streetkeepers, badgeporters, and headboroughs. Groups of robbers known as highwaymen rode through London's streets terrorizing people on the roadways, while burglars and footpads (thieves who rob people on foot) were able to carry out their actions with little interference (Bleiler 1976, v).

Some of the more economically stable areas were able to employ paid watchmen to patrol the streets; however, certain areas of town were havens for criminal activity and their citizens were unable to pay for private systems. A new office, called the magistrate, was reconstituted from the justice of the peace and was charged with administering watch organizations in their communities (Langworthy and Travis 2003, 60). In 1738, one of these magistrates, a former novelist, playwright, and attorney named Henry Fielding (1707–1754), was commissioned to supervise the Bow Street Court, an area of high crime. Fielding's predecessors in office, including his immediate predecessor, Sir Thomas deVeil, were able to make a fortune by taking bribes from the Bow Street's criminal element. In his books and plays Fielding had protested against the justice system extensively, and as a justice he refused to get involved in corruption (Critchey 1967, 20). Fielding sought to change the crooked system by instituting a professional police force to control crime in his area. Due to resistance from governmental officials, however, he opted to organize a group of former constables turned thief-takers to carry out investigations and bring suspects to trial (Bleiler, 1976, vi).

Fielding's thief-takers received no salary but did obtain rewards for the successful prosecution of cases. They were able to confiscate the offender's belongings and often received money from the victims of the crime. Upon Henry Fielding's death, his half brother John supervised this group, who came to be known as the Bow Street Runners, also known as the Flying Squad or the Bow Street Flyers. This plainclothes force carried hollow wooden staffs, called truncheons, that were adorned with a brass crown. The truncheons were hollow so that they could be used to carry

warrants and also functioned as symbols of their official authority. The Runners, always less than a dozen strong, were used to
guard the king and to investigate different types of criminal activity such as theft, post office and bank robbery, murder, assault,
and fraud. They were generally considered to be effective in their
duties and gained much renown throughout Great Britain. They
are often considered an early model for the country's famed detective agency, Scotland Yard (Bleiler 1976, vi–viii).

John Fielding, who was later knighted for his efforts, instituted a number of other changes in the Bow Street system. He organized a mounted patrol unit assigned to protect major
roadways, a foot patrol to patrol the streets, and mounted horse
patrols to serve the areas outside the city. In effect, he created a
tripartite system of preventative patrol. In addition, other innovations were instituted in London, including the Thames River
patrols in which officials patrolled the water in rowboats and on
foot in the wharfs. Even these changes, however, were not sufficient to meet the needs of an increasingly urbanizing nation
(Langworthy and Travis 2003, 60–63).

The inadequacy of eighteenth-century methods of law enforcement in England made it obvious that a new system of
policing was needed. In addition to their inability to control the
growing crime problem, the police forces were still seen as oppressive by many citizens. A new philosophy was needed to for-
mulate a more effective system of law enforcement. That
philosophy came in the form of a set of policies promoted by a
Metropolitan magistrate named Patrick Colquhoun. Colquhoun
argued for the separation of powers between the police and the
magistrates and justices. The Scot, who in 1797 wrote the popular *Treatise on the Police of the Metropolis,* was an advocate of the
utilitarian philosophy that advocated a preventive rather than a
punitive system of justice (Langworthy and Travis 2003, 63).

The beginning of the Industrial Revolution (early 1700s) was
a period of rapid population growth and movement to urban
centers. It was also a time of increasing crime rates. All of the
policing innovations installed during this period to deal with the
rising crime, however, were soon found to be insufficient. A new
system of policing was needed

Yet the modern era of policing did not begin until the early
nineteenth century. A member of the British Parliament named
Robert Peel desired to create a centralized force in 1785 but the
measure was aborted by the City of London, who did not want

such a police force. The idea did not go away, however, and it was resurrected by Peel's son, also named Robert, in the form of the Metropolitan Police Act of 1829. The young Robert Peel (1788–1859) had become an adroit politician and received an appointment to the position of home secretary. His new police force functioned independently of the magistrates and covered the areas directly surrounding downtown London; London proper was not included in the plan. Peel appointed two justices, later called commissioners, to lead the program. These two commissioners, retired military officer Charles Rowan and attorney Richard Mayne, were housed in a building that was previously used as a residence for the royalty from Scotland; the police headquarters thus became known as Scotland Yard (Trojanowicz and Dixon 1974, 25–28). The police force did not initially receive full acceptance by the citizens and were known as "peelers." However, the new police proved their worth to the communities in which they worked and received the more respected moniker "bobbies" in honor of their founder (Langworthy and Travis 2003, 68).

The tenets of the new law enforcement policy are referred to as the Peelian Principles:

1. The police force must be organized, firm, and organized in a military fashion.
2. The police will be under governmental jurisdiction.
3. Proof of police effectiveness will be found in lower crime rates.
4. News of criminal activity should be disseminated to citizens.
5. Police personnel should be adequately supplied in both time and area.
6. Police officers should maintain a calm and determined manner.
7. Officers should maintain a positive appearance.
8. Recruitment of qualified people and adequate training are necessary.
9. All officers will be provided a number.
10. Police offices will be located in areas centrally located and easily accessible.
11. Newly hired officers will have a probationary status.
12. Good record keeping is needed to correctly distribute police personnel (Germann, Day, and Gallati 1968, 60–61).

The innovations in the United Kingdom that culminated in the Metropolitan Police would eventually find their way to the fledgling United States. However, the social conditions of the young nation would contribute to a very distinct form of policing.

Policing in the Early American Colonies

The earliest known inhabitants of what was to become America were many different groups of Native Americans. The various indigenous tribes utilized an array of methods of social control. For example, tribes in the southern part of the country, such as the Cherokees, Choctaws, Seminoles, Creeks, and Chickasaws, had policing agencies to deal with internal disturbances and violations of codes of conduct within Indian land boundaries. The nomadic Cheyennes of the West had six different military societies that served as police in addition to having a military role. In time, and often in concert with federal troops, the Native American agencies adopted methods similar to those of Anglo-American police forces (Prassel 1972, 179–182).

Early Policing in the Northeast

Counties, adopted from the British shires, were established in the Northeast. Although counties were important, the local villages became the principal units of government because citizens had to band together in cohesive groups for protection. In some parts of the Northeast, the climate and soil were not very conducive to farming; so movement outside the villages was not a necessity (Folley 1980, 65–66).

Policing by the European settlers on American soil had some of the same practices as those in England. Prior to independence, charters granted in England governed the means of social control in the colonies. Although local concerns could be dealt with by the colonies, British law and custom superseded local attempts to control citizen behavior. The London Charter of 1606 provided for governance by a resident council in each colony that established local ordinances to follow the dictates of the crown, perform court duties, appoint local judicial officers, and provide other governmental services (Folley 1980, 64). The colonies would eventually gain independence from England, and, although they continued many of the British policing methods, America created its unique police structure that developed from the distinct traditions and the social conditions in three geographic areas: the northeastern and middle colonies, the southern states, and the western frontier (Langworthy and Travis 2003, 70).

In the northeastern part of the country, the New England colonies developed a strong industrial base, especially in the areas of fishing, timber harvesting, shipbuilding, and shipping. A large number of immigrants entered the area to work in these and other industries, and the populations of many of the cities grew rapidly. Prior to this influx, the system in place included a sheriff governing the county, marshals (who were similar to the British constables), and in some areas, including New York, Boston, and Philadelphia, a watch system. The sheriffs and marshals were actually more like entrepreneurs than government officials because they only worked daytime hours, they obtained fees from certain duties such as housing jail inmates and serving subpoenas, and they spent very little time on actual police work. The watch system was established in Boston in 1638, and soon similar measures were taken throughout the Northeast. In New York, citizens adopted the Dutch *schout* (nightwatchman) and the *ratelwatch* (rattle watch, a name that refers to the use of noise-makers to alert people of criminal activity and of the watchmen's approach). In America, the night watch was a patrol effort, and in some cities the watchmen were required to perform other duties such as calling out the current time and the weather conditions. Some cities even required the watchmen to tend to the city street lamps (Fosdick 1969, 59–60).

The watch system proved very ineffective because the watchmen were paid low or no wages and were therefore completely unsuitable for the work (Langworthy and Travis 2003, 71). The night watch was comprised primarily of men who worked during the day and supplemented their income with the night job. They eventually became the source of ridicule and derision because of their open drunkenness and sleeping on the job. The occupation became highly undesirable for trustworthy citizens, who often faced grand jury actions for failure to perform the watchman's tasks (Fosdick 1969, 59–61).

As the seventeenth century drew to a close, the changes in American social structure, which included urbanization and industrialization, brought together people from different class, racial, and ethnic backgrounds, often causing competition for jobs, social standing, and advantage. The competition often resulted in unrest and crime. Neighborhoods began to spring up that reflected the different ethnic and socioeconomic statuses of the people living and working in them. Prejudice and discrimination led to bitter and violent feuds in the street. Crime also became a major issue as fear of robberies and property crime became pervasive in the North during the early and mid-1800s and citizens armed themselves extensively to protect themselves (Johnson 1981, 17–25).

Early Policing in the South

The colonies in the South had a plantation economy due to the area's vast expanse of fertile land and favorable climate for growing crops and raising livestock. Unlike the settlers in the North, colonists in the southern states used the county as the primary unit of local government; this worked well in such a rural, agrarian society (Folley 1980, 65; Langworthy and Travis 2003, 73).

The southern institution of slavery contributed greatly to the early model of policing in the South. Since slavery was so pervasive in the region, it became a community effort to ensure that slaves stayed within the confines of the institution; in fact, laws restricted the slave owners themselves from being too lenient on the slaves (Friedman 1993, 87). Slave patrols, also called "patrollers" or the commonly used derivative "paddyrollers," were established to ensure that slaves would not escape or become involved in violent uprisings. The patrols traveled circuits and made sure that any slaves on roadways had the appropriate passes to be away from their home plantations. They also periodically visited plantations to check on the safety of the slave owners and to make sure that the owners were adequately enforcing discipline on the slaves (Langworthy and Travis 2003, 73–74). When there were increased fears of uprisings, the paddyrollers increased their activity (Friedman 1993, 87). For example, in Charleston, South Carolina, a group called the South Carolina Regulators was formed in the late 1760s for the purpose of controlling slaves (Friedman 1993, 180). The Regulators consisted of vigilante squads that remained a viable institution in the South into the nineteenth century. Slave patrols were not agents of the government, nor did they perform any crime prevention duties. True policing was primarily the responsibility of county sheriffs or, in some cities, of municipal police officers (Langworthy and Travis 2003, 73–74).

In the South, dueling became incorporated into the social structure. Despite laws against it, dueling was practiced to a sig-

nificant degree in the South, particularly in the mountainous regions. One of the functions of the early police in the region was
to keep a lid on the passion and violence that led to this type of
behavior (Friedman 1993, 178–179).

Early Policing in the West

The roots of Anglo-American policing in the West do not go back
as far as the colonial period, but it has a unique and interesting
history. One factor that influenced policing was the vastness of
the West. As settlers from the North and South moved westward
across the county, many of them with the hope of becoming
wealthy in the gold and silver mines, they began to settle in the
wide-open spaces of the American West and found the area more
suitable for ranching than for farming. The settlers formed themselves into villages and towns for protection, but, due to the wide
distribution of population, the county sheriff became the primary
governmental agent of law enforcement. With the municipal police responsible for law enforcement in the towns and the sheriff
responsible for enforcement in the rural areas, the West had similar characteristics of both the northern and southern states (Folley 1980, 66).

Another influence on the type of enforcement was whether
the settlers were from the North or South. Northern settlers preferred the municipal police, and southerners preferred the
county sheriff, based on their familiarity with their respective
systems (Langworthy and Travis 2003, 74). However, the West
was unique in that some of the areas being settled were already
states, others were under federal control, and still others were
under Indian control. The county sheriffs and municipal police
were responsible for the areas that were under state control; a
federal marshal and deputies were provided to areas that were
still territories; and Indians, with occasional assistance from soldiers of the United States Army, policed the areas that were still
Indian Territory (Johnson 1981, 89–90).

Still another influence was the diversity of people in the
West. As in the northern states, the West became a mixture of
people of different races and cultures. The Native Americans, European Americans, freed African Americans, Mexican Americans, and Asian Americans all competed over the newly
emerging resources of the West. Conflicts occurred not only between these groups but also between cattle ranchers and sheep

herders, between large cattle operations and small ranchers, between miners and mine owners, among other groups. People in this part of the country turned to four groups to maintain order and to handle criminal behavior: private citizens, federal marshals, merchants, and local police. Due to the concerns over lawlessness and the effectiveness of the police, local citizens and business owners frequently decided to take the law into their own hands, and vigilantism became a common way of dealing with crime (Johnson 1981, 90–103). Due to this image of frontier justice and to the tales that grew into legends of shootouts between federal marshals and notorious outlaws, the West took on a mystique that fascinated people in the East, culminating in numerous books and, later, movies.

The Evolution of American Policing: The Nineteenth Century

Municipal and County Police

The night watch of the 1700s was found to be inadequate in the nineteenth century. Major civil disruptions in most northern cities between the 1830s and 1870s erupted over issues of race and ethnicity, as well as economic problems or political disagreements. The violence was often so severe that some people of the era began to doubt if the new country, founded on democratic ideals, would survive (Walker 1977, 4). Mobs and gangs—with intriguing names like the Blood Tubs, Rip Raps, and Dead Rabbits in New York, Philadelphia, and Boston—appeared to be more in control, and greater in number, than the police. Rival gangs openly fought in the streets, especially during times of political activity such as elections. Even the volunteer firefighters struggled violently over the opportunity to fight the city's fires; many buildings burned down completely because the groups did not decide quickly enough who would fight the fire (Richardson 1974, 35). This chaotic situation was described in the book and later in the movie, both titled *Gangs of New York*.

The system of night patrol varied significantly from one city to another, but it usually covered the night hours of nine o'clock in the evening until sunrise, offering no coverage for the daylight hours. The riots and other disturbances made it apparent that measures for daytime coverage were needed. Boston started a daytime police force that operated separately of the city's night watch in 1838 and soon several other cities followed suit. In 1844, New York City integrated its day and night forces; this new system, which became the basis for the modern American police, served as a model for other cities such as New Orleans, Cincinnati, Boston, Philadelphia, Chicago, Baltimore, Newark, and Providence, which adopted prevention-oriented police forces in the 1850s and 1860s (Fosdick 1969, 66–67). The cities had differently sized police departments based on their populations, and, of course, New York's force was the largest (Friedman 1993, 149).

The early officers who patrolled the streets of the American cities dressed in plainclothes and carried only thirty-three-inch nightsticks. In 1855, some cities began requiring officers to wear regulation hats and caps. In New York, officers wore a medal around their neck to be used for their identification as police officers when making arrests or fulfilling other police duties; the medals were concealed at other times. Finally in 1856, the New York Police Department adopted a uniform policy, but it was strongly resisted by officers who felt it represented a militaristic and undemocratic type of organization. In addition, the uniforms were hardly "uniform" because police departments throughout the city opted for different styles. In the same year, Philadelphia required its officers to wear badges on the outside of their coats; it would be another four years before the full uniform was worn in that city (Fosdick 1969, 70–71).

Educational or experience requirements for the new recruits were negligible, and training in the ways of police work was likewise trifling and slapdash. The new uniforms adopted by many departments possibly brought about a more military style of training, and they certainly provided a very visible presence on the street. Much of the work of the early police patrol was to maintain order in the cities, and it often consisted of arresting vagrants, intoxicated citizens, and others who disturbed the peace. The lower socioeconomic classes primarily experienced the increasing power of the police because the deviant behavior of prosperous citizens was often ignored. Given the view that the control of the "dangerous classes" required most of the police's efforts, conflicts and distrust naturally grew between the police and citizens (Friedman 1993, 150–152).

In addition to controlling the unseemly actions of the populace, the police also adopted a service role by searching for lost children and placing the homeless in shelters, often in the police station houses. The station houses soon became overrun with those needing shelter, creating a chaotic situation. The construction of lodging houses for the homeless at century's end alleviated this problem for the police (Friedman 1993, 152).

Since violence had become a part of American life during this period, the use of firearms came to be accepted, as a dubious citizenry began to accept the idea that such a measure was the only way to maintain order. The use of firearms and their potential for deadly force against offending citizens was in distinct contrast to the London Metropolitan police, who had gained respect for their restraint in using firearms (Johnson 1981, 25–31).

Many of the problems of policing in America during the early years of police professionalism were due to the fact that the police were under the control of politicians. Two groups figured prominently in this arrangement: the urban entrepreneurs and the critics. The first group sought to control the activities of the police through patronage, and they were able to profit from the relationship between the police and the ward bosses who controlled them. The second group consisted of people with progressive ideas who sought reform in the criminal justice system (Johnson 1981, 55–71). The conflict between the two groups was one of governmental versus policing perspectives: The particularistic model (favored by the political machines) emphasized making case-by-case decisions on issues like hiring, promotion, and enforcement; the universalistic model (as favored by the progressives) promoted a meritorious system (hiring and promotion based on qualifications) and uniform policing based on legal standards (Langworthy and Travis 2003, 87).

Many people in policing became very rich in the 1800s. One such person was Alexander S. "Clubber" Williams, a captain in the New York City Police Department who gained fame as a brutal, insolent, and corrupt police administrator and later as a wealthy but vilified individual (Johnson 1981, 55–60). Williams is credited for giving the "tenderloin districts" their name: When discovering that he was going to a part of the city where vice and corruption provided the potential for a great deal of graft for unscrupulous police officers, Williams reportedly exclaimed that he would no longer have to settle for chuck steak but now was able to afford tenderloin (Reppeto 1978, 49–50).

It was not only the politicians and police administrators who reaped the benefits of a corrupt system; unscrupulous officers also took advantage. Patrol officers often ignored the vice going on around them and could frequently be found in saloons, pool-rooms, and brothels. Many detectives had an interesting scam. They received rewards from victims or bribe money from thieves, according to who made the better offer; in some cases there was an agreement between detectives and pickpockets to split the bounty (Johnson 1981, 61). It is understandable that the reputation of the police suffered to an incredible degree during this time.

The force opposing the urban entrepreneurs, the critics, came into prominence during the Progressive Movement of 1896–1917, a period when three major changes in ideology were taking place: (1) an emphasis on honesty and efficiency in governmental affairs, (2) an increase in authority for politicians and government officials, and (3) the use of people with specialized knowledge to handle specific social problems. The critics came from three different groups, all having the similar interest in promoting better police behavior.

One group of critics was commonly known as the "moralist crusaders" who were highly concerned with the evils of the day—prostitution, gambling, and alcoholism, as well as police corruption. People in this group promoted investigations into police affairs, and the first commission investigating the police, the Lexow Commission in 1894, examined graft activities among New York City police. The group was not very effective in controlling the activities of the police, however, because they were often up against solid political machines.

Another group of police critics was comprised of people who wished to improve police effectiveness and efficiency. This group often joined forces with other groups seeking reforms in the criminal justice system, such as the National Prison Association, whose committee on the police promoted a civil service system in which people were hired as police officers and promoted based on their merit rather than patronage.

An important change in policing in the nineteenth century was the development of the class of police officer known as the detective. Detective squads started in the largest American cities at midcentury and were charged with investigating crime, which often involved "going undercover" by covertly dealing with those involved in criminal behavior. The detective function derived its heritage from the thief-takers and constables of England. In time, the public became fascinated with the idea of these stealthy individuals. Detective novels became a popular form of literature, and fictional characters like Sherlock Holmes became fixtures of American nineteenth-century life (Friedman 1993, 204–208). But it was a real-life detective, Allan Pinkerton (1819–1884), who promoted the romanticism of the detectives by publishing over eighteen books from 1874 to1885 (Walker 1977, 22).

Out of necessity, the new field of forensic science also began during this century because criminal behavior became more prevalent and offenders more difficult to catch (Friedman 1993, 208). The phrase "forensic science" refers to all of the parts of the criminal justice system utilized in scientifically supported investigations that can effectively be used to prosecute offenders in a court of law (Nickell and Fischer 1999, 1). One of the primary advancements in the police departments of larger cities involved communications. As improved means of communication developed, agencies exchanged information about crimes and offenders.

A major problem experienced by the early police was the lack of any useful means to identify offenders. And so the new technology of photography found a use in law enforcement. Belgian officials had begun using daguerreotypes (early photographic pictures) in 1843, and France and the United States began using them within the decade. When the technology advanced to the point that prints could be made from negatives, the posting of offender's pictures in police station houses became possible. These pictures became known as "mug shots" because the pictures were images of faces (Nickell and Fischer 1999, 1). Victims and witnesses were asked to view the mug shots to determine the identity of offenders.

Another innovation to identify offenders was fingerprinting. No one person can claim to be the sole inventor of this technology; five people, working independently but around the same time in the 1870s and 1880s, posited the benefits of fingerprinting to the criminal justice system. Dr. Henry Faulds, a Scottish physician working in Japan, and Sir William James Herschel, a British magistrate working in India, both claimed to uncover the uses of the mysterious fingerprint, which appeared to be unique for each person. In 1880, the claims of these two people became noticed, and three others, famed British scientist Sir Francis Galton (another British magistrate), Sir Edward Richard Henry, and Argentine police statistician Juan Vucetich, who catapulted the process to fame. In actuality, this new science, at the time called dactyloscopia, had been discovered perhaps by much earlier peoples (Cronin 1977, 159–177).

At the same time, a worker in a French police department, Alphonse Bertillon, devised a method of taking precise measurements and descriptions of offenders' body parts (a science that would be labeled anthropometry), making notations of physical traits such as scars, and taking fingerprints for offender identification. The process, known as the Bertillon method, became customary procedure in many American cities (Friedman 1993, 208). This method would eventually prove to be overly tedious, and fingerprinting would eventually supplant it (Nickell and Fischer 1999, 8).

Major advancements in forensic detection were revealed in a book called *Criminal Investigation* by Austrian attorney Hans Gross. Gross advocated supplementing police work with practices derived from the disciplines of anthropometry, medicine, toxicology, serology, ballistics, mineralogy, ecology, and botany. Through his efforts at amalgamating these fields, he created the new field of criminalistics and gave it its name (Nickell and Fischer 1999, 9).

State Police

In the nineteenth century, states also started creating policing agencies. The Texas Rangers are often described as the first state police; however, at the time this group of settlers was formed in the 1820s, Texas was still a republic. The rangers were effective in protecting the rural communities in which they lived, and, when Texas declared its sovereignty in 1836, they took on additional duties, such as fighting the area's American Indians and later, in the 1850s, began to combat highway robberies, control slave escapes, and guard the border in an effort to keep out illegal aliens. The rangers gained much fame for their effectiveness in fighting crime; however, they were often ruthless in their dealings with certain groups, especially African slaves and Mexicans. Arizona and New Mexico started up state agencies based on the Texas Ranger model, and soon states in the East established state systems, although very different ones from the western rangers (Johnson 1981, 156–158).

Massachusetts also experimented with a state police agency in 1865, in response to citizens' fears of rampant alcohol abuse, especially by the state's Irish American population. A state force was assembled to govern such behavior because many citizens thought that local police agencies ignored what the majority considered alcohol drinking excesses. The state police in this form was short-lived; legislative changes abolished the agency and replaced them with rural detectives (Johnson 1981, 157–158).

Federal Police

In the 1800s, the federal government left most law enforcement responsibility to the states. However, some crimes—robbery of the U.S. mail, fraud involving the mail, and counterfeiting—were detrimental to the whole country's well-being. Since there was no national police and because states were unable to deal with federal crimes, federal agencies such as the Treasury and the Post Office developed their own enforcement arms to deal with them. The Post Office was one of the first federal agencies, created shortly after the new government began operating in 1789. The group of agents assigned to protect the national mail service, the postal inspectors, was the federal government's first police force. During the nineteenth century, the postal inspectors became well-known for their effectiveness and provided a model for other policing entities (Johnson 1981, 73–81).

The U.S. Secret Service, another federal agency, was formed after the American Civil War to combat crimes related to the national currency, most notably counterfeiting. Created in 1865, the agency assumed expanded duties two years later to investigate fraudulent activities against the government. A number of groups were targets of the new agency, such as distillers of illegal alcohol, smugglers, mail robbers, the Ku Klux Klan, and others. In 1894, it began providing protection to President Glover Cleveland on an informal basis. The responsibility to protect U.S. presidents became official in the next century (United States Secret Service n.d.).

Private Police

As businesses began to flourish in America during the nineteenth century, merchants often turned to private police or private security to protect their interests. The so-called express companies came about during the 1830s to ensure the safe transport of valuables, money, and, later, other items. Several private security agencies were formed during this time, including the investigative agency started by former Chicago detective Allan Pinkerton. Other notable companies during this period were Wells Fargo, Adams Express, and Overland Express (Lipson 1975, 23–32).

The benefits of private policing were direct and seemed more appealing to many businesses than paying taxes to a governmental entity that might be less effective in securing their interests. Most city police departments allowed a group of private citizens, called specials, to work as security officers for private firms. The specials were sworn in by police departments and wore almost identical uniforms to the local police, but they were employees of the private companies (Walker 1977, 29).

The railroads were a major employer of private security agents, especially because the railroads covered such a vast expanse of rural area. Allan Pinkerton's agency was hired by six different railroads in 1855 to protect the trains and also to monitor the actions of the railroad employees, particularly activities involving union involvement. Pinkerton's agency began providing security services to business in suburban Chicago; his Pinkerton Protective Police Patrol boasted its effectiveness in not only preventing crimes but also in discovering unscrupulous employee activity (Walker 1977, 30). As the nineteenth century neared its end, the railroad industry continued to grow at an incredible pace and private special agents, such as those employed by Baldwin-Felts Detective Agency, were responsible for investigating railroad crime, monitoring railroad stations and freight cars, removing hobos, preventing train fare fraud, and investigating allegations of equipment tampering. The last duty was the most important task of the railroad agents (Velke 2004, 19).

The Evolution of American Policing: The Twentieth Century

Municipal and County Police

The twentieth century brought new demands for local police. Labor-related conflicts increasingly dictated the use of police to keep the peace. In addition, the effect of prohibition on law enforcement was profound. In 1919, one year after World War I ended, state legislatures began voting on their support, or lack thereof, for the Eighteenth Amendment to the Constitution, which marked the beginning of the Prohibition Era (Edwards 2000, 73–85), making it illegal to produce, transport, or sell liquor. Congress passed a stringent enforcement of this prohibition, the Volstead Act, over presidential veto, and the states followed suit with similar actions on the state level.

Although considered by many to be an unenforceable legal action, Prohibition led to thousands of arrests by the police, although many of these cases were reduced to misdemeanor status. The prohibition of alcohol provided fertile ground for the period's gangsters, the most notorious being Al Capone. The period's organized crime bosses used the underground activity of bootlegging (a slang term for the manufacture, transport, and sale of liquor, also known as hooch), as a supplement to their other illegal crime operations. Prohibition was not the total impetus of twentieth-century organized crime, but it contributed to its growth (Friedman 1993, 339–341). The Eighteenth Amendment was repealed in 1933, almost fourteen years after America officially went dry (Edwards 2000, 75–85).

As new problems in fighting, preventing, and solving crime developed, policing strategies evolved in America. The large urban police departments initially looked to the London Metropolitan Police for guidance in developing their own methods, but soon they began to create their own strategies and then to borrow ideas from one another (Monkkonen 1981, 40). In the previous century, patrol work was performed initially on foot and later on horseback in some departments. When motorized cycles and automobiles were invented in the early part of the century, many police agencies used them, and their use became imperative because many of the people they were chasing were fleeing in automobiles. Motorcycles came into use in patrol work in Philadelphia in 1906, and automobiles were first used in Detroit in 1909 (Folley 1980, 72).

An innovative strategy that many police departments adopted in the early twentieth century was the establishment of specialized police squads. These often took the form of vice squads whose officers were trained in the enforcement of the vice laws at a time when vices—prostitution, gambling, and alcohol and narcotics abuse—were becoming worrisome to many citizens. The effect of these squads was to further remove police officers from specific communities to combat citywide problems (Langworthy and Travis 2003, 95).

The 1920s heralded a new era of police professionalism. Led by Berkeley, California, police chief August Vollmer, a new generation of innovative administrators appeared on the scene, insisting that their field is a profession and using the newest technological innovations to further their mission. Vollmer's contributions are legendary: He was the first administrator to hire college-educated officers as a matter of practice and the first to utilize a system of traffic signals. He used bicycles, motorcycles, and cars for patrol and equipped them with radios. He operated one of the first crime labs, utilized an early polygraph, and started a police academy. In addition, he was a professor, writer, and president of the powerful International Association of Police Chiefs, where he argued for a centralized criminal records agency, which would later be found in the Federal Bureau of Investigation (Langworthy and Travis 2003, 95–96).

Perhaps as important to the field, Vollmer was a mentor to the new generation of administrators to advocate professionalism, including O. W. Wilson, another highly innovative police manager and scholar. Wilson was one of Vollmer's "college cops" who went on to become chief of police of the Wichita, Kansas, police department in 1928, where he advocated the use of police cars for patrol work. He also served as professor at the University of California and Harvard University, and in 1960 he became the chief of police in Chicago (Friedman 1993, 360). In addition he was a prolific writer and authored the classic text, *Police Administration* (Langworthy and Travis 2003, 97).

Forensic science continued to be shaped by necessity, and many new advances in policing occurred during the early twentieth century. Due to the innovations of New York handwriting expert Albert S. Osborn, handwriting analysis gained legitimacy by being accepted in the courts. The nation's first fingerprint bureau was created in St. Louis after the technique was demonstrated at the 1904 World's Fair (Friedman 1993, 358–359). The first forensic laboratory in the country was developed in 1923 in Los Angeles under the guidance of August Vollmer (Nickell and Fischer 1999, 13). A highly modernized crime lab, complete with ballistics equipment, lie detector test, and X-ray capabilities, was established in Cincinnati in 1934 (Friedman 1993, 359). Scientific crime scene investigation procedures were advanced by a number of university faculty throughout the nation during the century. It was a British scientist, however, who in 1985 discovered the uniqueness of DNA structure that provides a "genetic fingerprint" for criminal investigation (Nickell and Fischer 1999, 11–12). The use of DNA testing in criminal justice was adopted throughout the United States and has proven to be one of the great innovations of recent times.

The 1950s brought new fears of crime, especially involving juvenile delinquency, as rates climbed during this period (Friedman, 1993, 449). The tumultuous 1960s brought new challenges to the nation's police departments. Called in to quell demonstrations over racial discrimination, the war in Vietnam, and other political issues, at the same time fighting a growing crime rate (and the resulting fear of crime), the police encountered a growing disconnection from the communities they served. In addition, increasing court-imposed restrictions on the police limited their ability to carry out their mission and had a marked effect on morale (Langworthy and Travis 2003, 97–99). So-called social wars were declared on drugs and poverty, and once again the police were seen as street-level enforcers of these policies. Many conflicts resulted from protesters' viewing the police as a military occupation force rather than peacekeepers.

By the end of the 1960s, a new philosophy of policing was obviously needed; the paramilitary, bureaucratic model was simply ineffective in dealing with the challenges of the decade and the perceived challenges ahead. The era of the community policing model, also called the community-oriented model, began as a result of the conflict in the 1960s and developed strength over the ensuing decades. The innovations and strategies of the previous professional era had succeeded in removing the police from the corrupting influences of the communities; they centralized power in the hands of well-trained, experienced administrators and gave the police a more favorable image than that of the earlier era. But now the police seemed too removed from their communities and citizens began to desire a return to the "beat cop" approach—a person to talk with on the street and a visible presence in the neighborhoods, rather than a detached official patrolling the streets in a police car.

The President's Commission on Law Enforcement and the Administration of Justice, drafted in 1967, saw this need and recommended better police–community relations. Crime prevention, rather than simply crime fighting, became a major focus. A holistic approach was adopted, and the officers on patrol became generalists rather than specialists. They adopted a problem-solving perspective in which the police, in conjunction with community members, identified specific community problems. In essence, the officers widened their scope of responsibility in order to deal with community problems (President's Commission on Law Enforcement and Administration of Justice 1967).

Some scholars see this community-oriented approach to police work as a return to an early model of American policing in which officers were tightly woven into the fabric of society. This approach causes concern among some due to the corruption that existed in the nineteenth century (Langworthy and Travis 2003, 100).

State Police

There were many changes in the state police agencies in the twentieth century, as well as in the municipal departments. Increased urbanization, industrialization, and immigration caused several states to create their own police forces to deal with a number of emerging problems. During the previous century, the Pennsylvania legislature had turned over law enforcement during violent coal mining labor disputes to private firms. The governor adopted a military-style police force to quell the labor and ethnic violence after a major strike in 1902. The new force was able to suppress the disturbances, but it was largely motivated by prejudice against ethnic and racial minorities. Other states adopted agencies based on the Pennsylvania model, but as labor disputes began to wane and as ethnic groups started assimilating in larger numbers after 1917, this model was no longer useful. Other changes were on the horizon that would force the state agencies to change (Johnson, 1981, 159–160).

Even the famous Texas Rangers took on a new mission at the turn of the century. Renamed the Texas State Rangers and placed under the state's Department of Public Safety, the reorganized agency began performing the same duties as the city and county police. Their image as crime fighters suffered initially but was restored due to their successful policing of the border towns that were experiencing rapid population growth (Hatley 1999).

The automobile had the greatest impact on twentieth-century state policing efforts. Originally an upper-class toy, the automobile soon sped along America's roadways in great numbers, thanks to mass production and affordability (Johnson 1981, 161–163). Many police agencies created state highway patrol forces to deal with the increasing number of motorists on state highways.

Federal Police

The federal government, which had a diminutive policing role in the nineteenth century, experienced remarkable growth in the next century. The United States Secret Service, which had been instituted in the previous century to combat counterfeiting and later to investigate fraud against the government, officially assumed in 1902 a role that it had performed informally: the protection of the president. As the century progressed, the agency assumed responsibility for the protection of the president's family, other high-ranking officials of the government, and visiting heads of foreign governments. In the 1980s, in addition to its other duties, the agency began investigating high-tech frauds involving credit and debit cards, computers, and identification documents. The next century would bring new challenges relating to computer fraud and international crime (United States Secret Service n.d.).

The primary federal policing agency during this time was the Bureau of Investigation (later renamed the Federal Bureau of Investigation, or FBI), which was part of the Justice Department. Created in 1908, the agency grew quickly with the addition of agents whose purpose was to investigate and prosecute offenders involved in the sex trafficking trade (white slavery). Another social problem, the burgeoning drug trade, became another focus. It was concerns over international affairs, however, rather than domestic issues that created a prominent role for the agency around World War I. A new unit, the General Intelligence Division, was created and J. Edgar Hoover was placed in charge. This division obtained information on suspected radicals and subversives; Hoover inflated the actual seriousness of the threats by this group and had his agents raid suspected hangouts (Johnson 1981, 167–168).

As director of the FBI, Hoover made the agency one of the best-known federal agencies. He created a highly qualified group of agents by raising law enforcement standards, and he championed several policing innovations such as founding the first federal criminal laboratory in 1932 and creating the National Police Academy three years later. A series of high-profile apprehensions of "notorious gangsters" in the 1930s, such as Pretty Boy Floyd, John Dillinger, and Bruno Hauptman, the kidnapper of the Lindberg baby, vaulted Hoover and the FBI to fame (Johnson 1981, 172–175). The agency's fame was also due in part to Hoover's use of propaganda, which played a large part in bringing his agency into the popular culture. Hoover was involved in the production of a number of movies and television shows that projected an image of the FBI as the nation's highly professional law enforcement agency. America's fascination with fictional detectives led to FBI agents being referred to as heroic figures, as G-men (government agents). These agents, who "always got their man," satisfied some of the nation's basic psychological needs (Powers 1983, 74). Hoover himself wrote nonfiction accounts of the agency and in the 1950s promoted himself as the icon of American traditional values. In his most popular book, *Masters of Deceit* (1958), the director expressed his view of the ultimate battle between an America with Christian values versus communist nations with satanic motivations (Powers 1983, 232–237). Soon the FBI had responsibility for espionage, counterespionage, and sabotage; Hoover's agency performed its mission in these areas admirably before and during World War II by stopping any major attempts at sabotage and by breaking up espionage rings (Johnson 1981, 172–175).

After the war, Hoover continued to gather intelligence on many people, including public officials and actors, and he contributed to the heightened postwar fears of communism. After the Red Scare, Hoover continued to gain power and attributed the growing protests from civil rights and antiwar groups of the 1960s to communist provocateurs (Johnson 1981, 175–181). Radical groups, lumped under the umbrella of the "new left," became the target of the agency, much as the communists had been in the 1950s and the Ku Klux Klan in the 1960s.

Hoover's long tenure as the FBI director, approaching almost 48 years, ended with his death in 1972, two years prior to President Richard Nixon's resignation from office following the Watergate scandal. The FBI had investigated the break-in, the subsequent cover-up attempts, and the related events that led to the national scandal (Federal Bureau of Investigation n.d.). Hoover's administration was controversial because his xenophobic tendencies found their way into bureau policy; however, he can be credited for increasing the level of professionalism and innovation in law enforcement (Friedman 1993, 271). Federal law enforcement suffered during the 1970s from a loss of prestige and prominence. However, the agency, under new leadership, promoted a more racially diverse workforce and recruited women as agents. New priorities were established as agency targets—people involved in organized and white-collar crimes—became a national concern. In addition, foreign counterintelligence became a new focus as incidents of terrorist activity increased at home and abroad.

Throughout the 1980s, the illegal drug trade and frauds involving savings and loan institutions were investigated. As the Cold War ended, agents were reassigned to domestic concerns, most notably violent crime. The ability to handle crisis situations became a prime concern as the agency became involved in controversial situations in the early 1990s, such as an incident at Ruby Ridge in Idaho in which a fugitive's wife was accidentally shot by an agent. Even more prominent in the media was the Waco, Texas, incident, in which agents responded to a group of heavily armed members of a sect called the Branch Davidians. The agents were unable to bring the event to a successful conclusion, and eighty people died as the compound was suddenly set on fire. Domestic terrorism also became a salient issue in the 1990s as the agency investigated several major acts: the bombing of the World Trade Center in New York in 1993, the Oklahoma City bombing in 1995, and the Unabomber attacks (Federal Bureau of Investigation, n.d.).

The use of technology continued to be a strong point of the FBI at century's end. The FBI's crime laboratory adopted the use of DNA technology, and the agency began investigating computer crimes, especially involving child pornography and other Internet crimes involving children. In the first year of the new century, however, the mandate changed again. Foreign terrorism became a major focus of the agency after the September 11, 2001 attacks in America (Federal Bureau of Investigation n.d.).

Private Police

Even though its founder died in 1884, the Pinkerton National Detective Agency was still a viable force in private security for railroads and industry in the twentieth century. Other agencies, such as the William J. Burns International Detective Agency, founded in 1906 by former Secret Service operative and later FBI director William Burns, also competed for a share of the private security market.

When railroads became nationalized during World War I, all private security agents became federal employees for the duration, becoming private investigators again at the war's end. Corporate leaders began using private security again, but the Great

Depression stifled the industry, with the unintended consequence that more educated people, needing work, entered the
field. World War II brought new opportunities in the form of
overseeing the transport of war materiel, patrolling beaches, and
diverting ships and submarines to specified areas (obviously,
great secrecy was needed for these operations). After the war, increases in crime over the next few decades promoted the expanded use of uniformed security personnel, whose use rate
increased whenever new fears of a crime wave arose (Lipson
1975, 35–57).

Policing Changes in Context

The profession of policing has had to adapt throughout its history. The earliest societies relied on informal methods of social
control to maintain order. As society became more complex, a
professional police force was created, based on the British model,
in the mid-nineteenth century. The early police became deeply
embedded in communities but also became heavily indebted to
political machines and acted to protect the interests of the
wealthy and powerful. Due to corruption, an increasingly adroit
criminal element, and technological advancements such as the
automobile, the police adopted a new philosophy of policing: the
professional crime-fighting model. Crime fighting required a
highly bureaucratic structure worthy of being accepted as a profession, and the military style was embraced. The strategy that
evolved and that was promoted by such noteworthy figures as J.
Edgar Hoover, O. W. Wilson, and William Parker was successful
in its attempts to maintain order but also created a distance between the police and the communities they served.

The professional model of policing proved unable to maintain social order during the social turbulence of the 1960s, as tensions over racial and gender inequality and the Vietnam War
continued to create a chasm between the mostly white, middle-
class male police and a citizenry that was becoming increasingly
diverse. The police were often perceived as agents of an oppressive government, and in many communities a quid pro quo
arrangement occurred. An increase in police force was met by an
increase in citizen resistance. For many, the collective persona of
the once esteemed police force took on the appearance of an occupying army, complete with battle gear, military strategies, and

plenty of armament. Police–community relations in many parts of the country became severely strained.

By the 1970s, the situation called for a new game plan. Community policing represented a return of the police to the streets by having officers working within communities and helping the communities deal with their unique problems through a collaborative effort. Problem-solving approaches and technical advancements have been put to use in crime prevention, rather than crime fighting, in an effort to make the police proactive rather than reactive. In spite of this change in philosophy and even with the successes of community policing, the police still primarily react to crime after the fact.

Working in a current ethos of increasing police visibility, increasing demands for technological innovation (especially in the area of criminal investigation), and a community orientation, all occurring in the looming shadow of terrorism, the police have been called on to address these contemporary concerns. Ironically, in the last few decades, the police have been heavily immersed in a community orientation, and now, especially since September 11, 2001, the demand for order and control has taken on an international focus.

References

Becker, Harold K., and Jack E. Whitehouse. 1979. *Police of America: A Personal View, Introduction, and Commentary.* Springfield, IL: Charles C. Thomas.

Bleiler, E. F. 1976. "Introduction." In *Richmond: Scenes in the Life of a Bow Street Runner.* New York: Dover Publications.

Cramer, James. 1964. *The World's Police.* London: Cassell and Co.

Critchey, T. A. 1967. *A History of Police in England and Wales 900–1966.* London: Constable and Co.

Cronin, John J. 1977. "The Fingerprinters: Identification as the Basic Police Science." In *Pioneers in Policing.* Edited by Philip J. Snead. Montclair, NJ: Patterson Smith.

Edwards, Griffith. 2000. *Alcohol: The World's Favorite Drug.* New York: Thomas Dunn.

Federal Bureau of Investigation. No date. "FBI History." Available at: http://www.fbi.gov/fbihistory.htm. Accessed February 28, 2007.

Folley, Vern L. 1980. *American Law Enforcement: Police, Courts, and Corrections,* 3rd ed. Boston: Allyn and Bacon.

Fosdick, Raymond B. 1969. *American Police Systems.* New York: Century Co.

Friedman, Lawrence M. 1993. *Crime and Punishment in American History.* New York: Basic Books.

Germann, A. C., Frank D. Day, and Robert J. Gallati. 1968. *Introduction to Law Enforcement and Criminal Justice,* 7th ed. Springfield, IL: Charles C. Thomas.

Hatley, Allen G. 1999. *Texas Constables: A Frontier Heritage.* Lubbock: Texas Tech University Press.

Hibbert, Christopher. 2003. *The Roots of Evil: A Social History of Crime and Punishment.* Phoenix Mill, UK: Sutton Publishing.

Johnson, David R. 1981. *American Law Enforcement: A History.* St. Louis, MO: Forum Press.

Langworthy, Robert H., and Lawrence F. Travis, III. 2003. *Policing in America: A Balance of Forces.* Upper Saddle River, NJ: Prentice Hall.

Lipson, Martin. 1975. *On Guard: The Business of Private Security.* New York: Quadrangle/New York Times.

Miller, Wilbur R. 1977. *Cops and Bobbies: Police Authority in New York and London, 1830–1870.* Chicago: University of Chicago Press.

Monkkonen, Eric H. 1981. *Police in Urban America, 1860–1920.* Cambridge: Cambridge University Press.

Nickell, Joe, and John F. Fischer. 1999. *Crime Scene: Methods of Forensic Detection.* Lexington: University Press of Kentucky.

Powers, Richard Gid. 1983. *G-Men: Hoover's FBI in American Popular Culture.* Carbondale: Southern Illinois University Press.

Prassel, Frank Richard. 1972. *The Western Peace Officer: A Legacy of Law and Order.* Norman: University of Oklahoma Press.

President's Commission on Law Enforcement and Administration of Justice. 1967. *The Challenge of Crime in a Free Society: A Report.* Washington, DC: U.S. Government Printing Office.

Rawlings, Philip. 2002. *Policing: A Short History.* Cullompton, UK: Willan Publishing.

Reppeto, Thomas A. 1978. *The Blue Parade.* New York: Free Press.

Richardson, James F. 1974. *Urban Police in the United States.* Port Washington, NY: Kennikat Press.

Trojanowicz, Robert C., and Samuel L. Dixon. 1974. *Criminal Justice and the Community.* Upper Saddle River, NJ: Prentice-Hall.

United States Secret Service. No date. "Secret Service History." Available at: http://www.ustreas.gov/usss/history.shtml. Accessed February 28, 2007.

Velke, John A. 2004. *The True Story of the Baldwin-Felts Detective Agency.* United States: John Velke.

Walker, Samuel. 1977. *A Critical History of Police Reform: The Emergence of Police Professionalism.* Lanham, MD: Lexington Books.

2

Problems, Controversies, and Solutions

The police are an essential institution in America. Although people often become irritated or upset when they feel the police are exhibiting too much control over their lives, they also feel safer knowing the police are around and depend on them for protection. They also expect the police to ensure traffic flows safely and to respond to emergency situations. They also depend on the police to investigate situations involving criminal behavior because of their expertise in these circumstances.

People are also intrigued by police. The fact that so many movies and television shows, both fictional and reality-type, have caught the public's attention reflects Americans' high degree of fascination with the police. Among the host of highly rated shows and series involving police work are the fictional shows (such as *Law and Order*-affiliated shows), crime scene investigation shows (such as *CSI, NCIS* [Naval Criminal Investigative Service], and *Criminal Minds*), and reality shows (such as *American Justice, Cold Case Files, Forensic Files,* and *City Confidential*). In addition, much of the news is dominated by stories involving the police. Obviously, people enjoy watching the police in action.

Although the police world is not always as exciting or glamorous as depicted in the media, it is unique and complex. The unique history of American policing and the present cultural demands on it give the "thin blue line" its distinctive flavor.

The Police Mission

Adopting a broad view of the police in terms of governmental philosophy, Delattre defines the American police mission as the performance of the police role in the country's "experiment in ordered liberty" (2002, 16). This definition refers to the function of the police in a democratic society of maintaining order while safeguarding individual liberty. If a society's policing apparatus is either excessively prohibitive or excessively lenient, instability results.

Reflecting a pragmatic, street-level approach to the police mission, an expolice administrator states that the mission of the police involves the performance of five distinct responsibilities: preserving the peace, protecting people and property, investigating crimes and arresting offenders, preventing crime from occurring, and enforcing laws (Bouza 1990, 1).

Other police scholars note that there are different functions, roles, duties, or various other terms to describe what the police do. Policing can be seen as having two primary functions—order maintenance and community service, along with a related set of duties.

Order maintenance has the associated duties of law enforcement, patrol, traffic control, and investigation; community service has the associated duties of acting as a community resource and providing crime prevention programs. Order maintenance refers to the function that helps promote a safe and lawful environment for the community in which the police work. While some scholars describe a separate police function of law enforcement, it can be argued that the actual enforcement of laws, which includes the arrest, apprehension, and prosecution of offenders, is actually a measure taken to ensure that social order is maintained; therefore it is part of the order maintenance function. The police provide order maintenance also through patrol work, traffic control, investigation of crimes, and other means.

The community service function is often seen as secondary to order maintenance, especially to the notion of crime fighting. However, it must be considered a major function because it comprises much of what the police actually do. Common activities of the police include serving as a community resource and assisting victims and potential victims of crime. The police are certainly part of a larger interdisciplinary network of providers of services to communities and can often be found working in crime prevention education programs, child advocacy programs, mentoring underprivileged children, and a host of other activities.

The Order Maintenance Function

Law Enforcement

The enforcement of criminal laws is a very important part of the law enforcement function. It is probably the responsibility most often associated with police work; in fact, policing as an occupation is often referred to as law enforcement. The actual enforcement of laws, however, entails much more than simply ensuring order through the apprehension and arrest of offenders, and it often overlaps with other areas of police responsibility.

Perhaps the law enforcement operations most frequently associated with the police are searches and seizures, and arrests. *Searches* consist of the examination of a a private area by governmental agents; *seizures* involve taking possession of items obtained in the search that can be used against the owner if criminal activity is found to be involved. In the United States, the search and seizure procedures used by the police create much debate. It is important in America, a country that historically has valued liberty and feared the possibility of an overly intrusive government, that searches not violate the rights of the citizens. The police are guided in this area by the Fourth Amendment to the Constitution, which provides that people cannot be searched without probable cause that a criminal offense has occurred. The 1961 case of *Mapp v. Ohio* established the exclusionary rule, which states that illegally obtained evidence cannot be used in court. There are some exemptions to the exclusionary rule, but police have to take care to use legally sound principles in searches and in the resulting seizure of possible evidence.

Another key area of responsibility of the police is the execution of arrests. The United States Supreme Court has interpreted an *arrest* as any substantial restriction on the ability of a person to freely come and go. Physical force to effect the arrest is unnecessary in this interpretation; a person who uses authority to verbally limit a person's ability to move about freely is making an arrest. In most cases, a warrant is required to effect an arrest, but the police are allowed to arrest a person if: (1) the offense is committed in the presence of an officer, (2) if the offense is a felony and probable cause exists, and (3) the act involves violence, even if the offense under investigation is a misdemeanor (Conser and Russell 2000, 383).

One of the aspects of the law enforcement function is the possibility of officers having to use to force for several reasons: to make offenders comply with instructions; to prevent potential harm to the officers, the offenders, or others; or to stop the attempts of a dangerous person to escape custody. The police use a continuum of force to ensure that the proper degree is used to contain a situation. Graduated sanctions for increasingly dangerous circumstances include:

- Verbal commands from officers
- Open-hand tactics or the use of what are termed "less lethal weapons"
- More forceful physical restraint measures
- Intermediate striking weapons, such as batons
- Lastly, deadly force, which is to be used by police only to protect their own lives or the lives of innocent people (Ortmeier 2006, 218)

The "tools of the trade" used by the police for law enforcement include both lethal and nonlethal weapons. The standard lethal weapon used by police officers has been a .38 caliber, six-shot revolver; however, because the police often encounter people with greater firepower, many agencies have adopted a host of other firearms (Dantzker 2003, 168–169).

Less lethal weapons are used when the police determine that deadly force is not needed. Different weapons are used for different situations, and none should ever be seen as the correct tool in all cases of offender resistance (Standen 2005). Examples of less lethal weapons include batons, chemical agents, stunning devices, distraction devices, and other immobilizing weapons. Batons are a descendant of the truncheon from the earlier days of the professional police and are used for striking when offenders are in close proximity to the officer and require physical intervention to control the situation.

Chemical agents, such as oleoresin capsicum (also called OC or pepper spray), contain the oil of hot peppers and are more effective than their early versions in the 1980s. Officers use these agents to stop offenders through the application of a spray, foam, or gel that is discharged from a canister, causing a burning sensation that normally stops offenders from aggressive activity

(Oldham 2005). Pepper spray causes offenders to experience eye irritation, tearing, and difficulty breathing when the spray is applied to the face, and it often prevents further activity until an arrest can be made.

Some less than lethal weapons stun offenders with an electric shock or with specially designed low-impact rounds. The stun gun is a weapon that looks similar to a flat flashlight with two electric prongs that produce muscle spasms and disorientation when contact is made and electric shocks are delivered (Ortmeier 2006, 214). The Taser (which stands for Thomas A. Swift Electric Rifle) was named after a character in a 1920s–1930s children's adventure series (Wrobleski and Hess 2006, 381). The weapon resembles a firearm, and most of the models used by police are in the form of a handgun. The weapon uses compressed nitrogen to discharge two electric darts that remain connected to the handgun; these darts deliver electricity into the body of offenders or on their clothing. When offenders are "tazed," the central nervous system becomes overwhelmed and uncontrollable muscle contraction occurs, causing temporary mobility of the suspect and giving officers time to contain the situation (Oldham 2005).

Another device often used by police is the Pepperball. The Pepperball weapon, often a handgun though other styles are in existence, uses compressed air to launch a projectile that is filled with OC powder and that stings offenders when impact is made. At that point, its effects resemble those of pepper spray. A shotgun version fires a projectile that looks like a badminton birdie and that can be used in any standard shotgun. Other stunning devices are projectiles (such as beanbags, rubber baton style rounds, or rubber balls packed into a cartridge) fired from handguns or shotguns that stun through impact. These devices are obviously less lethal than bullets (Oldham 2005).

Some devices cause distractions to allow officers to get control of situations. The flashbang is a grenade-shaped device that is hurled into dwellings or other areas, causing disorientation. The device makes a loud noise, produces a bright light that causes temporary blindness, and emits smoke. It is often used in hostage situations and in high-risk entry encounters that often involve the use of SWAT teams (Hess and Wrobleski 2006, 195).

Some other less lethal weapons used by the police are projectiles that use netting to stop fleeing offenders, foams that form around the offenders to stop movement, and bubbles that fill rooms where offenders are hiding. All of these have different uses and limited utility in various circumstances.

Some less than lethal weapons end up causing death for a variety of reasons, such as the poor physical condition of offenders, improper use by the police, or other unanticipated conditions. In spite of the potential problems, less lethal weapons are valuable tools and, when used properly, can achieve the desired objective without having to use deadly force.

Patrol

One of the primary duties of the police is patrol work, and 60 to 70 percent of a police officer's time is dedicated to this activity (Wrobleski and Hess 2006, 131). Patrol is often considered the backbone of a police department and is the most visible duty of the police. It is not only the duty that most connects the police and the public, it is also the one in which most police officers start their careers (Dantzker 2003, 67–68). Patrol has as its roots the practice of "standing guard" or "keeping watch," which was certainly practiced in the earliest societies and which had much utility in the military forces. The need for someone to patrol areas to observe possible criminal activity has been around as long as the need for social control measures. The duty for current policing agencies entails the vigilant observation of people and responding to situations involving crime, emergencies, or the need of other services.

The several different forms of patrol are foot patrol (the oldest form of patrol), mounted horse patrol, nonmotorized wheel patrol (bicycles, roller skates, and skateboards), automobile patrol, all-terrain vehicle (ATV) patrol, motorcycle patrol, water vehicle patrol, helicopter and airplane patrol, and patrol using canine units (often referred to as K-9 units) (Conser and Russell 2000, 258–269). A new form of motorized patrol makes use of the small, two-wheeled scooter-type vehicle called the Segway Human Transporter, or simply Segway, which was introduced in 2001. The Segway vehicle is guided by the movement of the rider and is being used by police departments not only for its transport benefits but also because it allows citizens greater accessibility to the police (Wrobleski and Hess 2006, 195–196).

Traffic Control

In traffic control, police officers have a number of assignments. Sometimes the traffic control duty is connected to patrol work and sometimes it is a separate activity. Traffic control includes the

enforcement of traffic laws, the direction of traffic flow, the provision of assistance to motorists, the investigation and documentation of automobile accidents, and the performance of
emergency services (Wrobleski and Hess 2006, 131). In addition,
the police are often responsible for educating the public about
matters of traffic safety; presentations are made to clubs, organizations, schools, and other groups about requirements such as
using seat belts, the use of reflectors, the wearing of safety gear,
and so on (Wrobleski and Hess 2006, 210).

Investigation

Another major duty of the police is the investigation of criminal
activity. This is a universal responsibility for police agencies, but
the size and intensity of the investigation process varies by department. As with patrol duty, investigation has been around for
centuries, even before the advent of the modern police force.
Upon receiving a request for an investigation of a criminal matter, an investigator (uniformed or plainclothes, according to the
agency) responds and initially completes a preliminary investigation by determining whether a crime has occurred, by ascer-
taining the people involved (either as suspects, victims, or
witnesses), and by reviewing the evidence. In addition, investigators review solvability factors, or the leads that will likely result in the determination of the offender's identity (Conser and
Russell 2000, 271–272).

Several investigative methods are used both at the crime
scene and in the crime laboratory. At the crime scene, investigators are responsible for securing the area; recording all observ-
able facts; photographing, measuring, and making a sketch of the
area; obtaining and identifying evidence; documenting a "chain
of custody," identifying each source handling the evidence; securing and storing the evidence; interviewing people who might
be involved; and assisting in the identification of potential suspects (Wrobleski and Hess 2006, 218–225).

Often the preliminary investigation is sufficient to uncover
the circumstances of the crime and to apprehend the offender.
However, if the results of the initial exploration do not meet this
end, a follow-up investigation is performed. The follow-up consists of reviewing previous evidence, conducting additional interviews, obtaining new information on potential suspects and
victims, collecting new evidence, and preparing for court
(Conser and Russell 2000, 272).

A common activity at the crime scene is the taking of fingerprints to determine the identity of criminal offenders. As they touch objects at the crime scene, people often leave behind fingerprints, which are made of sweat and body oils that seep from the grooves in the fingertips. All fingerprints are different due to unique patterns on the fingertips that are classified by fingerprint analysts as loops, whorls, and arches. If the offender's fingerprints are on file in a police database, the prints can quickly determine his or her identity. The prints are often invisible to the human eye ("hidden" prints are known as latent fingerprints) but can be detected through the use of fingerprint powders applied with a brush or chemicals, such as a certain glue that is fumed over the prints (Saferstein 2001, 395–418).

A new form of crime scene investigation involves the use of DNA testing. DNA (deoxyribonucleic acid) is part of a person's genetic material that, like fingerprints, are unique to that person. DNA samples can be extracted from blood, semen, sweat, saliva, skin cells, or other body material. It is often left at crime scenes and is obtainable from such items as weapons, clothing, cigarette butts, stamps, glasses or cups, bottles, condoms, and bed sheets (Saferstein 2001, 353–388). The analysis of DNA is quite complex but is performed in crime labs throughout the nation. As technology advances, the bugs are being worked out; for example, the length of analysis has been shortened due to the more effective use of computers in the analysis process. As DNA profile databases become more abundant, it will become harder for offenders to leave behind undetected traces of their identities. There have been many calls for a DNA database of all people, whether or not they have committed criminal offenses, but this is being met with resistance due to concerns of violation of civil liberties (Lane 2004, 176).

There are many other means of investigating criminal activity at crime scenes, such as the analysis of glass, soil, hair, fibers, paint, tire tracks, bullet comparisons, blood splatters, documents, vocal patterns, computers, drugs, and a host of other items (Saferstein 2001). Many police departments have specialized crime scene units (CSUs) that perform these investigatory services and that are composed of individuals well trained and often certified in investigations. Also, some detective units have specially trained personnel called profilers, who use behavioral analysis to develop a psychological profile of an unknown subject (referred to as an UNSUB), and some departments have begun using psychics to assist in investigations, especially in cold cases (that is, cases that have remained unsolved for a long period) (Wrobleski and Hess 2006, 227–228).

Other Order Maintenance Duties
Numerous other order maintenance duties are performed by specially trained officers, such as undercover detectives who pass themselves as people involved in covert criminal activity; vice officers who work offenses involving prostitution, gambling, pornography, and drug crimes; SWAT (special weapons and tactics) squads that handle critical situations in which guerrilla tactics, precision shooting, and night operations are needed; juvenile units that carry out policing activity with juveniles; and canine (K-9) units that use dogs to detect suspects, victims, drugs, weapons, explosives, and evidence, or to control unruly crowds and detain offenders (Wrobleski and Hess 2006, 228–238).

Community Service Function
The standard police motto is "to serve and protect." However, a tension often exists in policing agencies about whether their role is one of primarily social worker or crime fighter. The police often dislike the social worker label, but they rarely refuse to become involved when social service needs arise. The duty is one that requires much of a police officer's time and energy. The social service responsibilities are numerous and can involve assisting citizens who have locked their keys in their cars, transporting people to medical facilities, helping motorists with disabled vehicles, and talking to people with a variety of different problems and concerns (Dantzker 2003, 78). In addition, just a few of the community service demands placed on the police are giving information and directions to travelers, intervening in domestic situations, working with lost or neglected children, assisting in rescue or emergency operations, assisting in automobile license and vehicle registration, and conducting educational programs to schools and communities (Wrobleski and Hess 2006, 122).

The community service function is specifically addressed in the governmental report called *The Challenge of Crime in a Free Society* (President's Commission on Law Enforcement and the Administration of Justice 1967, 97–98), in which the authors suggest that the police are in a unique situation to observe the conditions that can be changed to make communities safer. The authors recommend that the police "make it their business" to report problems in city parks, on school playgrounds, in tenant buildings, or with city services such as garbage collection; these are considered important police concerns as well as the more traditional aspects of police work that involve crime fighting.

The World of the Police

The Police Mystique

Given the plethora of television shows, movies, and novels about the police and criminal justice, the American public is obviously fascinated with the romanticized police image. This fascination with the "police mystique" probably extends back to the occupation's beginnings. The advent of moving pictures and television produced early depictions of police work, though much of what appears in movies and on television shows is far from what most police experience. The Hollywood versions of police work can be compared to orange juice; the screen versions are akin to the concentrated type found in cans and only when the "water" of boredom, routine, and insider ritual are added is the real product accurately represented (Bouza 1990).

Even though the occupation of the police contains excitement at times, it often pales in comparison to the screen versions. The media focuses on the order maintenance function (the depiction of police as crime fighters who chase, arrest, and bring criminals to justice or who have the ability to investigate complex cases and solve them in one hour) rather than on the more common function of community service. The crime fighter image sells—it captivates audiences, whether they are viewing movies, the news, fictional police shows, or even the documentary-type reality police shows (Dantzker 2003, 3–6). Seeing this fictionalized representation is much more interesting than watching police officers respond to citizens complaining about animals in their homes, investigating discarded vehicles on the side of the road, or attending community meetings about local problems. To their credit, some reality police programs do depict some of these community service activities; however, the main focus is on the exciting fast-paced, action-packed fight against crime.

Real police also do not have the technological "toys" that many of their make-believe counterparts have on fictional television shows or in the movies. Despite our technological advancements in investigative equipment in recent years, the innovations are expensive and many police agencies simply do not have the money for them.

The Police Personality

Many scholars have explored the issue of a police personality, the idea that a distinct set of beliefs and behaviors can be found in police agencies. The police, as with other occupations, have a certain understanding of the world based on the social environment in which they live and work. This working personality affects the way they perform their duties and is influenced by certain occupational conditions inherent in police work: danger and authority. Officers are suspicious due to the vigilance required in dealing with people who might wish to harm them and due to their being on the watch for unlawful behavior. The police are often somewhat isolated from other people in that they feel uncomfortable dealing socially with those they come into contact with daily—both those who commit crimes and the citizens they serve. This isolation from others often makes officers turn to each other, creating a significantly higher level of solidarity than among many other occupational groups (Skolnick 1966, 44–70).

Individual officers often view their work uniquely and therefore have varying styles. Some officers focus primarily on the order maintenance function of the job; theirs is the *watchman* style. They use their discretion liberally in enforcing the law by concentrating on the offenses and situations deemed most detrimental to the social order, often ignoring minor violations that come to their attention. *Legalistic* style officers see the primary role of the police as making sure the laws are enforced in a formal manner, and they believe that performing their duties "by the book" is the correct way of handling criminal behavior or other police matters. Officers with the *service* style (often working in middle-class communities) see maintaining the community's moral codes as the primary role, are very involved with citizen complaints, but normally try to handle them in an informal manner (Wilson 1978).

The Police Subculture

The concept of a police subculture has been the subject of much discussion among scholars and has certainly found its way into popular culture, especially in books, movies, and television shows.

A *subculture* is basically a microcosm of the larger culture that possesses some of the culture's dominant features but also has its own unique and distinctive characteristics. In the case of the police, different dress, equipment, a specialized knowledge and training of crime and the criminal justice system, and intensified vigilance when relating to others while on duty all create unique subculture traits (Purpura 2000, 118). These traits often define the world of the police.

The police are distinctive in some important respects. Patrol officers normally wear uniforms while on duty; this creates a highly visible image of authority. The uniforms of the police normally catch the eye of people with whom they are in contact. The badge, representing the "shield," has special importance to the wearer as well as to the observer. (The police badge, originally made of copper, is probably the reason the police obtained the moniker copper or cop.) It is a source of prestige for many police officers to eventually possess the gold shield of the detectives. Workers in other occupations also wear uniforms but do not normally carry the image of police authority.

Uniformed police also carry their tools of the trade on their uniforms, always in plain view for citizens to observe. Officers are normally equipped with a firearm (a handgun that is either a revolver or semiautomatic pistol), a set of handcuffs, a pepper spray canister, and sometimes a stun gun. In addition, communications equipment is normally worn on the shirt. Again, although people of other occupations wear their tools in open view, such as construction workers, the tools of the police—including visible and potentially harmful weaponry—promote an image of power.

The police have specialized knowledge in the areas of crime and criminal justice. This knowledge is obtained from academy training, on-the-job training, in-house instruction, and sometimes college or technical instruction. Obviously other professionals also have a significant knowledge of the criminal justice system, such as attorneys and others in the court system, corrections officials, forensic scientists, and criminal justice educators; however, the combination of special procedural training and acquired street knowledge make a police officer's experience uniquely different from that of others in the criminal justice field.

The inherent danger involved in law enforcement causes police to have protracted levels of vigilance when dealing with those whom they are supposed to protect. Ordinary situations, such as approaching an automobile for a routine traffic stop, requires officers to be very cautious and especially cognizant of all aspects of their surroundings due to the potential danger (Purpura 2000, 118–119).

The police, as in many other professions, have developed their own specialized language, or argot, that separates their occupation from others. These terms tend to unify the police in their collective mission. Examples of "copspeak" include the terms "bad guys" for people who commit crimes, "black and whites" for police cars, "disorderlies" for people who violate laws against the peace, and "shooflies" for internal investigations officials (Philbin 1996). Often the jargon used by the police consists of euphemistic terms that serve an additional purpose of hiding truths that are psychologically difficult to candidly discuss. For example, corpses are commonly referred to as "stiffs" or "DOAs" (dead on arrival of the police); law violators, especially involving violent offenses, are labeled "perps" (perpetrators), who are arrested or "collared" (Bouza, 1990, 3); and victims of crime, again often of violent crime, are termed "vics." In addition, the phrase "eating your thirty-eight" (referring to a .38 caliber handgun) refers to officer suicide (Philbin 1996). More recent terms also reflect this argot: "Lawyering up" refers to a suspect's refusal to answer questions without an attorney present, and "rent-a-cop" refers to a private security officer. "Suicide by cop" is a term used to describe a situation in which people purposefully threaten the police or others, knowing that their action will likely result in death (Champion and Hooper 2003, 309–310).

The unique aspects of their occupation cause the police to have a perspective that is distinctive from many other career choices. All people and groups develop this perspective, often called a worldview, which colors how they perceive various situations. The worldview that constitutes the police subculture is unique in that it is characterized by an us-versus-them mentality—the "us" being the police brotherhood and the "them" being the citizens. The police subculture is sometimes called the blue fraternity or the blue brotherhood (although the terms are now inaccurate due to the number of "sisters" in policing).

Also, the development of the norms of the police begins with selection. Officers are hired based on a number of factors that have little if anything to do with the actual job, such as sexual orientation, gender role adherence, financial background, and others. The selection process ensures that people of a like background are brought into the occupation, often with little understanding of the marginalized groups with whom they will often be in contact (Kappeler et al. 1998, 88–89).

Developing a police subculture continues with training at the police academy, where those not fitting the police officer image (which includes a middle-class bias) are eliminated and those who follow the rules are rewarded. The paramilitary model further strengthens the value of group cohesion and contributes to an increased us-versus-them orientation. Training in the academy and on the job is focused on developing the recruits' practical rather than intellectual skills, because greater importance is given to firearms use, patrol techniques, and arrest and restraint methods. In addition, the telling of war stories to the young recruits by the older officers provides further socialization into the paramilitary structure of the police (Kappeler et al. 1998, 88–92). In other words, "cuff 'em and stuff 'em" techniques are emphasized over developing communication skills, even though the police perform more social work duties than law enforcement operations.

According to Kappeler et al. (1998), three general characteristics of the police subculture relate to the concept of *ethos*, or the "distinguishing character, sentiments, and guiding beliefs of a person or institution" (p. 97). The first is the ethos of bravery, the most salient of the three, which refers to the fact that officers face the potential of violent victimization when encountering others. The second is autonomy, which requires the use of discretion by the police when making decisions about whom and when to arrest and about when to use force; this ethos highlights the police role as gatekeepers. The third ethos is secrecy in which officers adopt an informal code that allows only certain information to be disclosed to outsiders.

Closely related to the police subculture concept is the *blue curtain* (Goldstein 1977, 202). This concept, also called the blue wall of silence, refers to an unwritten code of secrecy that is often maintained by the police to provide protection to other officers. Although other professions have similar codes of secrecy, the code among the police is often more closely upheld. Police supervisors often become entangled in the web of secrecy by promoting the departmental image above complaints of misconduct by outsiders. Good police work suffers in this type of environment (Delattre 2002, 394–395).

The police subculture appears to be perceived by many scholars, movie producers, and citizens as an entirely negative phenomenon. However, the high level of solidarity that is a part of the subculture can be seen as functional to the occupation because implicit in the work itself is the reliance on other officers to assist when needed, especially in life-threatening situations. The social isolation that also comes with the job is alleviated when other officers, with similar experiences and perceptions, become part of an officer's social network.

The Hazards of the Job

The police have jobs that put them into dangerous situations. A salient component of police work is the legally sanctioned ability to use deadly force if it is deemed necessary. *Deadly force* is defined as any type of force that will likely cause the death or serious injury of another person (Alpert and Fridell 1992, 12). The police are expected to use a graduated system of force when some level of force is needed to obtain compliance and to maintain safety. Deadly force is, of course, the most extreme measure and should be used as a last resort. Historically, the police in America, unlike their counterparts in Europe, have had much discretion in the use of deadly force, at least prior to the 1970s. The doctrine of the fleeing felon gave officers the right to shoot, or to use other means of deadly force on, anyone who ran from the police. This changed in the 1970s when many police administrators instructed their officers to use restraint in such cases. In 1985, the case of *Tennessee v. Gardner* stopped the use of deadly force when pursuing felons who are not presumed to be dangerous (Blumberg 1997, 507–530). The taking of a human life is not easy for most people, and many officers are psychologically traumatized after using deadly force. This is one of the top stressors police officers experience (Champion and Hooper 2003, 310).

Another area of police work that is dangerous and that is becoming increasingly controversial is the use of high-speed pursuits. Police officers are obligated to enforce the law, and this often means giving chase to people in automobiles who refuse to stop for the police or who decide to flee. During attempts to apprehend and possibly arrest suspects, high-speed chases endanger not only the lives of the officers, drivers, and passengers, but those of innocent people as well. The actions of the police are guided by court decisions, but police officers have to make important decisions on the scene about whether to begin or to continue pursuit. Factors that must be taken into consideration are the seriousness of the original offense; the speed involved; the location; vehicle, weather, and road conditions; the availability of accurate communications; and the laws and restrictions governing high-speed pursuits (Alpert 1997, 547–564).

As is expected, many aspects of police work make officers highly susceptible to the dangers of stress. The stress comes from the organizational work environment, which promotes feelings of irritation and humiliation that come from the close scrutiny of both the departments and the community itself, as well as from the potentially dangerous and psychologically harmful experiences the police undergo in the field. It is common for the organizational stressors to cause feelings of alienation for the officers or to cause aggressive responses to situations that would normally not require such a response. The dangerous and disturbing encounters often lead to a host of psychological problems, sleeping disorders, and alcohol abuse (Toch 2002, 5).

Due to the unpredictable nature of police work, officers often experience what is known as *burst* stress, or stress that comes from a single stressful occurrence, such as encountering a citizen with a gun. When an officer spends a lot of time engaged in tedious activities and then suddenly has to confront a critical, potentially life-threatening situation, the effects can be highly stressful. Officers experience the highest level of stress when they witness the violent deaths of partners or citizens. Posttraumatic stress disorder, suicide, substance use, and family problems that are related to the occupation can cause many officers significant problems (Champion and Hooper 2003, 297–320).

Police–community Relations

The term *police–community relations* refers to activities of police departments to ensure that a continuing line of communication exists between the police and the community. This dialogue should be based on genuine concern and on the ability of police, especially line officers on the street, to listen carefully to community needs. The movement to promote better communication was driven by the late 1960s social conflicts between police authority and the youth and urban poor (Farmer and Kowalewski 1976, 3–4).

Since the advent of the police forces in the United States, the relationship between communities and the police has been marked by conflict. At one point in their history, the police have traditionally been charged with keeping the activities of the "dangerous classes" away from the elite, with compelling members of this class to adopt the moral standards of the upper class, and with changing or at least concentrating the lower-class activities to ghetto areas. Now police come under pressure from the upper classes for not doing enough to shield them from the actions of the lower socioeconomic class. At the same time, the police are criticized by people of the lower socioeconomic classes, with whom the police mostly live and work, for using excessive and inappropriate force against them (Richardson 1974, 158).

During the 1930s, many rural African Americans and other minorities migrated to cities to escape the deleterious effects of the Great Depression. After World War II, another wave of migration occurred due to the economic recovery that took place after the war. It was during this period that the number of black people and other minorities in urban areas in the North and Midwest exceeded the number of minorities in the rural regions of the country. The consequences of this urban migration were overcrowded housing, unsanitary conditions in inner-city communities due to weak enforcement of codes, segregated residential and occupational conditions, and criminal activity. Most police officers in these minority neighborhoods were white and conditions were right for a festering hostility between these groups (Johnson and Campbell 1981, 101–113).

In the 1960s, violence erupted in many cities throughout the nation. Relations between the police and community became strained as riots exploded in many areas. As the conflict continued, many police tactics caused an exacerbation of the problem. Although brutality by the police was a complaint often cited by minority citizens, other grievances were more prominent, such as differential law enforcement practices directed at blacks and other minorities (especially involving protective services), and verbal and physical harassment. Another key issue involved discrimination in police work such as hiring, promotions, and general treatment of minorities in the field (Radelet 1973, 262). The level of aggressive conflict between policy and minority communities abated somewhat in the 1970s and 1980s as many programs in police-community relations were promugated by police forces throughout the country. The Rodney King incident occurred the following decade.

Citizen Review Boards

Due to the volatile situation between the police and community in many parts of the country during the 1960s, the President's Commission on Law Enforcement and the Administration of Justice (1967) issued a report recommending that the processing of citizen grievances and complaints should be adequately promulgated; however, the report advised against singling out the police and other governmental authorities. It also left guidelines for the institution of citizen complaints to local jurisdictions (President's Commission on Law Enforcement and the Administration of Justice 1967, 264–265).

Citizen review boards offer a way to examine police conduct through the use of citizen complaints. Normally a panel of citizens reviews the complaints by questioning officers and witnesses, developing conclusions about the legitimacy of the complaints, and recommending possible sanctions against the officer or officers if the complaints are found to be valid. Review boards are beneficial when there is a high level of community distrust in the police and when it is perceived that the police cannot adequately police themselves (Champion and Hooper 2003, 511).

Ethics in Policing: Police Misconduct

Varieties of *police misconduct* include police crime, occupational deviance, corruption, and abuse of authority (Kappeler et al. 1998, 20–25). *Police crime* involves the direct violation of existing criminal laws and, in its most serious form, the excessive use of force or drug violations. *Occupational deviance* refers to antisocial activities by the police that are made possible by the officer's position of authority: illegally taking impounded vehicles, taking money found during an investigation, conducting illegal searches, and so on. *Corruption,* or *graft,* refers to unethical activities that bring the police some personal gain, especially economic gain, and that are job related, for example, accepting bribes, embezzling funds, and extorting money. The *abuse of authority* involves the use of excessive force, psychological or emotional abuse, or legal abuse. These activities, in this classification system, obviously overlap to a high degree.

Another way to view police misconduct is through the concepts of nonfeasance, misfeasance, and malfeasance. *Nonfeasance* consists of actions by police in which officers fail to perform a legal duty, such as stopping and ticketing a speeder. *Misfeasance* involves actions in which officers fail to perform a legal duty in an appropriate manner, such as searching a house without a search warrant or other legitimate reason to do so. *Malfeasance* occurs when the police perform an illegal act, such as keeping money found in a drug raid (Albanese 2005).

Dealing with allegations of police misconduct is a two-stage process: (1) investigation of the activity deemed inappropriate and (2) determining punishment options if misconduct is determined. The police traditionally handled this process, but review boards of community members eventually became involved with both stages (Bayley 1994, 91).

Issues of Diversity in Policing

Race Relations and the Police

The issue of race has had a long and pervasive role in American history, and this is certainly true in law enforcement. Conflicts among various racial and ethnic groups have been reflected in the relationships between those given the authority to impose order and those who are subjected to such control.

Throughout the twentieth century, riots over issues of race were common in America, and law enforcement agencies played a part in these disturbances. Violent race riots erupted in 1917 in East St. Louis, Illinois, and in Houston, Texas; in Washington, D.C., Seattle, Chicago, Charleston, Longview, Texas, and rural Phillips County Arkansas in 1919; in Tulsa, Oklahoma, in 1921; in Harlem, New York, and Detroit in 1943 (Report of the National Advisory Commission on Civil Disorders 1968). The 1960s brought many riots, including those involving labor–management issues and war protests, in addition to continued racial conflict. Americans were able to witness the effects of police brutality against African Americans when Birmingham, Alabama, city police commissioner T. Eugene "Bull" Conner ordered high-pressure water hoses and dog attacks on a number of young people who were peacefully marching. Outbreaks of racial conflict in 1965 included the highly disastrous riots in the Watts area of Los Angeles.

The long hot summer of 1967 produced over one hundred and fifty civil disorders in the nation. The so-called ghetto riots occurred throughout the country in cities such as Tampa, Cincinnati, Detroit, Atlanta, and Newark, New Jersey, and they involved situations in which African Americans were arrested for basically minor offenses. Police brutality, prejudice, insensitivity, as well as a belief by black citizens that the police ignored their concerns, were cited as causes for the riots. Other factors that potentially contributed to the conditions were crowded and dangerous urban living conditions, worsened by the heat of the summer; a growing number of unsupervised young people on the streets; poor relationships and communication between police and the communities; and slow and unsuitable responses by the police (Report of the National Advisory Commission on Civil Disorders 1968). Although continued racial conflicts between police and black citizens continued in the next two decades, most of them were minor in comparison to those of the 1960s.

In the 1990s, however, the situation changed when one particular case created a firestorm of protest. In Los Angeles in March of 1991, motorist Rodney King and two passengers fled from officers of the California State Patrol, the Los Angeles Police Department (LAPD), and the Los Angeles Unified School District Police. When the car containing the three men was overtaken and stopped, the two passengers complied with police instructions, but the driver, a large and strong man, ran at the LAPD officers, who responded by subduing him with a stun device. The police then began beating and kicking him as he was lying on the ground while an amateur video camera operator, who was witnessing the event, captured the incident on tape. When the camera operator tried to discuss the videotaped event with personnel at the Los Angeles Police Department, the issue did not prompt much interest; so he turned the footage over to local television stations. The ninety-second tape was broadcast on local news and soon became a national story.

King ended up with numerous broken and fractured bones, broken teeth, and internal organ and brain damage as a result of the numerous blows that were dealt by the four officers. The officers went to trial for the charge of using excessive force, and a jury that had no African Americans heard the case. When the officers were acquitted of the charges, major rioting, violence, arson, and looting occurred in Los Angeles for five days. Other violent clashes broke out in other American cities. With the related fifty-four deaths and heavy property destruction, this became one of the nation's largest outbreaks of riot violence in the twentieth century. The four officers were later charged with civil rights violations and found guilty in a federal court.

As the twentieth century came to a close, relations continued to be strained between the police and black citizens. The issue of racial profiling came to the nation's attention as African American and Latin-American motorists were targeted simply because of their skin color. This practice was given the name DWB (driving while black/brown).

African American Police

African Americans have historically been excluded from equal opportunities in many aspects of American life, including employment. Entry into the various occupations was a difficult task, and policing, with its mandate to control the behavior of citizens, was especially difficult. The first black officers in America were employed in New Orleans as part of the city guard from 1805–1820. With its history of racial mixing, New Orleans was the home of many former African slaves who won their freedom due to their service as soldiers. Many such "free men of color" became members of the city guard because there weren't enough white men to serve on the force. The duties of this unit consisted primarily of controlling slaves, a function of the slave patrols in other Southern cities. The black city guard was discontinued and replaced with an all-white work force when the police became increasingly under political control (Dulaney 1996, 8–10).

After the American Civil War, the Black Codes were adopted by many Southern states. The purpose of these codes was to keep power from African Americans by denying certain rights, such as voting. In spite of the codes, a federal order by the U.S. military to restructure the New Orleans police department led to the employment of African American police officers for a second time. In the 1870s, other Southern cities followed New Orleans' model and began employing black police officers. Even though the number of black officers was low in the mid- to late 1800s, there was much resistance to their presence on police forces in any numbers, and, as the political winds changed by the early 1900s, black police officers in the South were virtually nonexistent (Dulaney 1996, 11–18). The number of African American police officers in the North also fell sharply during this time but began to rise after World War II; however, they were confined to working in areas in black communities and allowed to arrest only black citizens. Some African American police even had to ride in patrol cars marked "colored police" (Peak 2005, 358). Other officers were located in black station houses or "Negro substations" (Barlow and Barlow 2000, 229). In the 1950s, pressure from black communities and organizations caused a shift, and, by the late 1960s and early 1970s, the recruitment of blacks into the field began and relationships between police and minority communities improved (Barlow and Barlow 2000, 241–254).

Women Police

As with other male-dominated occupations, the entry of women into the police profession was difficult. The roots of the movement can be traced to the 1840s, when prison matrons were hired to oversee women inmates in some of America's penal institutions through the efforts of the American Female Reform Society and other groups. The philosophy of this movement carried over into policing in the 1880s. Prior to the 1900s, women were allowed in police departments through two routes: by having a background and training in social work or by being the widow of a police officer. Whichever route was taken, the duties of the police matron all conformed to the gender-based ideas of femininity. The matrons were responsible for working with female and juvenile offenders, assisting in missing persons investigations, and working with victims of sex offenses. They did not possess police powers or wear uniforms (Horne 1974, 26–27).

The movement had a moralist tone, following in the model of the American suffragists. The early women police officers include Lola Baldwin, employed by the Portland, Oregon, Police Department in 1905; Alice Stebbins Wells, appointed by the Los Angeles Police Department in 1910; and Mary Hamilton, who served as the first female police officer with the New York Police Department. These early female police officers promoted their roles as prevention oriented and nonthreatening to the male officer image. This tack might have been the downfall of the movement that peaked in the mid-1920s and quickly lost ground thereafter. The movement to establish women as a viable force in policing went into a sharp decline during the next three decades.

A new interest in the professional model of policing, with its emphasis on crime fighting rather than social work, contributed to its decline (Walker 1979, 101–111).

After World War II, women entered the occupation in greater numbers and with more responsibilities. In 1956, the International Policewomen's Association was reestablished as the International Association of Policewomen, and it promoted a new agenda: women police officers performing not in a matronly role but rather as crime fighters. The separate women bureaus that existed in the early years were incorporated into the regular police units. This did not happen without resistance from male officers, however. It would be another decade before women began performing the primary police responsibility of police patrol (Schultz 1995, 115–130). With the 1972 passing of the Amendment to the Civil Rights Act, women began entering the field, although the pioneering female officers had a difficult time in the culturally sustained masculine world of the police (Martin 1997, 363–366). As of 2004, women police represented almost 12 percent of all police officers (Federal Bureau of Investigation, 2004). As more women enter the field, especially in the administrative ranks, gender distinctions should lessen.

Other Minorities

Other racial and ethnic minorities in police work reflect the diverse nature of the American workforce. Native-American, Latin-American, and Asian-American officers, as well as officers with different ethnic backgrounds, contribute to the policing system that provides protection and service to communities that are similarly diverse. It is important that police agencies recruit from these groups, as they have in the case of African American and female officers.

Another growing population within the police workforce are gay and lesbian officers. Due to the antihomosexual sentiment among some police officers, perhaps due to their traditional middle-class, white, heterosexual perspective, homosexual men and women have often had a difficult time gaining acceptance from colleagues. Females seem to have an easier time gaining this acceptance from male officers due in part to stereotypes of the "masculine nature" of lesbians and the "feminine nature" of gay males. In an environment that values machismo, anyone seen as not possessing masculine qualities is often marginalized. Openly disclosing a homosexual orientation can prevent someone from being hired as a police officer and can lead to ostracism by other officers. Associations and organizations have been formed in some urban areas for gay and lesbian police (Barlow and Barlow 2000, 275–287). Time will tell if these officers will obtain acceptance into the field of policing.

The Changing Police Milieu

The Evolving Nature of Policing

Kelling and Moore (1991) provide a model of police evolution as it relates primarily to the sociopolitical factors that have influenced American law enforcement. In their first of the three eras of policing, the political period (1840–1930), the police were controlled by politicians who, to obtain votes, forced the police to engage in service-type work; this era was understandably filled with high levels of corruption. The second period, the reform era (1930–1980), saw a more professional and efficient police organizational structure that removed officers from political control but that also removed them from the communities they served. The third and present era, which began around 1980, is seeing a turn from a detached police force to one that has a symbiotic relationship with community citizens. The community policing approach that was ushered in during the current era has changed the nature of police work since its beginnings.

One way to consider policing evolution is to observe the changes brought about by technological advancements. Soulliere (1999) has proposed four stages of policing that illustrate how the changes in technology have influenced the field. The first stage (1881–1945) is highlighted by the technological introductions by the police innovator August Vollmer, such as mobile patrol, radio communication, polygraph technology, fingerprint and handwriting classification procedures, and the establishment of a forensics laboratory. The second stage (1946–1959) saw improvements in traffic control devices as well as instruments used to record blood alcohol levels in offenders. In the third stage (1960–1979), major technological innovations were adopted (primarily due to the recommendations of the President's Commission on Law Enforcement and the Administration of Justice), such as the 911 emergency call system, centralized dispatch systems, computer databases, and the increased use of computer-assisted technology. The forth and present stage, begun in 1980, has witnessed a number of technological advancements including telecommunication, mobile computing, expert systems, imaging, and biometric technologies.

Bayley (1998) reflects on seven changes in American law enforcement since the 1960s. First, today's police officers are at all levels more intelligent, more knowledgeable, and more sophisticated than officers of decades ago. Second, police executives are more innovative, better trained in police administration, and more desirous to leave their own unique legacies on their departments. Third, police agencies are more likely than their predecessors to make use of science, appreciate the value of the rapid dissemination of information, and understand the importance of evaluation. Fourth, police ethical standards have increased in recent years. Fifth, police forces are much more diverse in their composition than those of the past. Sixth, the police have had to become generally more familiar with advances in technology, forensics, and crime; this familiarity creates distinct changes in the organizational structure of law enforcement agencies. Last, the civilian review of police actions is becoming more accepted by the police, although acceptance is still a work in progress. Bayley does not accept the commonly held belief that major changes have taken place in the strategies used by contemporary police agencies; he instead posits that, while community policing is certainly a major focus currently, it is not as widespread or as novel as some suggest.

Current Police Philosophies

Current police philosophies can be organized under three headings: community-oriented policing, problem-oriented policing, and broken windows policing.

Community-oriented Policing

Community policing (or community-oriented policing) is the present ethos in American police work. Over time, as community members discovered that it was impractical to police themselves and that a more professional police force was needed, paid police officials were put in the communities to respond to crime. In the twentieth century, police agencies became even more professional and took as their primary focus the function of order maintenance through crime fighting. In some communities, the more professional police forces seemed to have gained legitimacy, but in others the police seemed too removed from the communities, causing great stress and conflict between the groups. In the 1970s, a new focus came on the scene: It reflected a move away from viewing the police as controlling the community to viewing them as partners with the community to prevent and combat crime.

Community policing, sometimes referred to as community-oriented policing, has a different philosophical and tactical orientation than the traditional crime-fighting model in that it elicits resources in the community in matters involving police policy. A definition of this approach to policing is provided by Friedmann:

> Community policing is a policy and strategy aimed at achieving more effective and efficient crime control, reduced fear of crime, improved quality of life, improved police services and police legitimacy, through a proactive reliance on community resources that seeks to change crime causing conditions. It assumes a need for greater accountability of police, greater public share in decision-making and greater concern for civil rights and liberties. (1992, 4)

Walker and Katz describe the components of community policing: decentralization, deformalization, despecialization, and delayerization. *Decentralization* refers to the attempts by community policing strategies to move decision-making power, both administratively and geographically, to the communities rather than maintaining a centralized police headquarters. *Deformalization* requires a dispensation of formal agency regulations and rules that thwart individual officer creativity and problem solving. *Despecialization* means a return to a generalist rather than a specialist perspective, by which the officers on the beat handle a variety of community problems and concerns. *Delayerization* refers to the "flattening out" of the police hierarchy structure so that there are fewer layers of administration between line officers and managers. This new form of policing was an attempt to rid the profession of the bureaucratic nature of the traditional model of policing (2005, 97).

The movement to a community-based model is often not an easy task for those trained in the traditional model of police work. To make this transition, officers need to develop skills in planning and organizing, problem solving, human relations and communications, and critical thinking. They also need to learn to utilize compassion and empathy in their dealings with the public (Champion and Hooper 2003, 21).

Problem-oriented Policing

Closely connected with the community policing movement is a philosophy known as problem-oriented policing (Goldstein 1990, 2001). The brainchild of police scholar Herman Goldstein, this idea is based on the fact that the police can be proactive through the early analysis of community problems rather than just reactive by responding to problems after they can cause serious damage. Problem-oriented policing is a strategy derived from street-level policing through the administrative structure that has as its primary goal the effectiveness of dealing with the problems discovered in the various areas the police oversee. It involves a close collaboration between police and citizens in an effort to uncover and adequately address problems that plague individual communities.

Beginning with an article in 1979, Goldstein proposed this new type of policing based on "end products" rather than just on police response to crime with little investigation into its causes (Eisenberg and Glasscock 2001). The model stresses that police should be active in identifying the specific problems in their communities, take a substantial role in addressing underlying symptoms of these problems, and enlist the aid of community resources to solve them (Ortmeier 2006, 170).

Perhaps the most salient component of the problem-solving philosophy is the *SARA process:* scanning, analysis, response, and assessment, This process requires officers to initially *scan,* or obtain information about a problem from a number of different sources, such as citizen surveys or community complaints. *Analysis,* the second step, is the intensive examination of the various characteristics of the problem with a consideration for underlying causes. The third stage is the *response* to the problem by the police that involves all available resources. The final phase in the process is *assessment,* in which response to the problem or situation is evaluated to see if the measures taken had the desired effect (Eisenberg and Glasscock 2001).

The problem-solving model gained influence over the next two decades, and many agencies in America adopted the approach; even London found favor with the model (Eisenberg and Glasscock 2001). Because of the growing interest in community policing during the same period, the two models merged, creating a philosophy of policing that had two primary components: a community orientation to crime and a focus on police problem solving (Bichler and Gaines 2005). Although the models both focus on community, the concept of community is somewhat nebulous; specifically, can federal and state policing agencies solve problems utilizing the "community" as a resource, or is this model only for use by municipal or county agencies (Quinet, Nunn, and Kincaid 2003)? In any event, the two models have become very closely related in policing philosophy, despite a slightly different focus.

Broken Windows Policing

Also closely connected to community and problem-oriented policing philosophies is *broken windows* policing. The assumption behind this policing strategy is that communities suffering from social disorder (a concept similar to the "disorganization" borrowed from the early criminologists around the turn of the twentieth century) contribute to high crime rates. Disorder, a natural occurrence in complex urban societies, is manifest in the presence of street prostitution, insistent panhandling, vandalism and graffiti, public drunkenness, and other indicators that a community is not appropriately handling crime. The metaphor of broken windows describes these conditions, which are normally misdemeanor offenses but which can cause fear and anxiety in citizens and lead to more serious problems.

The solution to the high crime rates is therefore to clean up the communities. The police, as key front-end players in the criminal justice system, can significantly reduce crime with an active patrol presence. This proactive strategy emphasizes crime prevention through patrol officers walking their beats, getting to know the small problems in the community (which will eventually lead to bigger problems if not corrected), and being active agents in increasing the quality of life for community residents. The restoration of order is a key element in broken windows policing; thus order maintenance is favored over crime fighting (Kelling and Coles 1996).

One of the by-products of broken windows policing is a model known as *zero tolerance policing,* as practiced in parts of America and in the United Kingdom, which seeks to aggressively enforce laws against the lower-level crimes of disorder such as graffiti, public intoxication, prostitution, and vandalism.

Although the more assertive style of enforcement is given credence by the broken windows philosophy, some suggest that it is merely "an iron fist in an iron glove" and that it only promotes police violence against citizens (Innes 2000).

Obviously, broken windows policing is a close fit with the community-policing and problem-solving policing strategies. All of these measures are proactive and community focused, and they all utilize prevention and order maintenance as ways of controlling crime. The community model is a marked departure from the reactive, centralized, crime-fighting strategies of the earlier professional model of policing.

New Approaches

There are currently a number of potentially valuable changes in the field of policing. In New York, which embraced community policing in 1984 and adopted a bottom-up approach to police management, the situation evolved that younger, inexperienced police officers found themselves in such a position of directing police responses to crime. This problem, as well as problems involving community boundary issues, prompted the nation's largest police department to adopt new procedures. Middle managers became responsible for finding new ways of dealing with crime and other community problems. Some of the goals were:

- Removing guns and drug dealers from the streets
- Effectively dealing with juvenile crime
- Adopting a domestic violence initiative
- Removing offenders and crime from public areas
- Returning ethnical credibility to the force (Champion and Hooper 2003, 448–449)

In addition, Police Commissioner William Bratton developed a program called CompStat in 1994. CompStat (computerized statistics) is an effort to make precinct commanders more responsible for problem-solving strategies to control crime through the use of computer-generated data on crime trends. The four components of CompStat are (1) the collection and review of crime data, (2) the development of strategies, (3) the deployment of available resources, and (4) evaluation. Biweekly meetings of the precinct commanders are held to review the problems and strategies used and to determine future courses of action. Other American cities have adopted similar programs with different names, such as Baltimore's CRIMESTAC (crime tracking and analysis) and Indianapolis's IMAP (integrated management of patrol) programs (Geoghegan 2006). Such an approach involving computer analysis and human problem solving could become a modern philosophy of policing that replaces community policing. Also, the components of the model could serve as an accompaniment to the community policing philosophy. It could, of course, simply be an idea that is used today and discarded tomorrow. Time will tell.

Another approach that is receiving some notice among police practitioners is the use of closed-circuit television cameras (CCTV) to observe the behavior of people in a surveillance area. This video policing effort has been in use in Great Britain since 1961, when cameras were installed in the subway system, but the concern for privacy has caused this system to be rejected in most American cities. However, Los Angeles, Chicago, and Philadelphia have surveillance systems in place. Program evaluations will determine their usefulness in this country (Maroney 2006).

Another potentially beneficial technology in police work involves global positioning system (GPS) devices. These devices track the movement of people, boats, cars, and other mobile objects. The GPS tracking system sends signals to a satellite that identifies geographic positions of people who are wearing monitors that are often attached to the ankle. The system is in use for people on pretrial release, work release, or under probation or parole supervision (Swager 2005). Several jurisdictions also use the device on juvenile offenders. Closely related to the issue of placing surveillance cameras in public areas, this measure involves the potential for societal rejection based on the idea of state-guaranteed privacy.

Intelligence-led Policing: The New Paradigm in Policing?

Although the community policing and problem-oriented policing philosophies comprise the mode of policing predominantly in use, a new model has entered the scene. Unlike the community approaches to policing, which constitute a dramatic change from their predecessor (professional policing), the intelligence-led model of policing employs components and philosophical goals of the community-oriented perspective. Unlike the community-oriented perspective, it emphasizes the use of intelligence to promote its goals.

Intelligence has long been used by military organizations to accomplish its missions, but, in the aftermath of the September 11, 2001 terrorist attacks in America, the idea of using intelligence became a prominent component of police work (United States Bureau of Justice Assistance 2005, vii). The need for intelligence to prevent future terrorist attacks on American soil was the impetus for using intelligence at the street level, but its use was applied to conventional crimes as well. "Intelligence" does not mean simple information; the term refers to information that has been collected and analyzed. Sometimes the information is gathered from and analyzed within the police agency itself, and in other cases the information is gathered from an outside party, then analyzed to determine where police resources may be best utilized.

The idea of using intelligence in law enforcement goes back to the early 1970s. During this period, the Law Enforcement Assistance Administration of the United States Department of Justice promoted the gathering of crime-related information and its dissemination to other agencies in all police agencies in the nation. Due to misuse by intelligence units in some police departments during the decade, a series of practical guidelines for police intelligence was introduced in federal programs and a few state agencies. The International Association of Law Enforcement Intelligence Analysts (IALEIA) was formed in 1980, and initiatives such as the Regional Information Sharing Systems (RISS) Centers and others were instrumental in bringing intelligence into police work (United States Bureau of Justice Assistance 2005, 5). After September 11, 2001, the use of intelligence in policing gained momentum.

At that time in England, a major development was underway with the Kent Constabulary. To combat an increasing problem with property crimes and a corresponding decrease in government criminal justice funding, the British police force began to prioritize police duties and was able to devote time creating and maintaining specialized intelligence units. The duties needing the least professional police response were farmed out to nonsworn personnel. This initiative, known initially as the Kent Policing Model, first used the term "intelligence-led policing," and the idea was adopted by the government in the form of the

United Kingdom's National Intelligence Model (United States Bureau of Justice Assistance 2005, 10).

The intelligence-guided model in the United States, as mentioned, seeks to incorporate intelligence with current community- and problem-based approaches. Criminal justice practitioners using this model differentiate the types of intelligence: *strategic intelligence,* which refers to long-term, broad-based processes; *tactical intelligence,* which refers to activity using intelligence to deal with direct, immediate concerns; *evidential intelligence,* which provides information needed to solve crimes; and *operational intelligence,* which applies long-term investigatory methods to numerous instances of crime in a given category (United States Bureau of Justice Assistance 2005, 3). The intelligence-led philosophy primarily involves gathering tactical intelligence related to criminal activity (including terrorism) and using it to catch offenders, to harden targets, or to prevention crime. The philosophy also uses strategic intelligence, which involves the planning and allocation of resources needed to carry out the mission and to provide all involved people with the information to successfully incorporate the model into crime-related policies (Carter 2005).

The intelligence-led model uses strategically gathered and professionally analyzed information about criminal activity to control and preferably prevent traditional crimes as well as terrorist activity. From its inception, the model has benefited from agencies called fusion centers that gather and share information on specific people, groups, or activities related to crime. These centers have sprung up in at least twenty-five states, with more currently in the planning or developmental stages. Also, several federal organizations are operating fusion centers.

Fully developed intelligence-led agencies have specialists known as intelligence analysts, intelligence officers, and intelligence managers. The personnel who occupy these positions are trained in crime research and criminal justice data analysis, and the agencies provide the resultant information to street-level police practitioners and managers. Although it is not feasible for all police departments to fund professional positions like these, there is a push for policing agencies to adopt information-gathering and dissemination methods as espoused by the model (United States Bureau of Justice Assistance 2005, 9–13). One of the problems that can easily occur is conflict between the professional analysts and the police officers due to difference in information orientation: Whereas the analysts' orientation is data driven, the officers possess an experiential-based knowledge, knowledge required "on the street." These problems can be overcome, however, through the training of both groups and with an emphasis on the benefits of the intelligence-led policing philosophy (Cope 2004).

Cope (2004) describes the five-stage process of intelligence-led policing. The first stage in the process is the acquisition of information by means of a substantial information infrastructure, which provides the police with the ability to obtain, store, and catalog information on crimes and offenders. The second stage is analysis, which converts the raw information to "actionable intelligence" by discovering patterns in the crime data and by connecting events or evidence to potential offenders or groups. Stage three consists of review, in which the information is prioritized to determine the criminal events that should be addressed most immediately. In the next stage, the actioning procedure, the information is acted on; tasking meetings by police administrators determine the actions to be taken, based on the data analyzed. The last stage is the evaluation process, which determines whether the measures taken to deal with the criminal activity are indeed effective. This five-stage intelligence-led process can be linear, simply progressing through the stages, or it can be used as a cycle in which the last stage of evaluation produces information that can be acquired, analyzed, reviewed, and acted on.

Ratcliffe (2005) proposes an alternate process—the 3i model, which posits that there are three factors in the intelligence-led paradigm. The first is *interpretation* of the criminal environment, in which aspects of crime in certain areas are evaluated through the use of a formidable intelligence structure, as well as the appropriate data sources and the means by which to analyze this data. The second is *influence* on decision makers, in which the appropriate people with power to implement change are made aware of the importance and proper use of intelligence in policing. The last stage is *impact* on the criminal environment, in which the tenets of intelligence-led policing create an actual decrease in crime.

Because intelligence-led policing utilizes a number of methods already in use by police agencies (such statistical information gathering, crime mapping, hot spot analysis, and other types of targeted enforcement, forensics, and criminal profiling) and because it is expected to work in tandem with current philosophical perspectives, it is questionable that this can be considered a new paradigm in policing. In other words, the eclectic nature of this approach makes it less easy to identify it as a new model of policing. In fact, its use of professional analysis and a strict division of labor, as well as the specific targeting of certain people (and potentially aggressive enforcement tactics), has some aspects of the professional, or paramilitary, style of policing that was replaced by the community orientations currently in use. The proactive nature of the intelligence-led model, however, distinguishes it from the professional model.

In any event, interest in this perspective appears to be gaining influence with police agencies across the globe, as reflected in the mission statements in police agencies from many countries. In England and Wales, legislation is in effect that requires all police forces to adopt the National Intelligence Model, which supports the policing philosophy. In Australia, all police organizational websites make reference to their intelligence-led or intelligence-driven approach. The police in New Zealand have also adopted the model as a major component of their service.

The fact that the intelligence-led approach is complementary to current models could possibly propel it to the forefront of policing in America. In 2003, the Secretary of the Department of Homeland Security Tom Ridge, in his address to the International Association of Chiefs of Police, acknowledged the National Intelligence Sharing Plan (NCISP), which adopts the intelligence-led philosophy (Ratcliffe 2005, 435–451). Through the efforts of the NCISP, state, local, and tribal police agencies have begun to reexamine their roles and adopt intelligence-oriented programs into their departments (Carter 2005). Such novel programs as CompStat, CRIMESTAC, and IMAP, as well as other programs that use information to drive police action, work well in the intelligence-led framework. Even older, more primitive methods of police work, such as the use of informants to provide information that can be put to use, are part of this philosophy; no technological advancement in policing has yet to supplant this traditional practice (Sheptycki 2000).

The Future of American Policing

There have been many changes in American police ideologies and practice through the years. It is interesting to speculate about potential transformations that will occur in the field over the next generations. The issue of whether or how long community policing will remain the dominant ideology is a key question. Some scholars (Crank 1995) believe that the focus on community policing will dissipate and that there will be a return to the traditional model of policing, while others (Friedmann 1992) believe that the community policing wave has just begun.

Other changes will be on the horizon for the police in America and indeed for police agencies throughout the world. Although it is impossible to forecast the future, one police scholar predicts these changes in American policing by the end of the first decade in this century:

- Technological advancements, including greater use of laptop computers and digital phone technology
- Better computer software, including voice-activated programs
- Improved computerized databases on criminal behavior
- Closed-circuit televisions and interactive video capabilities, especially involving court duties by the police
- Devices with "kill switches" to disable vehicles fleeing the police
- Other technological advancements such as jet backpacks for patrolling in the air, wrist radios, and satellite photography for investigations (Purpura 2001, 318)

A group of police futurists see the following as some of the changes in police work over the next few years:

- A business, rather than a military, model of management
- Customized policing based on the needs of individual communities
- Policing without borders
- Militarily tested advancements, such as satellite-assisted surveillance using global positioning satellites (GPS)
- Digital documentation of all encounters (Stephens 2005, 51–57)

Certainly the technological advancements that will be used by those committing crimes will require offsetting advancements by the police to combat them. It remains to be seen whether community policing will persist into the future or whether it will be replaced by some other policing ideology. It also remains to be seen if international events, such as those relating to terrorism, will cause policing to take on a more global nature. These questions will be answered in the course of time.

Responses by the police to meet these challenges will involve adaptation, and the police will adapt, as they have in the past. Three professional challenges for the police include the provision of effective services in a community policing environment; the ability to maintain a watchful eye over such growing concerns as terrorism, violence, drug abuse, gang activity, and white-collar crimes; and the development of a strong ethos of professional ethics to discourage misconduct (Conser 2000, 496–512).

References

Albanese, Jay. 2005. *Criminal Justice*, 3rd ed. Boston: Allyn and Bacon.

Alpert, Geoffrey P. 1997. "The Management of Police Pursuit Driving: Assessing the Risks." In *Critical Issues in Policing: Contemporary Readings*, 3rd ed. Edited by R. G. Dunham and G. P. Alpert. Long Grove, IL: Waveland Press.

Alpert, Geoffrey P., and Lorie A. Fridell. 1992. *Police Vehicles and Firearms: Instruments of Deadly Force*. Long Grove, IL: Waveland Press.

Barlow, David E., and Melissa Hickman Barlow. 2000. *Police in a Multicultural Society: An American Story*. Long Grove, IL: Waveland Press.

Bayley, David H. 1994. *Police for the Future*. New York: Oxford University Press.

Bayley, David H. 1998. *Policing in America: Assessment and Prospects*. Police Foundation. Available at: http://www.policefoundation.org/pdf/Bayley.pdf. Accessed March 1, 2007.

Bichler, Gisela, and Larry Gaines. 2005. "An Examination of Police Officers' Insights into Problem Identification and Problem Solving." *Crime and Delinquency* 51 (1): 53–74.

Blumberg, Mark. 1997. "Controlling Police Use of Deadly Force: Assessing Two Decades of Progress." In *Critical Issues in Policing: Contemporary Readings*, 3rd ed. Edited by R. G. Dunham and G. P. Alpert. Long Grove, IL: Waveland Press.

Bouza, Anthony V. 1990. *The Police Mystique: An Insider's Look at Cops, Crime and the Criminal Justice System*. New York: Plenum Press.

Carter, David L. 2005. "The Law Enforcement Intelligence Function: State, Local and Tribal Agencies." *Law Enforcement Bulletin* 74 (6): 1.

Champion, D., and Michael K. Hooper. 2003. *Introduction to American Policing.* New York: Glencoe/McGraw-Hill.

Conser, James A., and Gregory D. Russell. 2000. *Law Enforcement in the United States.* Gaithersburg, MD: Aspen Publishers.

Cope, Nina. 2004. "Intelligence Led Policing or Policing Led Intelligence: Integrating Volume Crime Analysis into Policing" *British Journal of Criminology* 44 (2): 188–203.

Crank, John. 1995. "The Community-Policing Movement of the Early Twenty-First Century: What We Learned." In *Crime and Criminal Justice in the Year 2010.* Edited by J. Klofas and S. Stojkovic. Belmont, CA: Wadsworth.

Dantzker, M. L. 2003. *Understanding Today's Police,* 3rd ed. Upper Saddle River, NJ: Prentice Hall.

Delattre, Edwin J. 2002. *Character and Cops: Ethics in Policing,* 4th ed. Washington, DC: AEI Press.

Dulaney, W. Marvin. 1996. *Black Police in America.* Bloomington: Indiana University Press.

Eisenberg, Terry, and Bruce Glasscock. 2001. "Looking Inward with Problem-Oriented Policing." *Law Enforcement Bulletin.* 70 (7): 1–5.

Farmer, Richard E., and Victor A. Kowalewski. 1976. *Law Enforcement and Community Relations.* Reston, VA: Reston.

Federal Bureau of Investigation. 2004. "Law Enforcement Personnel—Crime in the United States 2004." Available at: http://www.fbi.gov/ucr/cius_04/law_enforcement_personnel/index.html. Accessed March 2, 2007.

Friedmann, Robert R. 1992. *Community Policing: Comparative Perspectives and Prospects.* New York: St. Martin's Press.

Geoghegan, Susan. 2006. "CompStat Revolutionizes Contemporary Policing." *Law and Order* 54 (4): 42–48.

Goldstein, Herman. 1977. *Policing a Free Society.* Cambridge, MA: Ballinger Publishing Co.

Goldstein, Herman. 1979. "Improving Policing: A Problem-Oriented Approach." *Crime and Delinquency* 25 (2): 236–258.

Goldstein, Herman. 1990. *Problem-Oriented Policing.* New York: McGraw-Hill.

Hess, Karen M., and Henry M. Wrobleski. 2006. *Police Operations: Theory and Practice,* 4th ed. Belmont, CA: Wadsworth.

Horne, Peter. 1974. *Women in Law Enforcement.* Springfield, IL: Charles C. Thomas.

Innes, Martin. 2000. "An Iron Fist in an Iron Glove? The Zero Tolerance in Policing Debate." *Howard Journal* 38 (4): 397–410.

Johnson, Daniel M., and Rex R. Campbell. 1981. *Black Migration in America: A Social Demographic History*. Durham, NC: Duke University Press.

Kappeler, Victor E., Richard A. Sluder, and Geoffrey P. Alpert. 1998. *Forces of Deviance: Understanding the Dark Side of Policing*. Long Grove, IL: Waveland Press.

Kelling, G. L., and Catherine M. Coles. 1996. *Fixing Broken Windows: Restoring Order and Reducing Crime in Our Communities*. New York: Free Press.

Kelling, G. L., and M. H. Moore. 1991. "From Political Reform to Community: The Evolving Strategy of Police." In *Community Policing: Rhetoric or Reality*. Edited by J. R. Green and S. D. Mastrofski. Westport, CT: Praeger.

Lane, Brian. 2004. *The Encyclopedia of Forensic Science: A Guide to the Science Behind Crime Investigation*, 2nd ed. London: Magpie Books.

Maroney, Al. 2006. "Video Policing." *Law and Order* 54 (4): 66–68.

Martin, Susan E. 1997. "Women Officers on the Move: An Update on Women in Policing." In *Critical Issues in Policing: Contemporary Readings*, 3rd ed. Edited by R. G. Dunham and G. P. Alpert. Long Grove, IL: Waveland Press.

Oldham, Scott. 2005. "The Quest for Less Lethal Systems." *Law and Order* 53 (8): 94–100.

Ortmeier, P. J. 2006. *Introduction to Law Enforcement and Criminal Justice*, 2nd ed. Upper Saddle River, NJ: Prentice Hall.

Peak, Kenneth J. 2005. "African-Americans in Policing." In *Critical Issues in Policing: Contemporary Readings*, 3rd ed. Edited by R. G. Dunham and G. P. Alpert. Long Grove, IL: Waveland Press.

Philbin, Tom. 1996. *Copspeak: The Lingo of Law Enforcement and Crime*. Hoboken, NJ: John Wiley and Sons.

President's Commission on Law Enforcement and the Administration of Justice. 1967. *The Challenge of Crime in a Free Society: A Report*. Washington, DC: U.S. Government Printing Office.

Purpura, Philip. 2000. *Police and Community: Concepts and Cases*. Boston: Allyn and Bacon.

Quinet, Kenna, Samuel Nunn, and Nikki L. Kincaid. 2003. "Training Police: A Case Study of Differential Impacts of Problem-Oriented Police Training." *Police Practice and Research* 4 (3): 263–283.

Radelet, Louis A. 1973. *The Police and the Community*. Beverly Hills, CA: Glencoe Press.

Ratcliffe, Jerry. 2005. "The Effectiveness of Police Intelligence Management: A New Zealand Case Study." *Police Practice and Research* 6 (5): 435–451.

Report on the National Advisory Commission on Civil Disorders. 1968. Available at: http://www.eisenhowerfoundation.org/docs/kerner.pdf. Accessed March 1, 2007.

Richardson, James F. 1974. *Urban Police in the United States*. Port Washington, NY: Kennikat Press.

Saferstein, Richard. 2001. *Criminalistics: An Introduction to Forensic Science*, 7th ed. Upper Saddle River, NJ: Prentice Hall.

Schultz, Dorothy Moses. 1995. *From Social Worker to Crimefighter: Women in United States Municipal Policy*. Westport, CT: Praeger.

Sheptycki, James. 2000. "Editorial Reflections on Surveillance and Intelligence-Led Policing." *Policing and Society* 9 (4): 311–314.

Skolnick, J. H. 1966. *Justice Without Trial: Law Enforcement in Democratic Society*. Hoboken, NJ: John Wiley and Sons.

Standen, David. 2005. "Use of Force Options." *Law and Order* 53 (8): 88–92.

Stephens, Gene. 2005. "Policing the Future: Law Enforcement's New Challenges." *The Futurist* 39 (2): 51–57.

Swager, Brent. 2005. "GPS Monitoring Offenders." *Law and Order* 53 (9): 147–150.

Toch, Hans. 2002. *Stress in Policing*. Washington, DC: American Psychological Association.

United States Bureau of Justice Assistance. 2005. "Intelligence-Led Policing: The New Intelligence Architecture." Available at: http://www.ncjrs.gov/pdffiles1/bja/210681.pdf. Accessed March 1, 2007.

Walker, Samuel. 1979. "The Rise and Fall of the Policewoman's Movement, 1905–1975." In *Law and Order in American History*. Edited by J. M. Hawes. Port Washington, NY: Kennikat Press.

Walker, Samuel, and Charles M. Katz. 2005. *Police in America: An Introduction*, 5th ed. New York: McGraw-Hill.

Wilson, James Q. 1978. *Varieties of Police Behavior: The Management of Law and Order in Eight Communities*. Cambridge, MA: Harvard University Press.

Wrobleski, Henry W., and Karen M. Hess. 2006. *Introduction to Law Enforcement and Criminal Justice*, 8th ed. Belmont, CA: Wadsworth.

3

Worldwide Perspective

International and Comparative Criminal Justice

A comprehensive understanding of the American policing system requires an exploration of international and comparative criminal justice. *International criminal justice* refers to how countries deal with allegations of criminal behavior when the suspected offenders are from other countries and likely possessing different social customs and practices related to criminal justice. International criminal justice also seeks to resolve the conflicts between nations when significant differences exist in matters of social control, prosecution, and corrections.

Comparative criminal justice is the study of basic differences in criminal justice systems in various countries. No two criminal justice systems are the same, and the basic means of dealing with crime are determined by a variety of factors, including religion, traditional beliefs and practices, unique aspects of the country's history, the economic situation, and the nation's political structure.

A good example of international criminal justice analysis came in the highly publicized case of the "caning" of eighteen-year-old American Michael Fay in Singapore. In 1994, the young man was accused of graffiti vandalism of an automobile in Singapore, for which he received a ninety-day jail sentence and twenty-four lashes with a cane. Many in the United States were abhorred by this action because such an offense in America would have probably been punished much more leniently and would have resulted in a warning, restitution payment, or probation (Ebbe 2000,

1). It is also a common practice to require vandals, especially young offenders, to perform community service. Therefore, to many Westerners, the punishment for this particular criminal activity was excessive. The event revealed cultural differences in regard to social control measures.

Although the term "comparative" is used to describe the study of criminal justice in different geopolitical areas, Bayley (1999, 4) prefers the term "international," arguing that all science is comparative and that a better choice of terminology is to use "international" to refer to aspects of the subject under study or "transnational" for the study of activities that cross borders. However, the term "comparative" is commonly used in many disciplines, including criminal justice.

Transnational Crime

Important for adopting a worldwide perspective on policing, *transnational crime*, originally called transboundary criminology, refers to criminal activity that involves more than one county. The United Nations has identified certain acts that fall under this category of crime—internationally organized crime, terrorism, economic offenses, crimes against cultural heritage, and environmental crimes:

- International crimes consist of trafficking in drugs, weapons, industrial secrets, artwork, and human beings. Trafficking in humans is a growing problem and involves transporting people for the purpose of labor, prostitution, pornography, forced marriage, or involuntary military service (Reichel 2002, 43).
- International terrorism, a major concern especially since the September 11, 2001 attacks on the United States, involves terrorist activity in which the initiators conceive of a plan, direct their actions toward, flee to, pursue refuge in, or receive assistance from a nation or nations other than the one in which the acts occur (Reichel 2002, 44–45). In the case of the September 11 attacks, terrorists from a radical fundamentalist group with members in several nations directed acts against the United States.
- Economic crimes, which can benefit either corporations or individuals, are crimes such as transnational bribery;

the "dumping" of unapproved or banned productions on countries; and fraudulent practices with investors, institutions, or governments. Those involved in economic crimes also use the resources of organized crime to orchestrate their criminal acts.

- Crimes against cultural heritage often occur when a country's treasured historical artifacts are illegally obtained and often sold.
- Environmental crimes refer to a host of activities that result in the damaging of a country's ecosystem and include various forms of air, water, and land pollution that can also extend into other bordering countries, especially in the form of ozone depletion and acid rain (Reichel 2002, 43–49).

International Policing

More specifically related to policing, *international policing* encompasses several activities. One is the sharing of information between nations on a particular case involving criminal activity or for the purpose of crime data collection and analysis. In addition, surveillance activities in more than one country constitute a type of international policing. The collaboration of two or more nations in combating transnational crime—e.g., drug production and transport across borders—is another example of international policing. The use of liaison personnel to work between the involved countries is a vital component to this type of policing (Norman 1998, 93).

The Study of International and Comparative Policing

Bayley (1999) describes four important reasons for studying policing from an international or comparative perspective. The first involves the potential for the exploration of other policies and methods that can be beneficial in our own system of policing. Another reason is that a better understanding of how societies control the behavior of citizens gives greater insight into human behavior in general, which can help explain other facets of human reasoning and action. A third is that, from the study of the policing structures of other nations, information is extracted that can be used to inform and promote successful reform where such change is needed. The final benefit to a cross-national analysis of police systems is a better understanding of ourselves in relation to those of other cultures. Therefore, international study supplies not only greater insight into social-psychological aspects of policing and also a blueprint for practical policy change and implementation (Bayley 1999, 3–12).

Studying criminal justice and specifically policing, from both international and comparative perspectives, is important in our changing world. Comparative criminal justice helps us understand which policing measures are effective and which ones are not, provided appropriate research methods are used. Also, in a world that is becoming increasingly connected due to global media, travel, and communications—especially due to the recent concerns related to terrorism—understanding and dealing with the criminal justice systems of other nations in an international context are no longer a luxury for police agencies; they're a necessity.

No single international police agency discharges police duties throughout the world. A small number of organizations exist, however, to assist a group of member nations in matters involving law enforcement and investigation or crime. Interpol, Europol, the United Nations Office on Drugs and Crime, and the Schengen Agreement all represent attempts to create an international or regional policing framework.

Interpol

The agency Interpol, which is a shortened version of its true name—International Criminal Police Organization—is the largest organization with a global policing function. It does not provide direct police services, but it assists in the investigation of criminal activity by facilitating the exchange of information among its 184 member nations. Interpol adheres to measures that ensure respect for the cultural differences among its members (Norman 1998, 96). Interpol, headquartered in France, is the largest law enforcement organization in the world. Its member nations enjoy facilitation and coordination of police services, as well as the cooperation of policing agencies around the world.

The agency's precursor, the International Criminal Police Commission (ICPC), was formed in 1923 and headquartered in

Vienna, Austria. This agency was disbanded in 1945 but was reestablished and stationed in Paris in 1946 by five pioneer police officers. In 1956, the organization became known as the International Criminal Police Organization, later shortened to Interpol and a constitution was established.

Interpol's three major functions are (1) facilitating police communication throughout the world, (2) providing data access regarding criminal activity on an international basis, and (3) supplying field support services for policing organizations. The agency has established a global police communication system called the I-24/7 program that links the agency's General Secretariat in France to the member nations' National Central Bureaus (NCBs). Information on people suspected of terrorist involvement, perpetrators of child sexual abuse, and items determined to have been stolen are provided to the NSBs through a number of databases. Other information available through the database includes crime trend data and training in criminal justice methodology.

A unit whose function is to provide public safety against threats to individuals and nations, such as bioterrorism, aviation and maritime crime, and weapons of mass destruction, is also operated by the organization. The agency operates an antiterrorist unit, called the Fusion Task Force, that coordinates and distributes information on suspected terrorist actions. In addition, another unit, called the Command and Coordination Center (CCC), investigates fugitive activity, terrorism, organized crime, drug trafficking, financial crimes, and crimes involving advanced technology. In case of a terrorist attack or natural disaster, the CCC works in conjunction with the agency's Crisis Support Group to assist in rescue and victim identification tasks. In addition to involvement with these crimes, termed "priority crimes," Interpol also provides NCB support for nonpriority crimes such as genocide, war crimes, human rights violations, environmental crime, and police corruption (Interpol 2006).

Europol

Based in The Hague, Netherlands, Europol is a law enforcement organization for the nations in the European Union, similar to Interpol, but it is operated on a regional basis. It is a clearinghouse for information on matters involving criminal activity and terrorism, and it focuses on investigating organized crime syndicates.

The organization was formed during the Maastricht Treaty in 1992 and began operations on a limited basis in 1994. The new agency was known as the Europol Drugs Unit because the original mission was to combat drugs. In 1999, Europol became fully operational, and in 2002 it expanded its reach into matters of international crime.

Europol's mandate consists of supporting the member states in matters concerning drug trafficking, illegal immigration rings, terrorist activity, forgery and counterfeiting, human trafficking, vehicle trafficking, cyber crime, and other types of financial and organized crime. The agency operates a computerized system that allows the flow of information on matters of criminal interest to member nations as well as indexing and providing an analysis of the data (Europol 2006). As with Interpol, Europol does not have a single police agency with police powers but operates a system to facilitate cooperation and coordination among the contributing nations (Reichel 2002, 181).

United Nations Office on Drugs and Crime

The United Nations also has a program that deals with policing in an international format. The United Nations Office on Drugs and Crime (UNODC), previously known as the United Nations Office for Drug Control and Crime Prevention (UNODCCP), is the arm of the United Nations that is mandated with combating illicit drugs, terrorism, and other criminal activity. Vienna, Austria, is the headquarters of the program, and there are twenty-one field offices around the world, including a liaison office in New York. Approximately five hundred countries are affiliated with the international agency. The member nations create drug control policies that are responsive to their individual needs.

The United Nations, which supports many international programs to alleviate social suffering, created the Office on Drugs and Crime to facilitate coordination and to create a balanced approach to drug control and the resulting criminal activity. Toward that end, it enacts policies that prevent the production and trafficking of drugs and supports programs that aid in the prevention of drug use and the treatment for those who are addicted.

The UNODC has three major goals: (1) research and analysis of substance abuse issues; (2) the promotion of treaties and legislation to thwart drug activity, crime, and terrorism; and (3) cooperation among member nations through field-based drug enforcement projects.

The UNODC has a Global Program for Trafficking in Human Beings to stem the rapidly growing problems of trafficking in people for use in prostitution, slave labor, and the sex industry. The agency's Global Program against Transnational Crime provides member nations information, data, training, and strategies to fight organized transnational crime. A program aimed at suppressing corruption in governments and political organizations, the Global Program against Corruption assists members by implementing watchdog strategies. To combat the growing concerns over terrorism, the agency's Global Program against Terrorism assists members in enacting legislative policies designed to prevent and suppress terrorist activity. In addition, the Legal Advisory Program provides member states assistance in creating legal and structural components for antidrug, antiterrorism, and antiorganized crime programs (United Nations 2006).

Schengen Agreement

Another attempt at transnational cooperation for crime prevention and control is the Amsterdam Treaty, often called the Schengen Agreement after the city in Luxembourg where the treaty was signed. In 1985, the European nations of Belgium, France, Germany, Luxembourg, and the Netherlands entered into an agreement that allowed for external, rather than internal, border checks of people moving about the member nations. It provided a series of rules governing transport between these nations and stipulated the legal functions of the police regarding the movement of people across borders. It also created a system of extradition that promoted better cooperation among member countries on matters of extradition of offenders who cross borders and their subsequent prosecution. The cornerstone of the agreement, however, is the computerized system of crime data exchange that allows member nations greater control over the information than was possible through Interpol. The only members of the European Union that are not part of the Schengen Agreement are the United Kingdom and Ireland, who maintain their own border control systems. Nations other than those in the European Union, such as Norway and Iceland, are currently also linked to the agreement, which is now part of the legal and structural system of the Union (Reichel 2002, 182–183).

Policing Systems in Other Countries

Australia

Australia has a history of military-style policing beginning with the earliest force of marines that arrived from England in 1788 and that were sent to control the population of inmates transported to the island to serve their sentences. The early marine force begrudgingly adopted the police role and subsequently committed a number of acts of misconduct. They were replaced in 1795 by the Rum Corps, so named for their role in the illegal smuggling of alcohol. Police in this penal colony were exconvicts themselves who imposed heavy punitive control over the population. This country, with its vast frontier and convict inhabitants, mostly consisting of transported British and Irish inmates (Swanton, Hannigan, and Biles 1989, 11), experienced an increase in crime in the nineteenth century when gold was discovered. A more professional police force was formed in the mid-nineteenth century; however, conflicts between the police and community were common, especially in reference to labor strikes and corruption related to the enforcement of vice laws (Prenzler and Sarre 2002, 59).

Most of Australia's current police are federal forces. The Australian Federal Force is charged with the enforcement of federal laws such as certain types of fraud and drug trafficking, as well as contracting out standard police services to other jurisdictions in the Commonwealth (Prenzler and Sarre 2002, 53). A major feature of policing in the nation is the practice of single police departments' providing services to both urban and rural areas. Recruits normally begin their employment in the metropolitan regions and, as they gain experience, move to the rural sections of the country (Swanton, Hannigan, and Biles 1989, 13).

The early forms of policing in the country involved a large number of diverse duties, many of these (e.g., inspection of slaughterhouses, collection of various statistics, registering births) were outside of what one normally considers police duties. There has been a recent shift toward more specialized duties; however, the police on patrol normally tend to matters that will not result in criminal prosecution—a duty normally reserved for investigators. Private security agencies are popular in Australia, as well as the privatization of many service-related functions, causing concern for some that the country might institute a system of privatized police; this is probably an unfounded concern because basic law enforcement duties will likely remain with the public agencies (Prenzler and Sarre, 2002, 53–58).

Australia has traditionally used crime prevention methods in policing; however, the official response to crime until recently has been one primarily of crime fighting. Since the late 1980s, a number of specific crime prevention techniques have been in place, but the focus has been on the community dealing with problems related to crime. Standard police–community collaborations, such as a variety of "watch" programs and target-hardening initiatives, make up much of Australia's prevention programs (Cameron and Laycock 2002, 319–322).

Police commissioners, who individually determine their agency's command structures, head the state and territorial police agencies. In Australia, there is a marked distinction in status between commissioned officers, who are appointed by their state or territorial executive councils, and the noncommissioned officers, who are selected by the police commissioners (Swanton, Hannigan, and Biles 1989, 14).

Due to Australia's size, there are numerous police departments throughout the country with as few as one officer in rural areas to numerous officers in the metropolitan forces. This is similar to the variations in force sizes in the United States. In addition, the duties of officers in the small agencies encompass many activities. Australia's police forces are unique in that they are only state-based or terrority-based and single departments are often responsible for policing in both rural and urban areas. Communication is often poor between patrol officers and detectives, and this causes discontinuities in investigating crime. Relative to other nations, Australia's command structure has a smaller number of administrative and managerial levels—this creates a veteran crew of police managers but little incentive for lower-level officers to advance in the profession (Swanton, Hannigan, and Biles 1989, 13–15).

Australian police have had some problems in recent years regarding reports of misconduct (Reichel 2002, 177). In 1996, the federal police force was the focus of numerous allegations of serious misbehavior, such as corruption, drug trafficking, and child pornography, that resulted in incidents of insider whistle blowing and investigative committees.

Canada

Canada's present system of policing is highly decentralized with three levels of law enforcement—federal, provincial, and municipal—that are controlled by administrative structures at each level. Most people are familiar with the Royal Canadian Mounties, the federal force that is often compared to America's Federal Bureau of Investigation, but a number of other agencies exist in the country (Reichel 2002, 165–174).

Canada's early police forces mirrored those of Britain; constables provided police duties and were initially appointed by magistrates and later by police boards. After the Dominion of Canada was established (1867), a national police agency, the Dominion Police Force, was created to protect government buildings and to combat counterfeiting. A paramilitary styled police agency, known as the North-West Mounted Police, was formed to control the criminal activities of people on the frontier. This police agency merged with the Dominion Police Force in 1920 and became known as the Royal Canadian Mounted Police, the most famed of all Canadian forces (Terrill 2003, 123–124). The Mounties, as they are commonly called, have maintained close relationships with the Federal Bureau of Investigation in the United States due to the large number of people who flee to Canada to avoid capture and prosecution (Kurian 1989a, 51).

In Canada, police in the provincial and municipal areas may create their own forces or enter into a contract with the Royal Canadian Mounted Police. This unique format differs markedly from the shared governance between the state and municipalities in England and the fragmented system in the United States (Terrill 2003, 125).

At the top of the police hierarchy is the Solicitor General of Canada, who is a cabinet member of Parliament and a person who yields considerable power over the federal criminal justice agencies. This position provides direct supervision over the Canadian Security Intelligence Service, which is responsible for national security and the Royal Canadian Mounted Police, the sole national policing agency in the country. Most of the provinces have contracts with the Mounted Police; only Ontario and Quebec have their own provincial forces, which are headed by commissioners. Of the six hundred municipal police departments in the country, two hundred contract with the national agency while the others are independent; these forces have recently banded together to create regional forces to control costs and to become more efficient (Terrill 2003, 125–130).

While all police officers in Canada start out as uniformed patrol officers, as in the United States and England, recruitment and training standards are different among the national, provincial, and local agencies. Courses for technical training and management are offered in various academies, including regional programs (Terrill 2003, 134–135). New recruits are assigned to departments throughout the country except for the Northwest, where assignment is voluntary (Kurian 1989a, 56).

Canadian police have embraced a community-focused crime prevention model of policing. Local police mini stations and foot patrols are being increasingly used in the country. Special efforts are being made to deal with some of the police–community conflicts, especially those involving the nation's minority aboriginal people; community forums, youth summer programs, suicide prevention programs, and police recruitment programs are being used to reach out to this population (Terrill 2003, 127–133).

Perhaps the unique feature of Canada's police is the contract system. Eight of the country's ten provinces contract with the Mounties and, borne of a need to monitor governmental expenditures, it has proven to be a cost-effective system. Under the contracting system, local agencies spend a reasonable fee to the federal government, and in turn receive a highly organized force that has proven to be effective in controlling Canada's crime (Reichel 2002, 172–173).

China

China has a written history of almost 4,000 years, making it one of the world's oldest civilizations. It has a long history of autocratic rule and has been under a communist political and economic structure since 1949; from that time until 1978, China adopted an isolationist stance. In recent years, however, the country's potential to be a major force in world affairs has become evident (Terrill 2003, 549–551). Its unique past and culture have influenced China's system of social control.

The country's civil war (1945–1949), fought by the Nationalist Party (the Kuomintang) and the Chinese Communist Party, resulted in a regimented form of policing. These two groups were given the task of policing the nation during this struggle: Public security forces policed the base areas; the militia groups were responsible for the Communist-controlled border areas; and the People's Liberation Army (the military arm of the Communist government) was also used to maintain control. The Communists won the war and took control in 1949. A few years of instability gave way to a relatively calm period (regarding crime control) from the mid-1950s to the mid-1960s. When the Cultural Revolution took place from 1966 to 1976, ruler Mao Zedong encouraged a group of young activists called the Red Guard to engage in cultural and political revolution. The activists attacked the police and their headquarters, and the People's Liberation Army used their military might to maintain order. Upon Mao's death in 1976, Deng Xiaoping became the country's new ruler. Xiaoping took steps to modernize the county through interactions with the West. He also instituted modern police practices and made the police more accountable to the public. A viable police force was needed during this period due to changes in the economic structure that caused an increase in crime rates.

Current Chinese policing is defined by its three distinct elements: the Party Line, the Mass Line, and the Prevention Line. The Party Line, with its roots in both Confucianism and Communist Party tradition, emphasizes a system of policing based on moral and ethical behavior and the responsibility of police as providing a role model. The Mass Line is consistent with the Party philosophy and positions the police on an egalitarian level with citizens; this reflects the Communist desire for a classless society. The Prevention Line stresses the police role as one of crime prevention with a high level of community involvement.

Tanner (2005, 171–172) describes a controversial style of policing in China known as campaign-style policing. This involves a fixed-term targeting of special types of crimes, along with aggressive and punitive enforcement of these crimes. The campaign style results in rapid arrests of large numbers of offenders, followed by swift and severe legal sanctions. Due to the large amount of citizen involvement in this type of law enforcement, the Mass Line form of policing characterizes campaign-style policing.

The police structure in China is divided into five administrative organizations: (1) public security, (2) state security, (3) the judicial police serving the people's courts, (4) the judicial police serving the procurator, and (5) the police serving the country's prisons. A minister of public security, who oversees the administrative and operational divisions of a large force that provides patrol duties, investigations, security, traffic duties, specialized duties, and fire control, also heads the public security force. The state security police primarily combat governmental crimes such as espionage, conspiracy, and sabotage. The judicial police are security agents for the courts, serving papers and carrying out legal orders, including those involving the death penalty. The police of the prisons are correctional officers serving in the nation's prisons (Terrill 2003, 571–577).

Despite the fact that the country has historically enjoyed a fairly close relationship between the police and the public, China has never been known for its professional police forces (Terrill 2003, 580–585). In recent years, China has worked to improve the professionalism of the police. Numerous colleges offer coursework in the field of policing, and academies provide in-service training to recruits and officers. The police have adopted strategies to control the rising crime rates, traffic accidents, and increasing drug-related problems.

Controlling behavior informally is part of the Chinese culture, and local committees at the neighborhood, work, and school levels are formed to meet this end, in collaboration with the police (Terrill 2003, 571). Police departments in China currently have close ties to the community because community involvement is believed to be crucial to police success (Dai 2001, 156). A number of crime prevention measures involving citizens are being used in the country, such as neighbor watch programs, community newsletters, and "target hardening" strategies intended to make criminal activity more difficult. However, due to the rising crime problem since 1978, police are using more patrolling strategies, more punitive measures to control crime, increased efforts to thwart gang activity, and an overall more aggressive stance since the informal means of controlling crime appear to be inadequate for a changing nation (Lu and Miethe 2001, 109–111). The recent economic expansion experienced by China has contributed to the erosion of national traditions and has promoted a more professional and scientific type of police structure (Wong 2003, 223).

England

The influence of British policing, especially the professional police model of the 1829 Metropolitan Police as developed by

Robert Peel (see Chapter 1), had a major impact on policing throughout the world and is still in evidence in England today.

The top official in the British police hierarchy is the Home Secretary (also known by the longer title of Secretary of State for the Home Office), who is also a member of Parliament, acting in the capacity of a cabinet member of the prime minister. This position has many salient powers, including administrative input on matters of police management, monetary funding, and the formation of police standards throughout the nation's police departments. Under the Home Secretary are the chief constables and their assistants for the forty-one provinces; the chief police officials for the Metropolitan Police and City of London are given the title of commissioner. Another level of authority is vested in what are known as police authorities, a group of seventeen members consisting of politicians, lower court judges, and others appointed by the Home Secretary, who serves in an advisory capacity to the police forces. There are other organizations in the English police system, such as inspectors (who assess the effectiveness of the different agencies), a complaints authority (to investigate charges of police misconduct), and an intelligence service. Also, three associations represent the police on personnel issues; however, police officers in England cannot join unions, as is a common practice in America (Terrill 2003, 15–22).

Recruits all begin at the rank of constable and are able to advance to positions in administration and investigation by completing training and educational courses. There is a police college at Bramshill with a curriculum in police management, and several scholarships exist for officers desiring to attend the country's institutions of higher education (Terrill 2003, 24–25). It is imperative that officers are educated adequately in police work because all officers are required to justify their behavior or acts of omission (Lamford 1989, 406).

Crime prevention has continued to occupy a major focus in England, and strategies have been promulgated to achieve this end. All police forces have specialized crime prevention officers and a training academy exclusively designed for crime prevention. Also, officers practice proactive focused policing in high crime areas, especially when accompanied by neighborhood watch programs in which citizens take responsibility for monitoring their communities. Another strategy is the long-term assignment of beat constables to particular areas (Terrill 2003, 27).

Maintaining social control is important in England, as in all countries. The British forces do not emphasize the use of deadly force and still choose to rely on verbal and nonverbal language to contain potentially serious situations (McKenzie 1998, 67–71). This is in contrast to many of the world's police agencies, which resort to physical force to maintain order.

Officers in England, especially the urban police, suffer from feelings of alienation from the citizens they serve, although these perceptions are not entirely correct; many citizens see the police in a favorable light (Terrill 2003, 28–29). Greater criticism of the police comes from racial and ethnic minorities, and consequently programs have been created to bridge the gap between the police and the public, especially young minority group members.

France

The first police force in the nation was created in Paris in the tenth century. Following a model by the Romans, the position of Provost of Paris was established to use military forces, as well as watchmen and patrols, to enforce legal conditions. It was not until the seventeenth century, however, that a professional, national police was organized. The forces, which were headed by a position known as the Lieutenant General, were not only focused on law enforcement but also on other quality-of-life issues, such as fire control and street cleaning. To keep tabs on the citizenry, the police used a complex spy network. The Lieutenant Generals were not only the nation's chief law enforcement agents, they were also magistrates. After the revolution in 1791, the National Guard, which would later be called the National Gendarmerie, was formed. The Lieutenant General system was modified, and the chief law enforcement officers of the ninety-six counties became known as prefects who, unlike their predecessors, did not serve as magistrates. In 1854, a detective force called the Surete, with both uniformed and nonuniformed officers, was formed, and in 1966 the Surete merged with the Police of Paris to create the National Police (Terrill 2003, 211).

The present French system of policing is a national system with two primary forces: the National Police and the gendarmerie. The National Police force is the largest and is headed by the Ministry of the Interior, who has full oversight responsibility of the agency. The Director General is accountable for organizing and coordinating police field services. The chief law enforcement officer of the counties is the prefect who is directly in charge of local operations (Terrill 2003, 213–214).

The National Gendarmerie is the military police for the country's army, naval, and air force services, as well as the police agents assigned to law enforcement duties in small towns with populations fewer than 10,000 (Terrill 2003, 217–219). The gendarmerie falls under the Ministry of Defense, which is headed by an army general, called the Inspector General. This police agency is considered to be an elite police force, primarily due to their military training.

There are also a small number of municipal police in France. In an effort by former President François Mitterand, some forces have been created that are responsible to the city mayors. These officers have the authority only to provide patrol duties and cannot investigate crimes or make arrests; these duties must be performed by the National Police or the National Gendarmerie (Terrill 2003, 211–219).

French police focus on both proactive and reactive measures to control crime (Terrill 2003, 226–227). A recent push has been to the proactive type through the use of increased beat patrols, business security programs, and a program called tranquility vacations in which greater patrol and observation are given to residences during the summer months when people are on vacation.

The French police have a national system that varies distinctly from other Western systems, especially the American system, which has a highly decentralized structure. The police in France have strong historical connections to the judiciary and are often viewed by the public as having court functions (Terrill 2003, 220).

In recent decades the police in France have had to deal with rising crime rates, volatile group uprisings, juvenile delinquency, and a growing fear of terrorist activity. The police suffered from poor perceptions by the citizens, and relations between them have historically been strained. As a result, police administrators have taken measures involving police recruitment and professional training to enhance the appeal of the police to the citizens. The police culture is similar to the political culture in France in that there is an enduring love of freedom from oppression and at the same time a belief that police power is absolute (Terrill 2003, 220–228).

India

India is a densely populated area whose inhabitants speak eighteen different languages, as well as a number of regionally specific dialects (Raghavan and Sankar 2003, 114). The diverse and crowded nature of the country presents unique challenges for those in the criminal justice field. The functions of the Indian police are maintaining internal security, preserving order, social control, defense, social welfare, and enforcing laws through prevention and the effective prosecution of offenders (Diaz 1989, 172).

In early times, India used a version of the watch program in the rural areas in which a few watchmen, under the supervision of a village headman, maintained vigilant observation over their communities. This system, which was in place during the seventeenth century when the East India Company ruled the area, even had a provision to pay possible invaders a fee in an effort to prevent crime. Attempts were made to change the village policing scheme that was such a traditional part of rural Indian life, but the results were highly unsatisfactory and the former structure was resumed with minor modifications (Raghavan and Sankar 2003, 117–118).

The early professional police forces were modeled after the Royal Irish Constabulary in the mid-1800s after Charles Napier conquered the area. The Indian Police Act of 1861 provided a state-based police organized on a military structure. When India became independent in 1947 and organized itself as a republic in 1950, it primarily left the British structure in place (Diaz 1989, 171).

The twenty-five states in India have police departments that are headed by Directors General and supported by their deputies and inspectors. The states are divided into districts that are headed by administrators called Collectors. On a local level, police departments are supervised by Station House Officers (Raghavan and Sankar 2003, 114).

The crime rate in India has grown considerably in recent years, becoming a major concern for the nation's police and citizens. Given India's long history of community involvement in its efforts at social control, some rural communities still use a village-policing system called Village Defense Parties. Citizen committees, crime awareness and prevention programs, neighborhood watch programs, motorcycle patrol, and the use of the police beat system (in which officers use foot patrol on beats and extensively interact with citizens) are all initiatives toward crime prevention and community policing. A special challenge for India is religious-based conflict and the resulting violence, especially between the area's Hindu and Muslim population; efforts like the formation of citizen groups called the Mohalla Communities keep the police informed of developing tensions so that violence can be prevented (Raghavan and Sankar 2003, 123).

Due to the nation's increasing industrialization and commerce, India has increased its use of private security policing around residential neighborhoods. It has adopted other measures such as closed-circuit television in malls and hotels, along with security enhancement to prevent and investigate crimes (Raghavan and Sankar 2003, 126).

Ireland

Ireland has been an area of much internal conflict, and the role of the police as social control agents has obviously been affected by the national strife. The Irish police as a professional entity date back to 1822, when provincial police departments were formed in the country's northern, southern, western, and middle sections. These unarmed forces merged as the Irish Constabulary in 1836, the same year the Dublin Metropolitan Police was founded. The Irish Constabulary was renamed the Royal Irish Constabulary in 1867. These two police agencies were consolidated into the Garda Siochana (Guardians of the Peace) in 1922 when Ireland became an independent nation (Kurian 1989b, 190). Prior to the establishment of the Garda Siochana, Ireland's police structure was similar to the other police systems in the United Kingdom (O'Mahony 2000, 33).

The Garda Siochana constitutes the major police agency in Ireland and is the national police force. There are a number of specialized bureaus and units within the national agency, such the National Bureau of Criminal Investigation, National Drug Unit, National Crime Prevention Unit, and the National Bureau of Fraud Investigation. In addition to the Garda Siochana, there are also small, specialized local police agencies that possess limited authority and power such as the airport and harbor police (O'Mahony 2000, 39).

The national police agency is headed by a commissioner who reports to the minister of justice, who in turn has direct supervision over the police activities (O'Mahony 2000, 39) and who is assisted by a number of deputies and other assistants (Kurian 1989b, 190). The agency's philosophy is that control of citizen behavior is possible through noncoercive means; the police force is for the most part unarmed and until recent years has been effective in operating in this manner. Rapidly changing social conditions that have created increased criminal activity have caused some vigilante groups to assume the enforcement role of the police and have created strain between police and citizens, especially in the inner cities of the country (O'Mahony 2000, 39).

The national police have instituted a number of strategies to deal with drug abuse and other conditions that have contributed to disorganization in Ireland's cities. The establishment of a police–community liaison to deal with disgruntled citizens who take the law into their own hands has been a recent strategy. Internal problems involving employment conditions and complaints of maltreatment of citizens in the 1990s have created a challenge for the agency to repair public perception of the police (O'Mahony 2000, 39–41).

Israel

Israel is policed by the Israeli National Police (INP), a highly centralized state agency that came into being in 1948 when the country won its independence from England (Haberfeld and Herzog 2000, 60). Prior to that, the country was policed by the Palestine police force, operating under the Police Ordinance of 1926. The legal regulations of Israel are derivatives of British law, Ottoman law, and religious law (Kurian 1989c, 192).

As a national force, the police are centralized in a national headquarters governed by the office of the Ministry of Police. The highest authority is the inspector general, who reports directly to the ministry and who is normally a seasoned veteran in the field of police work. The national force is divided into three units with distinct responsibilities:

1. The patrol and training division is responsible for patrol duties and all training programs for the police.
2. The investigative division handles criminal activity not dealt with by the patrol and training unit.
3. The administrative section oversees personnel issues, communication, facilities and property, and supplies (Kurian 1989c, 192).

The INP was developed from the model of the British colonial police, which was a highly regulated, military-style force. This force further adopted a structure with an authoritarian style, forced discipline, stringent control over officer discretion, and a recognized distance between administrative and line staff. The headquarters of the state agency is presently located in Jerusalem and organized into six districts and thirteen subdistricts, comprised of nearly seventy police departments (Haberfeld and Herzog 2000, 60).

One of the benefits of having a national agency is that the force can respond very rapidly to situations that threaten national security. This is important in an area of the world with a history of international conflict, including terrorist attacks. Units specializing in internal security, antiterrorism, bomb response, border control, and special patrol police the state in an attempt to address the concerns over potential disturbance from other nations or governments. While this system has been effective in this mission, the rapid mobilization of the police in such a military fashion also has the unintended consequence of depleting certain areas of police resources when such an alarm is raised and officers are deployed to other areas (Haberfeld and Herzog 2000, 61).

The state police are fairly advanced in their use of technological innovation and compare favorably in this area to the nations in the West. Video motion-detection devices, traffic stop cameras, laptop-equipped patrol units, an automated fingerprint database, and DNA technology are all used by the Israeli police (Haberfeld and Herzog 2000, 64). The criminal identification division operates a number of laboratories that specialize in ballistics, forensic medicine, fingerprint analysis, document analysis, interrogation, and many other areas (Kurian 1989c, 194).

Since 1994, the INP has adopted community-oriented policing strategies (Haberfeld and Herzog 2000, 62). That year, a police unit called the Community Policing Unit (CPU) was established to institute community policing in the nation. The CPU trains its officers in community policing techniques and models and in crime prevention strategies, and it assists with program assessment. The CPU has instituted mini police stations in less populated neighborhoods and service centers in larger stations that provide many police services in one location. Allegations of officer brutality in Israel has prompted police administration to take action in recent years, such as the formation of commissions investigating police misconduct, to improve the stature of the local police, which has been worsened by media portrayal.

Japan

The police in Japan enjoy a lower crime rate than many other nations (Terrill 2003, 387). This has changed since 1991, however, as crime has increased somewhat. Of special concern is the rise of crimes of violence, which are more and more the result of organized crime in the country, and crimes involving illicit drugs. Even though the crime rate is growing, it is still relatively low and not a concern as in other areas.

Cultural aspects have an effect on national crime and the response to it. The Japanese have a tendency to define delinquency not as evil but as a condition in which individuals break from the culturally valued constraints of conformity. Therefore the response to crime is often less punitive than in many other nations (Terrill 2003, 373–375). The police are an integral part of the overall criminal justice system in Japan and have a unique policing style.

The Japanese model of policing has evolved through the years in a similar fashion to that of police systems in Europe, alternating between centralized and decentralized forms of administration (Terrill 2003, 377–381). The current system is based on the Police Law of 1954, although it has gone through other modifications since that time and maintains a very centralized focus through the establishment of a National Police Agency. Although it has a centralized agency, individual police forces, called prefectures, are scattered throughout the nation.

The bureaucratic structure of the National Police Agency consists of the Prime Minister at the top, who supervises the National Public Safety Commission, a group of six appointed members who serve five-year terms. This agency is given the administrative responsibilities of law enforcement budgetary oversight, police operations and training, traffic control, crime and offender data, and national disasters (Terrill 2003, 382–385).

The next level in the administrative structure is occupied by the National Police Agency, which directly supervises the prefectural forces located throughout the country as well as the National Institute of Police Science, the National Police Academy, and the Imperial Guard. The national agency is headed by a commissioner general and divided into five bureaus that oversee the administrative, investigative, traffic, and general law enforcement functions of the organization. In addition, district offices coordinate training and communications functions in different regions of the country.

The prefectural police comprise the next level and maintain some level of autonomy over the geographic areas they serve. The head of the prefecture is a governor, although a public safety commissioner who reports directly to the governor provides direct oversight of the prefecture. The exception to this structure is the Metropolitan Police Force of Tokyo, which is supervised by a superintendent general, along with directors who supervise different units.

An interesting feature of the Japanese system is the use of small mini police stations in the prefectures (Terrill 2003, 392). The mini units, called *koban* are operated by a few officers on rotating shifts. Some rural areas have only one-officer units and are referred to as *chuzaisho*. The citizens who work in concert with them in crime prevention programs view the officers in these small police offices in a positive manner.

Japanese police carry weapons but only while on active duty; at all other times the weapons are stored at the police office. The rate of firearms use by officers is very low compared to the United States, and the preferred method of controlling offenders is through the use of nonlethal technology. Also low in relation to their American counterparts is Japanese police misconduct, including the use of excessive force. However, the Japanese police have been under scrutiny by human rights groups for instituting harsh law enforcement measures, particularly involving warrantless arrests and overly aggressive interrogation tactics of suspects, who are often denied the right to counsel until after indictment. Also, the police are allowed to hold suspects for questioning for up to twenty-three days and can hold them longer if additional charges are brought. Opponents of these measures complain that police are given additional time to work on extracting confessions rather than on pursuing other avenues of investigation (Terrill 2003, 387–390).

Mexico

Mexico has long been perceived as possessing one of the world's most corrupt police forces with the levels of corruption pervading the ranks. A major challenge of the nation has been to counter this perception and to make the police more accountable and professional (Reichel 2002, 73).

In its organizational structure, the Mexican police organization has federal, state, and municipal systems, with overlapping jurisdictional levels (Kurian 1989d, 258). The federal system has as its primary agency the Federal Judicial Police (Policia Judicial Federal) that has single departments in the larger cities and regional officers for the rural areas. A director who supervises the commanders of the thirty-one states heads the Federal Judicial Police.

The state agencies operate in a variety of different structures, but a common organizational form has state police agencies divided into the State Judicial Police (Policia Judicial Estatal) and the Public Safety Police. The preventative police department, a division of the Public Safety Police, has two subdivisions: the transit police, who handle traffic-related crimes and traffic control, and the metropolitan police, who deal with crime control and the investigation of both minor and major crimes. The investigation of major offenses by the metropolitan police is then turned over to the State Judicial Police director (Reichel 2002, 174–176).

Combating drug trafficking has been an ongoing challenge for Mexican authorities. In addition to conventional enforcement strategies, the nation has adopted a holistic approach involving a crime prevention component that deals not only with the crime of drug trafficking but also with the sociological, psychological, medical, toxicological, fiscal, and other related issues. The community is involved through campaigns and others efforts to educate the citizens on the danger of drugs and to direct the activities of youth to more prosocial activities (Talboado 2003, 195–206).

As noted earlier, many of the police forces in Mexico have gained notoriety for corruption, brutality, and criminal activity in recent years. In 2000, the country's then newly elected president vowed to institute changes in the country's police through the restructuring of departments and breaking of political ties in order to professionalize the nation's police (Reichel 2002, 176).

There have been recently instituted reforms at the federal level. One is the 2001 establishment under the presidency of Vicente Fox of a new national investigative unit called the Agencia Federal de Investigaciones (Federal Agency of Investigation), which replaces the corrupt Policia Judicial Federal (Federal Judicial Police), Another is the creation of the Policia Federal Preventiva (Federal Preventative Police) in 1999 under President Ernesto

Zedillo, which assumes the control of crime throughout the country. Finally, the Secretaria de Seguridad Publica del Distrito Federal (Secretariat of Public Security of the Federal District) is charged with controlling crime in Mexico City, an area that has the nation's highest crime rate (Reames 2003, 2).

Russia

In 1917, Russia embarked on an attempt to establish a communist society, but by the late 1980s citizen dissatisfaction with the earlier Soviet form of government culminated in the dissolution of the system in 1991. Russia is now highly industrialized, although technologically it stills lags behind other nations. It is a nation rich in natural resources and inhabited by a people loyal to their country (Terrill 2003, 441–443). With a long history of citizen repression, Russian has experienced an evolving system of policing.

Russia has a long history of violently oppressive police forces. Under the leadership of Ivan the Terrible, a force known as the Oprichnina was formed around the mid-sixteenth century that was well-known for its terrorist activities. Other rulers maintained similarly distinctive police forces, and by 1917 the police agency known as Cheka used executions to promote the cause of the new Communist Party; the Cheka was disbanded in 1922. A state police force known as the Committee for State Security (better known to Westerners as the KGB) was formed by Communist Party leaders in 1954. The agency used espionage, subversion, and terrorism to promote communist ideology across the globe. The agency was disbanded in 1991 when the Soviet Union collapsed and the new Russian Federation was founded (Terrill 2003, 457–464).

Another police force used in Russia during the Soviet years was the militia. This group provided law enforcement and order maintenance for the new government and also performed investigations, intervened in economic and technical crime, monitored citizen movement, and provided driver education. When the Soviet Union was disbanded, the militia groups remained and a new focus on controlling street crime was instituted (Terrill 2003, 464–467).

Another type of police in Soviet Russia consisted of ancillary forces of volunteer citizens whose purpose was to protect property, defend the nation, and maintain stability. Workers, farmers, and young people often volunteered for this service but interest waned for this program even before the dismantling (Terrill 2003, 467–468).

The oppressive strategies of the police under the Soviet Union have changed under the new regime, though understandably citizens remain skeptical of the police. A large number of officers were dismissed from employment in the 1980s due to a massive exposure of police corruption that resulted in a campaign for restructuring. High crime rates, economic problems, and a changing police force will determine how effective Russia can maintain order under its new government.

Sweden

Sweden has traditionally had a devotion to social welfare programs, and this emphasis on a nationalized system is reflected in its police structure. Its historical emphasis has been on neutrality in military matters, which has allowed time to focus on domestic issues (Terrill 2003, 287–289). Therefore, much time and effort have been given to instituting crime prevention practices and to social work methods in its police forces.

The policing system in Sweden prior to the mid-nineteenth century was similar to those of many other European nations— characterized by disorganization and decentralization (Terrill 2003, 300–303). Watchmen, constables, firefighters, and military forces served municipalities at various times. This changed as the century progressed and officers were responsible for investigating and prosecuting minor offenses. Specialized units were formed and professionalism among the ranks became a priority. It wasn't until 1965 that the idea of nationalizing the police, which had already been considered for decades, became a reality.

The Ministry of Justice is at the top of the police hierarchy in Sweden and is part of the national cabinet. The person occupying the justice minister position is a civilian with much power over basic police administration. The primary unit that governs direct police policy is the National Police Board, which includes a committee headed by a commissioner, a deputy, and eight members. Also, specialized forces have a host of functions including drug traffic enforcement, corruption investigation, forensic investigation, and international crime control. Counties separate the twenty-one local police districts, but the National Police Board is responsible for police functions in them (Terrill 2003, 303–305).

Historically, Sweden has been a long-time proponent of crime prevention in policing. Beat patrol officers have been used since 1959, and neighborhood police stations, used in many towns, have proven to be successful. Other local programs and legislation as well have provided evidence of a local crime prevention program: for example, a six-hour temporary detention for anyone considered an immediate danger to the public; an Operation Identification system using a number given to each citizen at birth; and random roadside sobriety checks, in effect in Sweden for a number of years. Since 1996, Sweden has instituted a national program for crime prevention, recognizing that the government is ultimately responsible for crime control, that the underlying cause of crime must be addressed, that a local approach to crime control is the most effective, and that citizens must also be involved in crime prevention. The social police reflect an attempt by police agencies to mix social work aspects with police work, especially with juvenile offenders (Terrill 2003, 308–313).

On a national level, Sweden became involved in a crime prevention program in 1996 with four core values:

1. The government has the ultimate responsibility for crime prevention.
2. Crime policy should include measures that explore the social problems leading to crime.
3. Attempts to attack criminogenic factors should be used at the local level.
4. Strategies to prevent crime should include citizen involvement (Terrill 2003, 312).

An Overview of World Policing Systems

As the previous review of world policing systems shows, there is a marked difference in the ways that nations carry out the functions and duties of the police. An understanding of these variations, especially in relation to the American system, is important. A review of these differences can benefit students of the criminal justice system, particularly students of policing.

The United States has more separate police forces than any other nation in the world. It is such a highly fragmented and decentralized system that even counting the number of individual forces is problematic. The Federal Bureau of Investigation lists the number of municipal police personnel at around 580,749 (with approximately 451,737 sworn officers) and sheriffs' departments personnel at around 330,274 (with approximately 174,251 sworn officers). The FBI also lists the number of federal officers with police powers as approximately 106,354 (Bureau of Statistics 2006). However, it is obvious that determining the exact number of agencies (including federal, state, county, city, private security, campus, and a host of specialized forces) is a very difficult task.

Harper (2005) notes that counting the various police forces is a demanding and frustrating endeavor, commenting that, if a business is likewise unable to count all of its departments, it will surely fail. The American system has federal, state, county, and municipal agencies and a large number of specialty forces that often overlap by geographic jurisdiction (e.g., municipalities are located in counties, counties are located in states, states are located in the nation), and this overlap routinely causes conflict in the areas of police law enforcement and investigation. The complex arrangement in American policing has been described by Lab and Das (2003) as "easily the most extreme case of a decentralized multiple uncoordinated system" (171). Thus, although this fragmented system is the case in the United States, it varies greatly from those in other countries.

If the United States is an extreme example of decentralization of its police agencies, many other countries are examples of a centralized system. Whereas Mexico's decentralized police structure resembles that of America to some degree, the structures of the French and Swedish forces are highly decentralized. Many nations have a national police in addition to other police forces, but most do not have the overlapping levels of authority characteristic of the United States system.

Every nation has a political and social history that has affected the structure of its police force. Revolutions, wars, invasions, and changes in political and economic organization have produced systems of social control that have evolved as needed. Also, cultural aspects reveal changes in police structure. In the United States, the so-called rugged individualism and fear of excessive government intrusion among the citizenry are certainly at least partially responsible for the nation's unique system of separate and disjointed agencies. In addition, the division of labor that is so highly valued in America puts the onus of social control on the police, bestowing responsibility on this specialized profession. This is in contrast to the systems of many nations (notably Asian countries) that value social cohesion and possess a desire to assist in the social control of individuals rather than to leave the responsibility to a group of people whose occupation is to control deviant behavior.

As nations industrialize, crime rates tend to rise and create new challenges for the police. And, as the world becomes more of a global community and countries become more aware of the activities of others, police forces may tend to become similar. It is also likely that criminal patterns will also become more similar. By taking new ideas and adapting them to fit into a nation's cultural identity and other factors, police systems throughout the world can possibly become more effective in controlling crime.

References

Bayley, David. 1999. "The World Stage." In *Policing Across the World: Issues for the Twenty-first Century.* Edited by R. I. Mawby. London: University College London Press.

Bureau of Justice Statistics. 2006. Available at http://www.ojp.usdoj.gov/bjs. Accessed March 2, 2007.

Cameron, Margaret, and Gloria Laycock. 2002. "Crime Prevention in Australia." In *The Cambridge Handbook of Australian Criminology.* Edited by Adam Grayear and Peter Grabosky. Cambridge: Cambridge University Press.

Dai, Yisheng. 2001. "New Directions in Chinese Policing in the Reform Era." In *Crime and Social Control in a Changing China.* Edited by Jianhong Lui, Lening Zhang, and Steven Messner. Westport, CT: Greenwood Press.

Diaz, S. M. 1989. "India." In *World Encyclopedia of Police Forces and Penal Systems.* Edited by George Thomas Kurian. New York: Facts on File.

Ebbe, Obi N. Ignatius. 1996 (2000). "The Purpose of Comparative and International Criminal Justice Systems." In *Comparative and International Criminal Justice Systems: Policing, Judiciary, and Corrections.* Edited by O. N. I. Ebbe. Boston: Butterworth-Heinemann.

Europol. 2006. "Fact Sheet on Europol." Available at: http://www
.europol.eu.int/index.asp?page=facts. Accessed March 2, 2007.

Haberfeld, Maria, and Sergio Herzog. 2000. "The Criminal Justice System in Israel." In *Comparative and International Criminal Justice Systems: Policing, Judiciary, and Corrections*. Edited by O. N. I. Ebbe. Boston: Butterworth-Heinemann.

Harper, Hill. 2005. "Counting Police Agencies Is Hard to Do." Paper presented at the annual meeting of the Criminal Justice Association of Georgia, Savannah, Georgia.

Interpol. 2006. "About Interpol." Available at: http://www.interpol
.int./public/icpo/default.asp. Accessed March 2, 2007.

Kurian, George Thomas. 1989a. "Canada." In *World Encyclopedia of Police Forces and Penal Systems*. Edited by George Thomas Kurian. New York: Facts on File.

Kurian, George Thomas. 1989b. "Ireland." In *World Encyclopedia of Police Forces and Penal Systems*. Edited by George Thomas Kurian. New York: Facts on File.

Kurian, George Thomas. 1989c. "Israel." In *World Encyclopedia of Police Forces and Penal Systems*. Edited by George Thomas Kurian. New York: Facts on File.

Kurian, George Thomas. 1989d. "Mexico." In *World Encyclopedia of Police Forces and Penal Systems*. Edited by George Thomas Kurian. New York: Facts on File.

Lab, Steven P., and Dilip K. Das, eds. 2003. *International Perspectives on Community Policing and Crime Prevention*. Upper Saddle River, NJ: Prentice Hall.

Lamford, T. G. 1989. "United Kingdom." In *World Encyclopedia of Police Forces and Penal Systems*. Edited by George Thomas Kurian. New York: Facts on File.

Lu, Hong, and Terance E. Miethe. 2001. "Community Integration and the Effectiveness of Social Control." In *Crime and Social Control in a Changing China*. Edited by Jianhong Lui, Lening Zhang, and Steven F. Messner. Westport, CT: Greenwood Press.

McKenzie, Ian K. 1998. "Policing in England and Wales." In *Law, Power, and Justice in England and Wales*. Edited by I. McKenzie. Westport, CT: Praeger.

Norman, Paul. 1998. "The European Dimension." In *Law, Power and Justice in England and Wales*. Edited by I. McKenzie. Westport, CT: Praeger.

O'Mahoney, Paul Douglas. 2000. "The Criminal Justice System in Ireland." In *Comparative and International Criminal Justice Systems*.

Prenzler, Tim, and Rick Sarre. 2002. "The Policing Complex." In *The Cambridge Handbook of Australian Criminology*. Edited by Adam Grayear and Peter Grabosky. Cambridge: Cambridge University Press.

Raghavan, R. K., and A. Shiva Sankar. 2003. "A Community Policing Approach to Crime Prevention: The Case of India." In *International Perspectives on Community Policing and Crime Prevention*s. Edited by Steven P. Lab and Dilip K. Das. Upper Saddle River, NJ: Prentice Hall.

Reames, Benjamin. 2003. "Police Forces in Mexico: A Profile." Center for U.S. Mexican Studies. Available at: http://www.repositories.cdlib.org/usmex/prajm/reames. Accessed April 16, 2007.

Reichel, Phillip L. 2002. *Comparative Criminal Justice Systems: A Topical Approach*, 3rd ed. Upper Saddle River, NJ: Prentice Hall.

Smith, Ken. 1979. *Australia*. New York: Mayflower Books.

Swanton, Bruce, Garry Hannigan, and David Biles. 1989. "Australia." In *World Encyclopedia of Police Forces and Penal Systems*. Edited by George Thomas Kurian. New York: Facts on File.

Talboado, Walter Beller. 2003. "Crime Prevention Policies and Civic Morals in Mexico." In *International Perspectives on Community Policing and Crime Prevention*. Edited by Steven P. Lab and Dilip K. Das. Upper Saddle River, NJ: Prentice Hall.

Tanner, Murray Scott. 2005. "Campaign-style Policing in China and Its Critics." In *Crime, Punishment, and Policing in China*. Edited by Borge Bakken. Lanham, MD: Rowman and Littlefield.

Terrill, Richard J. 2003. *World Criminal Justice Systems: A Survey*, 5th ed. Cincinnati, OH: Anderson Publishing Co.

United Nations Office on Drugs and Crime. 2006. News page. Available at: http://www.unodc.org. Accessed March 2, 2007.

U.S. Bureau of Justice. 2006. "Bureau of Justice Statistics." Available at: http://www.ojp.usdoj.gov/bjs/. Accessed March 2, 2007.

Wong, Kam. 2003. "Crime Prevention in China: A Community Policing Approach." In *International Perspectives on Community Policing and Crime Prevention*. Edited by Steven P. Lab and Dilip K. Das. Upper Saddle River, NJ: Prentice Hall.

4

Chronology

This chapter provides a chronology of the major events that have influenced policing practices in America. It shows the evolution of ideas and associated law enforcement measures that have emerged in an effort to control crime. Although much of this information is presented elsewhere in the book, especially in Chapter 1, a chronology provides the sequential context for these events.

1780 BCE In Babylonia, the codified laws of King Hammurabi define criminal violations and punishments. The laws, which are preserved in basalt, are based on *lex talionis,* the idea that punishment for crime should be retaliation in kind; for example, if person steals, his hand might be cut off, or if she lies, her tongue might be taken out. The regulations in the code number almost three hundred, and the penalty of death is reserved for twenty-five of them.

1350 BCE Pharoah Hur Moheb creates a police force in Egypt to safeguard water transportation on the Nile River.

450 BCE The Roman Twelve Tables are implemented, codifying criminal, civil, and religious laws. Originally ten tables, the codes classify certain activities as crime (e.g., murder, theft, and sorcery) and stipulate punishments, such as crucifixion, burning, beating, and drowning. The two other tables that are added offer additional

450 BCE (*cont.*)	crimes and punishments. The tables, made of brass, are placed on the walls of the Temple of Jupiter for public viewing.
27 BCE	The Praetorian Guard (the privileged corps) and the Urban Cohort are created in Rome by Augustus. These early forms of police are, in essence, military organizations charged with guarding the emperor's palace and maintaining order.
14 BCE	Emperor Augustus creates the Vigiles (watchmen of the city), a group of officials whose job is to control fires and to maintain order in the cities. They are formed due to the ruler's concerns of destructive fires and the criminal activity occurring in Rome. They later become responsible for making arrests, capturing escaped slaves, and guarding the public baths.
529 CE	The Justinian Code is completed. In Rome, Emperor Justinian desires to create a less complicated system of laws than those in place. He commissions scholars to make a simpler code, which is later expanded to include two additional legal works.
700s	The frankpledge system is begun in England and France. Also known as the tithing system, this plan makes teams of community citizens and families responsible for observing criminal behavior and apprehending violators.
865	In France, a special security force of marshals is formed to enforce the law. They are the forerunners of the Gendarmerie.
1066	The Norman Conquest occurs in England. Government officials are used to carry out the wishes of the king to collect taxes, assemble armed forces, and control crime. Constables and shire reeves supplement the frankpledge system. Shire reeves (later known as sheriffs) have great power, and judges travel throughout the county holding trials. (Counties [shires] had been in existence at least since the Anglo Saxon period.)

1215   King John signs the Magna Carta in England. This document is created under pressure, in an effort to avoid a rebellion by people growing tired of the king's excessive control over their lives. It takes much legal power away from the king and creates the rule of law. The document establishes many provisions that eventually find their way into American law, such as the right to due process, the right to trial by jury, the right to a speedy trial, and limitations on punishment.

1285   The Statute of Winchester in England provides for the watch and ward system of day and night watches by citizens in walled cities. It also places more power in the hands of the constables. Initially a position of prestige, the constable loses much status over time as less and less competent people fill the position.

1300s   At midcentury, the Justice of the Peace position is added to the criminal justice system in England. Originally conceived as an assistant to the shire reeve, the Justice of the Peace eventually becomes a supervisor of both the shire reeve and the constable. The constables' duties evolve into supervision of the watch and ward system, serving warrants, and apprehending offenders.

1631   The first night watch in America is formed in Boston on April 12. This primitive method of controlling deviant behavior requires volunteers to observe suspicious activity and report it to authorities. The citizen volunteers are required to perform the service or pay a fine for noncompliance; many of the community members elect to pay fines rather than perform the duty.

1658   The first paid watch system is begun in New Amsterdam (later renamed New York).

1700s   Some states in the southern United States, specifically South Carolina, Virginia, and North Carolina, enact slave patrol legislation that seeks to legally control the activity of slaves and to prevent escapes and uprisings. The slave patrols that are established as a result of the legislation have law enforcement responsibilities

1700s (*cont.*)	including investigating traveling persons, interrupting slave meetings, and searching slave quarters.
1750s	Henry Fielding, a magistrate in London, establishes the group that will become known as the Bow Street Runners in London. This group, also known as the Bow Street Flyers or the Bow Street Flying Squad, is often considered the world's first professional detective force. Upon Henry's death, the group comes under the control of his half brother John.
1767	The first organized vigilante movement in the United States is formed in South Carolina; the group eventually becomes known as the South Carolina Regulators.
1785	The first American police commissioners are appointed in Boston.
1789	The first federal law enforcement agency, the United States marshals, is created by an Act of Congress, and appointments are made by George Washington. The marshals' duties include the service of legal papers to carry out the directives of legal and political authorities, but not traditional police duties.
1797	Patrick Colquhoun's *Treatise on the Police of the Metropolis* is published. The book influences Robert Peel in his establishment of the London Metropolitan Police.
1829	The United States Postal Service is created. This is the first federal agency granted law enforcement authority, charged with policing crimes involving the mail service.
	The London Metropolitan Police, the world's first modern police agency, is established by Sir Robert Peel in his Metropolitan Police Act. This new style of policing, based on Peel's principles of policing, is duplicated in other nations, most notably the United States.

1832   François Vidocq becomes the director of the French detective agency known as the Surete.

1835   In America, the Texas Rangers are formed. While many consider this group to be the first state law enforcement agency, Texas is still a territory of Mexico at this time.

1844   New York City becomes the first American city to combine its day and night watch programs. This new structure is based on Robert Peel's Metropolitan Police model.

1845   All of the New York City Police Department's precinct stations are connected by telegraph.

1850   Henry Wells and William Fargo establish the American Express Company to protect freight services from theft. Their shotgun riders on the trains become part of the American landscape.

1851   The vigilante group known as the San Francisco Committee of Vigilance is formed in California to control the crime and corruption that developed in the area as a result of the gold rush. It also attempts to control the activities of newly arriving immigrant groups. The Vigilance Committee is responsible for several lynchings and other acts of violence. The 1851 committee disbanded after one year, came back into existence in 1856, and disbanded again in the same year when its members were officially elected to office.

1855   Allan Pinkerton founds the Pinkerton Detective Agency as a private security company to protect railroads. Pinkerton goes on to achieve fame not only as a lawman but also a writer.

1856   The New York City police department becomes the first modern American police force to require its officers to wear uniforms.

1860s   Police departments in several major American cities briefly come under state control during the early to mid-1860s.

1865   The United States Secret Service is created. The initial function of this agency is the investigation of counterfeiting crimes. It is later charged with protecting the president of the United States and other political figures.

1866   New York Mayor William "Boss" Tweed gains political control of New York City and begins a period of pervasive governmental corruption. Police misconduct becomes commonplace during this time. The era ends when Tweed is incarcerated in 1871.

1867   Police telegraph call boxes go into use in New York City.

1870   The Standing Committee of the National Prison Association endorses a crime prevention and social work approach for the police rather than an order maintenance or law enforcement orientation. The crime prevention/social work approach changes dramatically in the next century with the development of police professionalism.

1878   The Posse Comitatus Act is passed, placing limits on the power of the government to use armed forces in law enforcement.

    The first telephone system is established in Washington, D.C.

1880s   The new technique of identification by fingerprinting is developed by a number of people at nearly the same time.

1881   The Chicago Police Department installs the first police telephone booths.

1883   The Pendleton Civil Service Reform Act, which created civil service, is passed. This act ends the spoils system, which allowed political figures to appoint friends and others to federal government positions based on personal and political ties rather than on qualifications and merit.

        In France, Alphonse Bertillon identifies his first repeat offender through the use of his system of identifying criminals by using body measurements begun in the late 1870s; this method is called the Bertillon method.

1886   The Haymarket Riots occur in Chicago. The riots are started over labor tensions and result in a bomb killing an officer and others at the scene.

1887   The Bertillon system of anthropometric identification, which used body measurements to identify offenders, is implemented by the New York City Police Department.

1891   The Immigration and Naturalization Service (INS) is founded as part of the federal Justice Department. It is the department's first bureau dealing with law enforcement matters and is charged with enforcing laws governing the admission, deportation, and naturalization of non–United States citizens.

1893   The National Chiefs of Police union is formed to allow police administrators around the nation to meet and discuss innovations in the field. The name changes to the International Association of Chiefs of Police (IACP) in 1903.

1895   Theodore Roosevelt becomes the police commissioner of New York City. He institutes many innovations such as a bicycle patrol, a telephonic communications program, a recruit training program, and merit pay. Roosevelt also works to make the system less corrupt during his three years in office.

1898	The National Bureau of Criminal Identification is opened in Chicago. This office uses the Bertillon method to track criminal offenders.

1900s   Telephotography comes into use in several police departments, permitting the transmission of photographs between departments.

1905   The Pennsylvania State Constabulary is created. Although other states have already begun experimenting with state policing systems, the constabulary is unique and fairly comprehensive. The unit has a mounted force and substations scattered throughout the state. Other states follow this model.

1908   The Bureau of Investigation (later renamed the Federal Bureau of Investigation) is formed during the presidential administration of Theodore Roosevelt. The agency has jurisdiction over more than two hundred categories of federal offenses, including kidnapping, embezzlement, bank fraud, civil rights violations, drug charges, and others. The agency is also charged with providing investigation services, particularly crime lab and psychological services, to requesting agencies.

The first formal police training academy is created in Berkeley, California, under the leadership of August Vollmer.

Lola Greene Baldwin is hired by the police department in Portland, Oregon, one of the nation's first female police officers.

1910   Alice Stebbins Wells is hired by the Los Angeles Police Department, becoming the nation's first full-time, salaried female officer. Her appointment paves the way for female officers in other cities, although their roles are initially very limited.

1912   Isabella Goodwin becomes the first female detective. She is employed by the Los Angeles Police Department, and her duties consist of investigating crimes involving juveniles and women.

A series of silent comedy movies by the Keystone Company depict police officers as bumbling idiots. The Keystone Kop movies continue for a few years, and the name comes to represent incompetence in police work for generations.

1914   The Berkeley Police Department (California) becomes the first American police department to have all officers supplied with police cars.

1915   The Fraternal Order of Police is created in Pittsburgh by two police officers. The organization is generally received well and not specifically viewed as a labor threat by police administrators.

1916   The University of California at Berkeley becomes the home of the first university-level police training school.

1919   The Boston Police Strike takes place after nineteen police officers are fired due to their membership in a union calling itself the Boston Social Club. Over a thousand officers strike in protest over the dismissals. The state militia is called in to quell the chaos after days of rioting, and new officers are hired to replace the dismissed police. The officers take the case to court but the dismissals are upheld. Legislation is passed in Massachusetts that prohibit people in public service from striking, and several other states follow.

1921   The polygraph (also known as the lie detector) is first used in law enforcement in Berkeley, California. This was a project of August Vollmer.

1922   August Vollmer becomes president of the International Association of Chiefs of Police.

1923   The International Criminal Police Organization (Interpol) is created to facilitate the exchange of information

1923 (*cont.*)	among member nations regarding criminal activity across international borders.
1924	J. Edgar Hoover becomes the long-term director of the Bureau of Investigation, later named the Federal Bureau of Investigation (FBI). He institutes major technological innovations and takes an aggressive crime-fighting stance that gains the agency respect worldwide. His methods come into question during the latter part of his leadership as violations of constitutional rights are raised. Hoover serves as agency director until 1972.
1926	The first radio system is used in police cars in the Berkeley Police Department (California). This system was one-way, however; officers could only receive communication from dispatch.
1927	The United States Custom Service becomes a federal bureau. The agency has been in existence for many years before becoming a bureau and is charged with investigating crimes involving the illegal transport of contraband across U.S. borders.
1929	Eliot Ness becomes the leader of a group of federal law enforcement agents who become known as the Untouchables. They create great interest in federal law enforcement, becoming immortalized in books, movies, and television in later years.
	The Pennsylvania State Police become the first agency to use a statewide teletypewriter system.
1931	The Wickersham Crime Commission (formally known as the National Commission on Law Observance and Enforcement) releases its report of the investigative unit created by President Herbert Hoover in 1929. The report states that police corruption and brutality, especially regarding the use of the "third degree," pervade United States police departments. The report also provides guidelines for police administrators, technological advancement, and record

keeping, recommending crime prevention units in police departments and the proliferation of state police agencies. Despite some resistance, the report establishes a foundation for police reform.

1932   The Uniform Crime Reports (UCR), a project of the International Association of Police Chiefs, is put into place. The program is formulated to gather statistical information on crime from local police agencies. In addition, the FBI opens its Latent Fingerprint Section and a crime laboratory for examining ballistic evident.

1933   The Bayonne Police Department (New Jersey) initiates a two-way police communications system.

The first baccalaureate program in criminology is offered at the University of California at Berkeley.

1935   The National Police Academy is opened by the U.S. Justice Department. This center provides police administrators with prestigious and highly sought-after training by FBI agents.

The FBI opens the National Training Academy to provide training for state, city, and county law enforcement officials.

The first baccalaureate program in police administration is started at Michigan State College.

1950   The Kefauver Commission (officially named the Senate Special Committee to Investigate Organized Crime in Interstate Commerce) reports the prevalence of organized crime and exposes widespread corruption, especially in the form of bribe acceptance, among police officers.

William Parker becomes the Chief of Police of the Los Angeles Police Department. He is credited with reorganizing the department by forming a highly professional police force with a paramilitary structure. Later

1950
(*cont.*)
many suggest that his techniques are responsible for the chasm between the LAPD and inner-city residents, manifested in the riots that erupt in the 1960s. He remains at the helm until 1966.

Police Administration by O. W. Wilson is published. This book becomes the standard text for students of police management.

1955
The police–community relations movement begins. This movement to improve the image of the police comes about as a response to citizen criticisms of police organizations and certain administrators.

1961
Mapp v. Ohio establishes the exclusionary rule, which provides police with guidelines for making reasonable searches.

1964
Many demonstrations erupt over the Vietnam War, sometimes causing violent conflict between the protesters and the police. The protests continue into the early 1970s. Tensions begin to grow between protesters and the police, who are seen by many Americans as using excessive levels of force.

1965
A race riot in the Watts area of Los Angeles results in thirty-six deaths and nearly nine hundred injuries. The violence soon spreads to San Francisco, with six deaths and two hundred injured there. A chasm between the predominantly minority citizens and primarily white police officers widens as riots continue. The perception of a double standard of treatment by the police fuels the growing conflict.

President Lyndon B. Johnson declares a war on crime and appoints the President's Commission on Law Enforcement and Administration of Justice.

1966
Miranda v. Arizona establishes safeguards to protect citizens against self-incrimination when being questioned by police. This decision results in the well-known Miranda rights that officers recite to suspects.

1967   The National Crime Information Center (NCIC), operated by the FBI, becomes operational. The center
provides information on criminals and criminal behavior in the following categories: wanted persons,
stolen firearms, stolen vehicles, stolen license plates,
and other identifiable stolen items. By the end of the
year, the agency processes approximately two million
transactions.

Race riots occur in one hundred and fifty cities in the
United States. Many of the riots occur in inner-city
minority communities, and pressure mounts for
politicians and police administrators to find a peace-
ful solution in the midst of racial strife between officers and citizens.

The Challenge of Crime in a Free Society, the report of the
President's Commission on Law Enforcement and Administration of Justice, is published. This report focuses on the crime problem, the protests of the era,
and police conduct. It is the first report to identify the
criminal justice establishment as a system, comprised
of law enforcement, the courts, and corrections. It recommends that these interrelated parts should function
as a cohesive single unit and that more police–
community partnerships should be set up.

1968   *Terry v. Ohio* establishes the guidelines for the police's
stop-and-frisk searches, which allow officers to con-
duct a cursory pat-down search of people to determine if weapons are present.

The death of Martin Luther King, Jr. results in riots
and protests in nearly one hundred and seventy cities
in the United States. Many minority groups, including the Black Panther Party, begin to believe that Dr.
King's philosophy of nonviolence is unproductive
and that the police will continue to act violently and
unfairly against them if they take a posture of nonviolence. These groups decide to take up arms and defend themselves against what they consider racist
and corrupt activity by the police.

1968
(*cont.*)

The National Democratic Convention in Chicago erupts in demonstrations and major violence. The televised event, which results in hundreds of injuries including physical harm to nearly two hundred police officers, is called a police riot by some writers.

The Kerner Commission (also known as the National Advisory Center on Civil Disorders) conducts an examination of riotous activity. The commission is established due to the high level of civil unrest of the period, especially regarding racial matters.

The Law Enforcement Assistance Administration is created by Congress to fulfill the mandate of the Omnibus Crime Control and Safe Streets Act of 1968 (often referred to as the Safe Streets Act or the Crime Control Act) by providing financial assistance to criminal justice agencies.

1970

Four students are killed at Kent State University in Ohio by National Guard soldiers who were brought in to quell demonstrations on the campus. This event reignites controversy regarding the role of social control agents in containing citizen demonstrations through force.

The Federal Law Enforcement Training Center (FLETC) is opened in Washington, D.C., to provide training to all federal law enforcement officers except the FBI. The center is relocated to Glynco, Georgia, in 1975.

1972

The Bureau of Alcohol, Tobacco, and Firearms (ATF) is formed as a federal bureau charged with enforcing laws dealing with illicit alcohol and tobacco manufacturing, distribution, or sale and illegal firearms activity.

The Knapp Commission (established by New York City Mayor John Lindsay) produces its report detailing the prevalent abuse of power by police officers of the New York Police Department. The Commission is prompted by NYPD officer Frank Serpico's allegations of police corruption.

1973   The Drug Enforcement Agency (DEA) is created and becomes the primary federal agency responsible for combating the burgeoning drug problem in the United States. It is charged with the investigation and enforcement of drug laws nationally and internationally.

Two hundred and sixty-eight law enforcement officers are killed, making this the single deadliest year for the police in recorded history.

1979   In Atlanta, twenty-nine young African Americans are murdered between 1979 and 1981. Fear and racial conflict grip the city, and the police are confounded by the elusiveness of the subject. Wayne Williams is arrested and subsequently sentenced to life imprisonment for two of the murders.

1980s   New police initiatives involving community policing, problem-oriented policing, and zero-tolerance policing are implemented on a large scale throughout the nation's cities.

DNA testing, a new extension of forensic science, becomes a major new tool for detectives, ushering in a new age of criminal investigation.

1982   *Broken Windows* is published. Written by James Q. Wilson and George Kelling, this book describes the theory by the same name positing that socially disorganized communities invite crime through the visible manifestations of condemned houses, abandoned automobiles, homeless people, overt prostitution, and other things that suggest that the residents are unconcerned with controlling crime. The authors recommend that police officers should aggressively deal with nuisance-type crime in order to prevent major crimes from occurring. The work is highly influential and police departments throughout the nation adopt a broken windows model of preventive policing.

1990s
An alarming number of school shootings occur in several states, including Washington, Alaska, Mississippi, Kentucky, Arkansas, Pennsylvania, Tennessee, Oregon, Virginia, Georgia, New Mexico, and Oklahoma. The highest-profile event happens at Columbine High School in Littleton, Colorado, where two students go on a shooting rampage and kill thirteen people before killing themselves. This sets the stage for debates on juvenile access to handguns and bullying in schools.

1991
Motorist Rodney King is beaten by officers of the Los Angeles Police Department. The event is recorded on film by an observer and turned over to a local television station. Four of the officers are indicted for police brutality.

1992
The four indicted police officers in the Rodney King incident go to court and are found not guilty. Riots begin and last for five days, resulting in over forty deaths and over two thousand injuries. The rioting spreads to other cities in the United States.

1993
Two of the four officers in the Rodney King beating are convicted in federal court for civil rights violations and sentenced to thirty months' incarceration.

A compound at Waco, Texas, is burned after a standoff between members of the Branch Davidian religious cult and federal officers. The exact cause of the fire in the compound is under speculation. Approximately eighty people are believed to be killed in the incident.

1994
The Murrah Federal Building in Oklahoma City is bombed by Timothy McVeigh and Terry Nichols, resulting in one hundred and sixty-nine deaths and over eight hundred injured. This event, the deadliest terrorist action on American soil until the September 11, 2001, attacks, occurs exactly one year after the Waco, Texas, incident. McVeigh is executed in 2001.

The Violent Crime Control and Law Enforcement Act is passed. This act establishes the Police Corps program, provides funding opportunities for community policing initiatives, increases penalties for a number of criminal offenses, strengthens antiterrorism policy, and provides changes in the treatment of police officers engaged in corrupt activities.

1996   A bomb explodes during the 1996 Olympic Games in Atlanta. Eric Rudolph, who has been placed on the FBI's most wanted list, remains a fugitive until 2003. He is found that year by a police officer in North Carolina and is found guilty in 2005, when he is sentenced to life in prison.

2001   On September 11, nineteen terrorists, members of a group known as Al Qaeda, hijack three commercial airplanes. The planes are then flown into two key targets that symbolize America's financial and military institutions: the World Trade Center in New York City and the Pentagon in Washington, D.C. A third plane, probably intended to strike a target that represents America's governmental institution—the White House—crashes into a field in Pennsylvania after passengers on the plane manage to thwart the terrorists on board. Nearly three thousand people lose their lives in the attacks. Many New York City police officers and other emergency personnel lose their lives or experience injury in attempting to rescue survivors from the World Trade Center. The attacks start the American War on Terrorism, which brings about major changes in policing policy, expands the need for knowledge of comparative policing, and requires local and state police agencies to become engaged in terrorism preparedness.

In October, Congress creates the USA Patriot Act in response to the September 11 attacks. The Patriot Act provides greater ability to intercept communications information to federal officers, gives regulatory powers to combat violations of federal financial law, and attempts to thwart terrorist activity and remove terrorists

2001
(*cont.*)

from the country. The Act becomes controversial, with some critics claiming that the provisions are not adequate to deter terrorism and others claiming that it allows federal officials to commit civil rights violations.

2002

The Homeland Security Act of 2002 is created on September 20, establishing the Department of Homeland Security. The executive department has a mission to prevent terrorist attacks in the country, make the county less vulnerable to terrorist attacks, and lessen the damage created by such an attack if it occurs and assist in recovery efforts. The new department is created to establish a single agency whose sole responsibility is the protection of citizens from terrorist activity. While other agencies have this responsibility from different perspectives, a single structure is desired in the wake of the September 11 attacks. In addition, the department creates the Homeland Security Advisory System, a five-level colored diagram with the designations of green (low risk of terrorist attacks), blue (general risk), yellow (elevated risk), orange (high level), and red (severe risk).

2005

In August, a hurricane given the name Katrina hits the Gulf Coast, creating much damage in Louisiana and Mississippi. In New Orleans, levies constructed to prevent flooding are breached, causing massive flooding. People living in the inner-city areas are stranded for days. The New Orleans Police Department experiences great stress, causing officers to leave the force. Looting and violence occur downtown, and officers are directed by the mayor to direct their efforts more to controlling disorder than to search and rescue.

2006

In August, the national security level is raised to red, the highest level, after several arrests are made in London regarding another possible attack on several commercial airplanes. Although the attempts are focused on planes flying from Heathrow Airport, American authorities take extra precautions about items brought aboard planes, especially liquids, since disguised liquid explosives are said to be used.

5

Biographical Sketches

M any people have had a significant impact on the field of policing. It would be well beyond the scope of this text to mention all of them, but it is possible to list some of the most prominent figures. The following are concise biographies of some of the pioneers of policing.

Harry Anslinger (1892–1975)

Harry Anslinger was a contemporary of FBI Director J. Edgar Hoover and is best remembered as the long-term director of the Federal Bureau of Narcotics who launched a massive campaign against illicit drugs in America. Anslinger was a part-time railroad employee who developed an interest in solving crime. His personal observations of the devastating effects of narcotics use on the lower-class people in his hometown in Pennsylvania put into place a lifelong desire to eradicate drug use in the nation. Anslinger worked with the federal government, beginning in the World War I period and serving in a variety of positions in several regions of the world. In 1930, the Federal Bureau of Narcotics was formed to deal with the growing concern over illicit drug use in America. Anslinger became acting director of the new agency and, that same year, the permanent manager. He immediately went to work fighting drug trafficking and placed a special emphasis on marijuana. His aggressive antimarijuana campaign put out a significant amount of misinformation about the effects of the drug. As was the case with Hoover and his war on communism, Anslinger used the media to gain public support for his cause by relating many social ills to drug use. Also like Hoover, Anslinger had incredible longevity in his position—in his case, thirty-two years. America has had many drug czars, but Anslinger has the distinction of being the nation's first.

Lola Greene Baldwin (1860–1957)

Some consider Lola Baldwin to be the nation's first female police officer; much controversy exists, however, because Alice Stebbins Wells is considered by others to have this distinction. While who truly deserves the honor is in question, Lola Baldwin's legitimacy as a pioneer police officer is not. A native of New York State, she moved with her husband and children to Portland, Oregon, at the turn of the twentieth century. She began working with young "wayward" or displaced women, including area immigrants, and was instrumental in creating a juvenile court in the city. Baldwin worked as a volunteer probation officer and vice agent, and, when her volunteer position ended, she asked for and was given a paid position as a police officer in 1908 at the age of forty-eight. This position was distinct from those of the male officers and Baldwin preferred it this way. She did not wear a uniform or badge, and she was housed in the YMCA building rather than the police headquarters. She performed more in a social work capacity than in a crime-fighting capacity. She went on a crusade to rid the city of brothels, dance halls, nightclubs, and even movie theaters, which she felt contributed to the sexual exploitation of young females. Due to her efforts in Portland, Baldwin was selected by the federal government to keep prostitutes from military installations in the West at the onset of World War I. After the war, she returned to her position as a police officer in Portland, where she continued her fight for wayward youth and women. She traveled around the country promoting the inclusion of women in police work but retained her ideas about the social service role of women. She retired in 1922 but continued her active work for social issues.

Samuel Battle (1883–1966)

Samuel Battle has the distinction of being one of the earliest African American police officers in the modern police era in

America and the first black officer in New York City. The son of former slaves in North Carolina, Battle moved north to Connecticut to attend a training school. He moved to New York City, where he worked as a train porter and later took the police officer civil service examination, despite the fact that African Americans were certainly not encouraged to apply for law enforcement occupations. Battle passed and started his career, where he was met with the disapproval of his fellow officers. He refused to make waves, however, and was assigned to the primarily black community known as Harlem. Due to his fine performance as a police officer in the area, which included rescuing a white officer from an angry mob during a racial disturbance, he was promoted to sergeant in 1926, although this process took longer than that of his white counterparts. Battle achieved another milestone when he became lieutenant in 1935, the NYPD's first person of color to hold the rank. He became an early pioneer in community policing by forming organizations to keep young people out of legal trouble. Battle was appointed the city's parole commissioner in 1941, a truly significant accomplishment during this era. He worked diligently to quash the racial discord that was rampant in the early 1940s and was successful in curbing the violence. He retired in 1951 but continued to work with underprivileged youth in crime prevention efforts.

Alphonse Bertillon (1853–1914)

In the field of criminalistics, few pioneers' work measures up to that of Alphonse Bertillon of France. His system of anthropometric description, which involved exact measurements of an offender's body parts for greater ease in identification, paved the way for more serious scientific forensic criminal investigation. Bertillon was an unusually precocious individual, born into an intellectual family that cultivated a curious young mind, especially in matters of medicine, anthropology, and statistics—areas that would serve him well in later life. He studied medicine but failed to obtain an academic degree. He secured employment at the Prefecture of Police of Paris, where he was given a low-status job as records clerk, where he was responsible for putting arrestee data into a filing system.

Noticing the slapdash method of maintaining offender files and the unscientific manner of recording offender characteristics of the period, he began a new system of cataloging body measurements, markings, tattoos, and other features to have a better system of recognition. In an age when poor identification resulted in many offenders' release from the criminal justice system or improper sentences, his system became a major success, resulting in the detection of many recidivists. Bertillon's system included not only a record of physical measurements but also photographs and fingerprints. He thus increased the effectiveness and efficiency of the outdated filing system for ease in retrieval. Bertillon's system was initially not accepted by many police officers, who objected to crime fighting through the use of a measuring device. However, his system became incredibly popular throughout Europe and the rest of the world. In France, Bertillon's name was spoken with the same reverence as his contemporary, Louis Pasteur.

William Burns (1858–1932)

Few people in the late nineteenth or early twentieth century gained as much celebrity in the field of criminal investigation as William Burns. His immaculate dress reflected his background as a tailor, and his interest in acting supplemented his interest in cracking cases with dramatic style. He was a contract detective until he obtained a part-time position with the Secret Service in 1891; in five years the position became permanent and his devotion to work was evidenced in the way he went to extremes doing undercover work, including moving away from his family for extended periods to chase criminals. He received an appointment in the Department of the Interior in 1903, where his investigative work resulted in the conviction and imprisonment of key government and political figures in the West. He left the government and started his own agency in 1910. His investigation of labor disputes, which pitted Burns against famed attorney Clarence Darrow in high-profile cases like that of Leo Frank, gained Burns as much fame at the time as his contemporary, Allan Pinkerton. Burns became head of the Bureau of Investigation (later renamed the Federal Bureau of Investigation) from 1921 to 1924, but the Teapot Dome Scandal, which ruined the careers of several key government officials, including some Bureau of Investigation agents, caused him to resign. Burns retired and died eight years later. The detective agency, which still bears his name, continues to exist even though the Burns family no longer has a business interest in it.

Patrick Colquhoun (1745–1820)

Patrick Colquhoun was a Scottish merchant who later became a pioneer in British policing. Colquhoun, the son of a government officer, went to the United States at age sixteen, returned to Scotland in 1766, and later moved to England where he became a magistrate. Convinced that London possessed a large population of lower-class habitual street criminals, he envisioned a police force like the Bow Street Runners on a much larger scale. The magistrate studied law enforcement extensively and sought to establish a police force that would prevent crime. In 1795, he published the highly influential *Treatise on the Police of the Metropolis,* which would be reprinted and reedited numerous times over the next several years. The magistrate was concerned about the theft of commercial ships by a group of thieves who were nicknamed the mudlarks, and in 1800 he published a treatise on the need for a marine police force. Under his guidance, London established the Thames Police Act of 1800, which created the Thames Police Office that was quite effective. In 1797, Colquhoun was given an honorary law degree by the University of Glasgow. He continued to publish works on criminal justice and politics, serving as magistrate until shortly before his death in 1820 at age sixty-six.

Wyatt Earp (1848–1929)

The image of the ideal law enforcement officer on the Western frontier has long been exemplified by Wyatt Earp. Although much of his renown is probably due more to legend than fact, Earp was certainly a key figure in policing during the cowboy era. He began his career in 1870 in Missouri as a constable, and in 1874 he served as a deputy marshal in Wichita, Kansas. He later became a marshal in Dodge City, and his reputation as a no-nonsense lawman grew. He moved to Texas and later to Arizona, where he and his brothers decided to enter a career in mining.

The Earp brothers became the town marshals and began a contemptuous relationship with Sheriff Johnny Behan. An out-and-out conflict erupted in 1881 when the Earp brothers had a gunfight with cattle rustlers who had connections to the sheriff. The shootout was the infamous gunfight at the OK Corral in Tombstone, Arizona, and became the material for the legend of the lawless Western frontier and Wyatt Earp. Earp was not the paragon of virtue he is made out to be in the numerous tales, songs, movies, and television shows depicting the legend. His influence on law enforcement in popular culture is indisputable, and his image is certainly one of the field's most enduring.

Henry Faulds (1843–1930)

Henry Faulds was a Scottish physician and missionary working in Japan who, after developing a keen interest in the fingerprints found on ancient pottery, published an article in the journal *Nature* in 1880 on how the analysis of "skin furrows" could be used in criminal investigation. Faulds himself had already used this method to solve two cases in Japan. After the publication of the article, Faulds drew a response from a magistrate in India named William Hershel, who claimed that he had been using fingerprints in criminal investigation much earlier. Faulds defended his legitimacy as the "inventor" of fingerprint analysis and attempted to gather support from police agencies, including the famed Scotland Yard, to set up fingerprint laboratories, but his requests were dismissed. Faulds continued to produce scholarly articles on the subject while maintaining his place as the originator of dactyloscopy. (*See also* William James Hershel, Francis Galton, Edward Richard Henry, Juan Vucetich.)

Henry Fielding (1704–1754)

Henry Fielding was a former playwright who became a magistrate in the Bow Street area of London. Fielding, who had gained fame as the author of *Tom Jones*, decided to enter law as an attorney and was appointed to the position of magistrate. Fielding took the new task very seriously because crime rates were increasing in the rapidly growing British cities. The magistrate assembled a group of exconstables to function as criminal investigators; these nonsalaried employees were called thief-takers and received financial compensation through rewards from the victims and the confiscated possessions of the offenders. These investigators, also known as Fielding's people, were under the control of the magistrate and eventually received a small stipend for their services. Fielding's detectives later gained fame as the Bow Street Runners. Fielding was able to use his writing skills to produce a series of pamphlets on crime and crime prevention. His most notable of the pamphlets is *An Enquiry into the Cause of the Late Increase of Robbers,* published in 1748, which reported that the causes of theft included too many lazy immigrants into the area, governmental corruption, and inept constables. Fielding also created the *Covent Garden Gazette,* a publication that gave descriptions of people wanted for crimes as well as explanations of the crimes. Fielding also placed flyers detailing crimes and wanted persons in newspapers with a request to contact him if people had relevant information. Henry Fielding died a young man at forty-seven but was succeeded in office by his half brother, John Fielding.

John Fielding (1721–1780)

Although blinded at age nineteen as the result of an accident, John Fielding was a businessman in London who also studied law with his half brother Henry Fielding at the Bow Street police office and who worked as his assistant. When Henry died in 1754, John became the magistrate. John had been an instrumental part of many of Henry Fielding's innovations, and he continued them and instituted a few more during his tenure as Bow Street Magistrate. John Fielding also stressed preventative crime control and organized two types of patrol: a mounted horse unit and a foot patrol. Fielding also founded a police bulletin called the *Police Gazette* that dispensed information about criminal activity and wanted offenders. John became known as the Blind Beak of Bow Street who, despite his disability, visited crime scenes to assist in solving area crimes. A popular notion developed in London that John Fielding could recognize over three thousand criminals by the sounds of their voices. The Blind Beak, Sir John Fielding, died in 1780.

Francis Galton (1822–1911)

By the time Sir Francis Galton had entered the fury over the legitimacy of dactyloscopy's true discoverer, he already had renown
as a highly successful scientist. Galton, also well-known as
Charles Darwin's cousin, had a strong interest in aspects of hered-
ity and genetics, and, when called upon by the Royal Institute to
deliver a speech on the Bertillon System in 1888, he elected to
focus on fingerprinting rather than on other aspects of Bertillonage. Building on the work of Henry Fauld and William Hershel,
he began an investigation of the subject after contacting Hershel.
His examination culminated in his seminal work *Finger Prints*,
published in 1892. In this volume, Galton provided a typology of
fingerprints, including the now famous classification of arches,
loops, and whorls. Soon afterward, Scotland Yard began utilizing
fingerprints in its anthropometric classification system. Fingerprinting had now gained legitimacy and found its way into main-
stream criminal investigation as a result of the scientific
contributions by Galton. In 1894, Galton turned over the reins of
dactyloscopy to Edward Richard Henry. (*See also* Henry Faulds,
William James Hershel, Edward Richard Henry, Juan Vucetich.)

Pat Garrett (1850–1908)

Patrick Floyd Jarvis Garrett, better known simply as Pat Garrett, is
another legendary lawman from the Old Western frontier and best
known for his pursuit and killing of perhaps the most legendary
outlaw of the period, Billy the Kid. Born in Alabama and raised in
Louisiana, Garrett moved west as a young man where he worked
as a cowboy in Texas. He continued west to New Mexico, where
he ran a saloon. As sheriff of Lincoln County, New Mexico, he was
charged with hunting down twenty-one-year-old Henry McCarty,
also known as Billy the Kid or, as he was better known at the time,
simply the Kid. In 1885, Garrett, a tall man with a gunslinger's
reputation, deputized two people and went to Fort Sumner, New
Mexico, on a tip that the renegade was hiding there. Billy the Kid
walked up on a startled Garrett who was able to respond more
quickly than the equally startled outlaw and shot the Kid dead.
The news of the death of Billy the Kid made Garrett a legend, and
this legend grew as the years passed. Garret published his account

of the incident in a book with the lengthy title *The Authentic Life of Billy the Kid, Whose Deeds of Daring and Blood have Made His Name a Terror in New Mexico, Arizona, and Northern Mexico,* written at least in part by Ash Upson. Garrett later dabbled in politics and law enforcement, again becoming a sheriff in another county. He also organized a unit of the Texas Rangers and became a customs official, appointed by Theodore Roosevelt. In his last years he became a rancher and was killed in an incident involving livestock on his ranch.

Daryl Gates (b. 1926)

Although Daryl Gates is probably remembered best as the police chief of the Los Angeles Police Department during the Rodney King beating and the subsequent riots in Los Angeles and other cities across the country, he is also credited with a number of innovations that are now standard in police work. Gates was a strapping young man when he used the GI bill to obtain a degree in public administration while working as a police officer with the LAPD. Although he took this route simply to pay the bills, he had no intention of making policing a career. He became the chauffeur for the LAPD's famed chief, William Parker, eventually adopting some of Parker's aggressive police tactics.

Gates took his job seriously and quickly rose through the ranks despite making several controversial comments involving race. As a detective, he worked on several famous cases, such as the death of actress Marilyn Monroe, the assassination of Senator Robert Kennedy, and the Charles Manson murders. He was also involved in the violent riots that shook the Watts area of Los Angeles in 1965. As a result of his involvement, he became known as an authority in riot control. As police administrator, Gates promulgated a series of innovations that have become a staple in police work, such as the special weapons and tactical (SWAT) units, structured units that use military tactics to bring crisis situations under control, and the Drug Abuse Resistance Education (DARE) program, in which police officers provide drug education to school students. When LAPD officers were acquitted of the Rodney King beatings and riots were sparked, Gates was criticized by many people for not keeping the situation under control. Gates left the LAPD in 1992.

Herman Goldstein (b. 1931)

Police scholar Herman Goldstein is the originator of one of the field's most popular innovation strategies: problem-oriented policing. Goldstein started out as a young assistant municipal administrator in Portland, Maine, concerned with efficiency in city government. He began to study the city's policies on police administration alongside famed police management expert, O. W. Wilson. He obtained a few other government positions before ending up in Chicago in 1960 as assistant to Wilson, who had become the city's chief of police. He worked with Wilson in this position for four years and during this period developed ideas about police operations and administration, which he published in academic journals. In 1964, he accepted a professorship at the University of Wisconsin Law School; this appointment reflects the prestige Goldstein was enjoying at the time since he did not possess a law degree or a Ph.D. While at the university, he served on several high-profile commissions such as the pivotal President's Commission on Law Enforcement and the Administration of Justice (1964–1968), the Kerner Commission on race riots (1967–1968), and the Knapp Commission that investigated corruption in the New York City Police Department (1971–1973). He also published the classic book *Policing a Free Society* in 1977, and two years later he published an article called "Improved Policing: A Problem-Oriented Approach," in which he outlined a new style of policing that advocated a holistic, proactive approach to police work. In this model, the police are active participants in discovering the root causes of crime, working with the communities to solve these problems. This approach became connected with the broader philosophy of community policing that has characterized policing since the 1980s. Goldstein retired from his position at the University of Wisconsin, but his problem-oriented style of policing continues in many departments throughout the nation.

Hans Gross (1847–1915)

The criminal investigators of today owe much to the pioneer, Hans Gross. Gross, an Austrian attorney who practiced law in the 1870s, became concerned about the technical application of investigation by police officers. He completed a significant amount of self-study in the areas of physics, medicine, psychology, and other forms of science, as well as photography in relation to their potential utility in assisting the police in their detective work. Gross contended that no crime scene is devoid of some type of clue that, if appropriately observed, will lead investigators to the perpetrator. Gross believed that investigating officers should be provided with forensic knowledge along with advanced technology for use in convicting criminals.

In 1883, Gross published a handbook called *The Manual for the Examining Magistrate: A System of Criminalistics* and in 1898 founded a journal called *Archives for Criminal Anthropology and Criminalistics.* Gross went on to become a professor of law and continued to publish more volumes on the techniques of criminal detection such as his prominent work, *Criminal Investigation,* released in 1906 with an English translation. Gross's scholarly work and his ideas about criminal investigation in his era, including the concept of modus operandi (method of criminal activity), bloodstain analysis, and other forensic techniques, later became hallmarks of forensic science.

Beverly J. Harvard (b. 1951)

The distinction of being the first African American woman to head a big-city police department belongs to Beverly Harvard. Harvard was born in Macon, Georgia, and received her degree in sociology from Morris Brown College in Atlanta. In 1973, she began her career as a police officer with the Atlanta Police Department. She worked her way up through the department hierarchy, holding a number of administrative positions such as the chief affirmative action officer, executive protection officer, director of public affairs, and deputy chief of the three major divisions in the department: career development, criminal investigations, and administrative services. In addition, Harvard became the first woman in the department to graduate from the Federal Bureau of Investigation's National Academy in Quantico, Virginia. She was promoted to chief of police in 1994 and instituted a number of changes in the department including additional services for juveniles, a domestic violence unit, a firearms task force, and an improved citywide communications system with the fire department. She was the chief during the 1996 Olympic Games in

Atlanta and was responsible for coordinating all law enforcement measures for the event. A strong advocate of community policing, Harvard sought to put the police more in contact with the people they served. She left the office in 2002.

Edward Richard Henry (1850–1931)

In 1873, a young British magistrate collector with the civil service stationed in India, named Edward Henry, began a career that would eventually lead to his appointment as inspector general of police in Bengali in 1891. Within two years, the administration integrated Bertillonage into his police operations. Although the system was successful in solving many criminal cases, the system was cumbersome and lacking in organization; the technology to match the existing prints to those of suspects was not in place at the time. After visiting Sir Francis Galton in 1894 to gather ideas on the problem that perplexed even the eminent scientist, Henry returned to India and continued to try to devise a cataloging system. He accomplished this and even extended Galton's fingerprint classification system. By 1898, the Indian police agency replaced Bertillonage with Henry's fingerprint cataloging system. In 1901, Henry was summoned to Scotland Yard to serve as assistant commissioner of police of the metropolis and as director of the criminal investigation department; he also used his new cataloging system at the agency. Henry's classification scheme was quickly adopted throughout Europe and the United States. (*See also* Henry Faulds, William James Hershel, Francis Galton, Juan Vucetich.)

William James Hershel (1833–1917)

While working in India as a civil service employee and later magistrate, William Hershel of Britain used the ancient ritual of handprint inking on legal documents to determine accurately the correct recipients of pension payments. Many of the native Indians were illiterate and the conventional use of fingerprints was unavailable; so the misrepresentation of claimants, resulting in fraud, was common. Hershel used inked handprints, which inadvertently had cultural significance to the Indians, because he had determined that the prints varied remarkably among individuals and that they changed very little as people aged. He reported these finding to his superiors, who were not interested in his claims.

After reading Dr. Fauld's article in *Nature*, Herschel submitted a letter, which was published in the subsequent edition of the journal. The great debate had begun on fingerprinting's originator. It continued through the years and Hershel's claim received a boost when acclaimed scientist and fellow countryman Francis Galton came to his defense in his claim as the true originator of the new field. (*See also* Henry Faulds, Francis Galton, Edward Richard Henry, Juan Vucetich.)

J. Edgar Hoover (1895–1972)

The Federal Bureau of Investigation has had seventeen directors since its inception, none nearly as well-known or as controversial as John Edgar Hoover, who headed the organization for forty-eight years. Hoover was a young lawyer who began his career with the Justice Department in 1917, becoming the director of the General Intelligence Division the following year. He worked his way up the ladder to become assistant to the Attorney General, and, when the Bureau of Investigation absorbed the intelligence division, Hoover became assistant director of the agency and in 1924 he became the director.

Hoover set out to make the organization more professional, removed several agents, and ordered background checks, intensive interviews, and physical testing on all new recruits. Given the freedom from political influence, the new director embarked on a campaign to eliminate organized crime, and he tracked and brought to justice such high-profile figures as John Dillinger, Machine Gun Kelly, Ma Barker, and Bonnie and Clyde. Hoover also relentlessly pursued suspected agents of espionage and subversion during his tenure, causing much criticism that he violated civil liberties with his methods of intelligence gathering. However, during his tutelage, the Federal Bureau of Investigation made tremendous advancements in the areas of computer and laboratory technology, police training, and forensic investigation. Hoover's long term of service as the FBI director ended with his death in 1972.

George L. Kelling (b. 1935)

The community-oriented policing philosophy in its modern form, which has been the dominant model in American law enforcement for over two decades, can be in large part attributed to George Kelling. Kelling, who received his Ph.D. from the University of Wisconsin, is currently a professor at Rutgers University and a fellow at Harvard's Kennedy School of Government. His work at the Police Foundation produced two pivotal studies. The first is his study of police officers, called the Kansas City Prevention Patrol experiment, that found that, contrary to popular views, a police presence does not necessarily prevent crime or make residents feel safer. The second study, called the Newark Foot Patrol Study, found that foot patrol likewise did not significantly reduce crime, although residents felt safer and more positive toward the police. Kelling's ideas on policing, which were developing during the Kansas City and Newark studies, culminated in a landmark 1982 article published in the *Atlantic Monthly* called "Broken Windows: The Police and Neighborhood Safety," coauthored with James Q. Wilson. The article described the ideas of broken windows policing and set the stage for the development of community policing. A book published in 1996, called *Fixing Broken Windows: Restoring Order and Reducing Crime in Our Communities*, coauthored with his wife Catherine Coles (and containing a foreword by James Q. Wilson), further outlined the broken windows model. The model has been met with some criticism; however, the impact of his research and his ideas on police work has been significant.

Greg MacAleese (b. 1947)

Greg MacAleese combined his skills as a journalist with his experiences as a police officer and created a novel idea to get the public more involved in helping police solve crimes and locate suspects; this idea has been used in many cities and has inspired a major television series. MacAleese was born in Canada and moved to New Mexico with his family as a teenager. He received a degree in journalism from the University of New Mexico in 1969 and worked with the *Albuquerque Tribune* and the Associated Press as a sports writer. He left journalism due to the stress involved in constantly having to meet deadlines and embarked on a career in policing because he thought his experiences would provide good information for future books. He started as a beat patrol officer with the Albuquerque Police Department in 1973 and moved into criminal investigation, for which he had a passion. In 1976, after working on a violent crime case, MacAleese decided to reenact the event on a local television station with the hope of getting tips from viewers. The case was solved and the show, called *Crime Stoppers,* became very popular with viewers and quickly spread to other states across the country and eventually to other countries as well. The hit television show *America's Most Wanted* was based on the idea, continues to have massive appeal with audiences, and has led to the solving of many crimes. MacAleese worked at other criminal justice positions and continued to work with *Crime Stoppers,* but eventually opted go into the private security industry.

Eliot Ness (1903–1957)

Like Wyatt Earp and others who conjure up the image of the Western lawman on the frontier, the name "Eliot Ness" evokes the persona of the G-man, the gangster-chasing federal agent of the Prohibition Era. Ness, a 1925 graduate of the prestigious University of Chicago, initially worked as an insurance investigator. During the Prohibition Era, the manufacture, sale, and use of alcohol were prohibited, and the criminalization of spirits created fertile soil for organized crime syndicates, which in turn caused the creation of new agencies in law enforcement to control them. Ness developed an interest in policing and began taking courses in criminology at the university to gain a better knowledge of the subject, and at the same time he participated in alcohol raids. He was hired as an agent with the Treasury Department in 1926, where he developed a reputation as a serious, incorruptible officer.

He was charged with tracking down the notorious gangster, Al Capone, and set out on this task with vigor, much as Pat Garret did in his pursuit of Billy the Kid in the frontier West many years earlier. To pursue Capone, Ness formed a group of a dozen law enforcement officers and tracked him for two years; Capone was eventually captured and charged with tax evasion. Ness and his crew, dubbed the Untouchables, gained much fame in the 1930s. Ness left the bureau and coauthored a book about his experiences called *The Untouchables,* which was developed into a television series and movies over the years since then. Even though the image of the incorruptible, crime-fighting G-men, as represented in these stories, did not totally reflect reality, the public was fascinated with this new image of the police as promoted by Ness and the Untouchables.

William H. Parker (1902–1966)

William Parker made an undeniable imprint on the field of policing and specifically on police professionalism. As the chief of police with the Los Angeles Police Department (LAPD) during the years 1950 until his death in 1966, he followed the path of August Vollmer and his own contemporary O. W. Wilson in demanding a higher level of professionalism in police work. He was born in South Dakota and moved to California (as did his friend Wilson), where he entered the LAPD and worked his way up the police hierarchy. He took a leave of absence when he worked with Wilson in organizing a European police force during World War II but returned to the LAPD; in 1950, he became the agency's chief. Parker emphasized vigorous officer selection and training in his attempts to build a police force modeled on the military structure. He was adroit at marketing a highly favorable image of his agency and used the media very effectively to meet this end. Parker was able to showcase his department's image through a very popular radio and later television series, *Dragnet*, achieved through his personal connection with the show's originator, Jack Webb. The chief, however, had a continuing conflict with many African American citizens who felt his aggressive style of policing was a means of oppression. The violent Watts riots and other outbreaks of racial strife in Los Angeles during his tenure have been viewed by many as a revolt against Parker's policing style.

Robert Peel (1788–1850)

Robert Peel is the world's most noted police pioneer in that he is attributed with creating the first true police force in the world. Peel was born in Lancashire, England, to a middle-class household. His father, of the same name, was a manufacturer who became a member of the British Parliament and who was later knighted; the title "Sir" was passed to young Robert upon his father's death. The younger Peel was educated at Oxford University and afterward embarked on a career in British politics. He was eventually selected Home Secretary and, due to a rising crime problem, wanted a professional police force to combat it. The idea of a professional force was unpopular in England because many thought such a force would be a detriment to freedom, as they perceived the oppressive police force in France to be. Peel was successful in getting his Metropolitan Police Act passed in 1829, a feat attempted by his father many years earlier. This act revolutionized policing by separating police and magistrate functions and by providing police officers with uniforms, small batons called truncheons, and assignments to patrol beats. Though initially viewed with skepticism and sometimes contempt, the officers, popularly called peelers, won the respect of citizens for their use of restraint during potentially explosive outbreaks. The force, known as the London Metropolitan Police, was guided by Peel's principles of policing, which formed the basis of professionalism in the field. His innovations won him the title "father of modern policing," and his officers later received the often used nickname bobbies as a testament to his influence.

Allan Pinkerton (1819–1884)

Allan Pinkerton is the name most often associated with private security in the annals of police history. He and his private detective agency, reinforced by the company logo of the all-seeing eye, have made an indelible mark on private investigation in America. Born in Scotland, Pinkerton's father was a police officer; however, a law enforcement career was not initially the young man's occupational choice. When forced to flee Scotland due to his political beliefs, Pinkerton settled in Dundee, Illinois, near Chicago, where he ran a cooperage. When a counterfeiting ring interrupted area business endeavors, Pinkerton became a deputy sheriff to pursue the counterfeiters. He left Dundee for Chicago in 1850 and was hired by the Treasury Department to investigate counterfeiting incidents because of the reputation he had gained in Dundee. He formed a special private police force to deal with railroad crime and was also hired as a postal agent. The Pinkerton's Protective Police Patrol was created in 1857 and contracted out private security services to local businesses. The agency grew and covered an area encompassing five states. After some successful high-profile investigations, Pinkerton's fame grew and agencies were established in other cities during the 1860s. The master detective wrote a handbook on criminal investigation, followed by sixteen detective stories. Even after his death the agency continued through the efforts of his sons, but the focus was more on private security than on investigation.

Theodore Roosevelt (1858–1919)

Although best remembered as the twenty-sixth president of the United States and leader of a military group known as the Rough Riders during the Spanish-American War, Theodore "Teddy" Roosevelt was at one time New York City's police commissioner. Roosevelt, born into a wealthy family in New York, overcame childhood sickness to become a robust athlete and later a well educated political figure. He was elected to the state legislature, and later he received an appointment to the United States Civil Service Commission at a time when the spoils system was rampant. (The spoils system was the practice of obtaining public positions on the basis of personal connections and money.)

Roosevelt was able to secure the police commissioner position in 1895, and he immediately set out to change the corrupt system of law enforcement in the city. He gained fame by using midnight rambles to observe police behavior on his own nightly rounds. He exposed dishonest cops all the way to Police Chief Thomas Byrnes, a notoriously corrupt police administrator, and Alexander "Clubber" Williams, a notoriously violent police officer. Roosevelt was a progressive commissioner and used modern police advancements such as bicycle squads, firearms training, and an early version of the broken windows style of policing by increasing the policing of nuisance behaviors. His tenure as commissioner was only two years and he had bigger ambitions, but Roosevelt's term as the top administrator of the country's largest police department is remembered as a time of professionalism and reform in a troubled period of policing in the nation's history.

Frank Serpico (b. 1936)

A book published in 1973 and a movie release in the same year made "Serpico" a household name and a term synonymous with

whistle-blowing in police work. If it had not been for the coura-
geous action he took to deal with police corruption, he probably
would have received no fame, and the corruption that was going
on in the New York Police Department would have possibly not
been exposed. Serpico was a young, idealistic cop with the NYPD
in the 1960s with a strong desire to become a detective. He refused to accept the gratuities normally offered to the police in return for protection. He transferred to the plainclothes division in
1966, where he was exposed to even greater acts of corruption,
including bribes and payoffs involving drug and gambling operations. His refusal to become involved with this activity, along
with his unpolice-like appearance consisting of the long hair and
hippie clothing normally detested by the police at that time,
made him a pariah among his fellow officers.

After he continued to be confronted with corruption, he
tried with no success to report the misconduct through appropriate channels. He gave his story to the *New York Times* in 1970 and
the whole affair went national. The Knapp Commission was
formed to investigate the complaints, and the activity of the
NYPD was exposed. Serpico was shot in the face during a drug
bust in 1971, and many believe that the failure by his partners to
protect him was a show of their disapproval of his whistle-blowing. Serpico left the force after the incident and moved out of the
country. He later returned to New York where he still gives
speeches against police corruption.

Bruce Smith (1892–1955)

Bruce Smith never served as a police officer, but he had a tremendous impact on policing during his lifetime. During the 1920s
through the 1950s, Smith was one of the most prominent police
scholars in America. He was one of the few civilian reformers to
have an impact on the field, through the efforts of professional police, such as August Vollmer, O. W. Wilson, and William Parker,
who promoted his reform ideas. A large, outgoing, and well educated New Yorker, Smith had a law degree but never practiced
law. Instead he began completing research projects using the survey method in various police organizations, including the FBI, the
Institute for Public Administration, and the International Association of Chiefs of Police. The survey method involved a comprehensive analysis of police agencies; Smith performed the surveys

of police departments in New Orleans, Chicago, and other cities. He was also instrumental in launching the Uniform Crime Report (UCR) system, a standardized crime reporting system in the 1920s. As a result of his affiliation with political leaders and the FBI on this project, he became close friends with J. Edgar Hoover, the long-term agency director. In the late 1930s and 1940s, Smith was actively involved in police reform, and he especially took up the cause decrying the use of the third degree, an accepted practice of police violence during interrogation. He was also the author of three texts, including the seminal *Police Systems in the United States* in 1940. He was in the process of completing a fourth book at his death in 1955.

Eugene François Vidocq (1775–1828)

Sometimes referred to as the world's first master detective, Eugene François Vidocq established many methods of criminal investigation that are still in use today, including psychological interrogation techniques, detailed crime records, mug shots, and the detailed study of criminal offenders to solve crimes. Born in France, Vidocq ran away from home as a youth to embark on a life of adventure and assumed a number of positions, such as street performer, soldier, and sailor. He also became an escape artist, not for entertainment but to escape his detention in local jails for assaulting a police officer. Vidocq became well-known for this skill and escaped for the last time in 1779, when he later assumed a new life as a legitimate clothes seller. He turned himself into the police ten years later when he was faced with growing fears of being turned in by his underground acquaintances.

Vidocq agreed to be an informant for the police, setting in place a short but extremely eventful career as a detective. His personal knowledge of criminal activity and the Paris criminal element suited him well in his development of a force of investigators known as the Surete. Vidocq used excriminals to make up this group. His innovations include the introduction of record keeping of criminal files in a card index format, criminalistics, ballistics, shoe and foot impressions in plaster of paris, and improved surveillance techniques. In 1828, a new prefect of police (police chief), disdaining the idea of using exconvict investigators, relieved Vidocq of his duties. Vidocq published in memoirs in 1828 and later formed a private detective agency. The master detective died in 1857 in poverty due to a series of lawsuits that depleted his savings. A legacy to his great skills can be found in America in a group called the Vidocq Society, a volunteer organization (by invitation only) of investigators who pursue cold cases (those left unsolved after many years).

August Vollmer (1876–1955)

August Vollmer is the person most often associated with police reform and professionalism in America. Born in New Orleans and raised in Germany and the San Francisco Bay area, Vollmer was a feed store merchant in Berkeley who served in the military during the Spanish-American War. A prominent citizen in Berkeley, he received a job as postal carrier, where he learned a good deal about the citizens in the community. He was encouraged to run for town marshal by citizens concerned about crime in the area; he ran and obtained the position, which later became the office of chief of police. He was able to reduce the incidence of gambling, a major problem at the time, and then turned his attention to modernizing the police force. He started the bicycle patrol; brought traffic light technology to Berkeley; used automobile patrols, polygraphs, and assessment instruments for new recruits; started a forensic lab; and started the first police academy in conjunction with the University of California. He advocated college education for his officers and developed a degree program in criminology for them; in fact, he often used college students (termed college cops by people in Berkeley) as part-time officers. He also held key law enforcement organization positions, authored books, contributed to the Wickersham Commission report, and served as professor of police administration at the University of Chicago and the University of California. For all of his contributions to the field of law enforcement, he has often been called the father of American policing.

Juan Vucetich (1858–1925)

Austrian-born Juan Vucetich moved to Argentina where he began his employment as a police officer. Although possessing a low level of education, Vucetich's natural proclivity for mathematics provided him with an appointment to director of the police statistical bureau, where he was given the responsibility of establishing a criminal classification system. He used the standard Bertillon system but sought to devise a better one based on fingerprint analysis. Vucetich worked tirelessly to establish such a system and was able to do so in less than two months.

His system was adopted by the La Plata police department, making his the first officially accepted fingerprint identification classification system, predating the Henry system. However, anthropometry was still the only accepted system, and Vucetich fought unsuccessfully to install his system for years. In 1894, a new police chief allowed him to implement his system in lieu of anthropometry. In 1904, his text on fingerprinting, *Dactyloscopia Comporada*, was published. His scheme gained much credibility when the Academy of Sciences honored it as the best criminal classification system; five years later the system was adopted nationwide. A growing public distaste for the system caused the government to abandon it. Vucetich, who had labored so vigilantly to implement the system, was exiled and died a few years later in poverty. (*See also* Henry Faulds, William James Hershel, Francis Galton, Edward Richard Henry.)

Joseph Wambaugh (b. 1937)

The police have been depicted in movies, television, and books in a number of ways throughout the years; they have been cast as bumbling buffoons, as totally unscrupulous egoists, as overly aggressive super cops who relish killing suspects, and as unblemished, incorruptible automatons. Police author Joseph Wambaugh can be credited with bringing a more realistic image of the police to the American reader and viewer. The son of a police officer, Wambaugh served a stint in the Marine Corps and began employment with the Los Angeles Police Department (LAPD) in 1960 while a college student at California State University. He was a patrol officer and later a detective who observed the exciting field of police work and witnessed the Watts riots in 1965. As he pursued his master's degree, he wrote a number of short stories and quit the force when it was suggested that he write a book of his experiences. He quit the force to write full-time and wrote a novel about three LAPD officers called *The New Centurions*, which was published in 1971 and later made into two television projects. He continued to write novels, including his best seller, *The Choir-*

boys, which was made into a major motion picture. Wambaugh, who was frequently not always happy with the translation of his work into the screen version, also supervised a major television series that ran during the 1970s called *Police Story*. He also produced some nonfiction work, such as the critically acclaimed *The Onion Field*, published in 1973. Wambaugh's writing skills helped bring realistic police work to a public anxious to understand this fascinating field.

Alice Stebbins Wells (1873–1957)

Was Lola Baldwin or Alice Stebbins Wells the country's first female police officer? In 1910, Wells was hired by the Los Angeles Police Department as a full-time police officer with full police powers. Wells had petitioned some prominent people in Los Angeles to provide her with the appointment. She followed in the footsteps of the early prison matrons and other women who worked in the criminal justice field but who were not given responsibility for regular police duty. Although she was a sworn officer, she was housed away from the male officers and was expected to work primarily with women and children by keeping them away from the evil elements of the day. This social service responsibility was fine with Wells due to her strong moral and religious beliefs. She frequented movie theaters, dance halls, arcades, skating rinks, city parks, and other places in an effort to ensure they were safe for women and children. She became a popular figure in the city and soon other cities began hiring female officers. (Unfortunately the trend did not continue, and it was decades before women in policing became acceptable.) In 1915, a group formed the Internal Association of Policewomen (IAP) in Baltimore and elected Wells as its president. Despite the decrease in interest in women police that would soon occur, Wells was a true trailblazer and reformer.

James Q. Wilson (b. 1931)

Respected police scholar James Q. Wilson emerged on the scene during a chaotic period of riots, rebellion, and disorder. The fact that many political leaders sought his advice during such a period attests to his influence in the criminal justice field. Wilson was born in Colorado and raised in California. He received his Ph.D. in political science in 1959 and became a member of the University of Chicago's faculty. His research interests included race and urbanization, not criminal justice; in fact, he received no academic training in criminology and had no major interest in the field. The University of Chicago, however, had one of the nation's first criminology programs and commanded the respect of many political figures. In 1961, Wilson took a position at Harvard University, where he made many important professional connections. When President Lyndon B. Johnson took an aggressive stance toward the growing crime problem and sought a blue chip panel of crime experts, Wilson was included. Wilson's performance on the President's Commission on Law Enforcement and the Administration of Justice (1966–1967) resulted in his appointment to task forces on crime and justice. He gained much notice in 1968 with the publication of his book, *Varieties of Police Behavior*, in which he outlined his oft quoted typology of police officers—watchmen, legalists, and service officers—a classification taught now in almost all introductory criminal justice and policing courses in the nation. He continued working on criminal justice committees and in 1974 he published *Thinking About Crime*, a book that appealed to many political figures of the era. A journal article published in 1982 and coauthored with George Kelling, called "Broken Windows," helped usher in the era of community policing. Wilson retired from Harvard in 1987 and returned to California, where his advice and ideas on the criminal justice system are still actively sought.

O. W. Wilson (1902–1972)

Orlando W. Wilson, one of August Vollmer's college cops, would become one of the leading experts on policing, particularly on police management. Wilson was born in South Dakota but moved with his family to Berkeley, California, where he enrolled at the University of California. Wilson had to work to pay his way through college and became a police officer in the city police department under Vollmer, who was also teaching courses in criminology at the university. Wilson graduated with his degree in criminology in 1924 and, upon Vollmer's recommendation, began his employment as the chief of police in Fullerton, California. He would also serve as police chief in Wichita, Kansas, from

1928 to 1939 where, following his mentor Vollmer's lead, he instituted a number of innovations, including marked patrol vehicles, improved communication systems, polygraphs, and a crime laboratory. Wilson entered the military during World War II, where he served as a colonel and chief public safety officer in Europe. He taught courses in police administration at the University of California from 1939 to 1960 and served as dean the last ten years he was at Berkeley. In 1960, Wilson accepted a position as the chief of police in Chicago. He retired from public service in 1967 and moved near San Diego, California, where he died five years later. He published a number of works on police management, the most important of which was *Police Administration*, first released in 1950, which became the standard text in the field. Wilson was a strong supporter of police professionalization who sought to thwart corruption in the departments he supervised. He influenced generations of police managers as an administrator, professor, and scholar.

6

Facts and Data

This chapter consists of pertinent information about the field of policing in America. It contains tables and figures presenting data from government researchers. All tables and figures are located at the end of this chapter.

Police Personnel

This section provides information about the personnel makeup of federal, state, and local municipal police offices and sheriffs' departments.

Federal Police Agencies

There are approximately 106,000 federal law enforcement personnel, based on 2004 data; these officials carry firearms and have arrest powers. The numbers of these employees and their primary functions are shown in Table 6.1.

Additional information about federal police officials in 2004:

- Of all federal officers, 16.1 percent were women and 33.2 percent were members of a racial or ethnic minority.
- The largest employers of federal officers, accounting for 63 percent of the total, were the:

  -U.S. Customs and Border Protection (28,200)
  -Federal Bureau of Prisons (15,361)

-FBI (12,414)

-U.S. Immigration and Customs Enforcement (10,691)

- About half of all federal officers were employed in:

-Texas (14,633)

-California (13,365)

-The District of Columbia (9,201)

-New York (8,159)

-Florida (6,627)

- Nationwide, there were 36 federal officers per 100,000 U.S. residents, including 1,662 per 100,000 residents in the District of Columbia. There were more than 60 per 100,000 residents in Arizona, North Dakota, Vermont, Montana, New Mexico, Texas, and Alaska. There were fewer than 10 per 100,000 in Wisconsin, New Hampshire, and Iowa.

State and Local Police Agencies

The United States has an abundance of various types of state and local law enforcement agencies:

- As of June 2000, state and local law enforcement agencies had 1,019,496 full-time personnel, 11 percent more than the 921,978 employed in 1996. From 1996 to 2000, the number of full-time sworn personnel increased from 663,535 to 708,022.
- As of June 2003, local police departments had 580,749 full-time employees, including 451,737 sworn personnel. Sheriffs' offices had 330,274 full-time employees, including 174,251 sworn personnel.
- From 1987 to 2003, minority representation among local police officers increased from 14.6 percent to 23.6 percent. In sheriffs' offices, minorities accounted for 18.8 percent of sworn personnel in 2003, compared to 13.4 percent in 1987.
- From 1996 to 2000, total employment by local police departments was up an average of 2.1 percent per year. Sheriffs' offices increased their number of employees by 3.5 percent per year. (U.S. Department of Justice, Bureau of Justice Statistics, *State and Local Law Enforcement Statistics*)

Table 6.2 gives a breakdown by state of the full-time state and local law enforcement agencies and employees based on June 2000 figures.

Table 6.3 provides information about the types of agencies that employ police personnel (both full- and part-time) and differentiates between sworn and nonsworn employees.

Figures 6.1 and 6.2 show the rise in the number of full-time police officers and sheriffs' departments from 1987 to 2003. It is easy to see the increase in both types of agencies, even though the number of police department officers is considerably larger than those of sheriffs' offices

Tables 6.4 and 6.5 provide information about the numbers and percentages of full-time sworn officers and full-time civilian employees in police departments and sheriffs' offices.

Tables 6.6 and 6.7 provide information about the largest police departments and sheriff's offices in the country. New York City has the largest police department, and Los Angeles County, California, has the largest sheriff's department.

Sworn and nonsworn reserve or auxiliary officers are utilized in police departments and sheriffs' offices throughout the nation and provide a valuable resource in law enforcement. The numbers of these officers are shown in Tables 6.8, 6.9, 6.10, and 6.11

The numbers of officers in police departments and sheriffs' offices are broken down by gender and race in Tables 6.12 and 6.13. White males make up the majority of police officers; these figures are extremely consistent in both police departments and sheriffs' offices.

The changes in the number of female and other minority police officers and sheriffs' deputies are shown in Figures 6.3 and 6.4. A slow but consistent growth is occurring in female and minority hiring and retention in police departments, but both have experienced decreases in sheriffs' departments since 1997.

There are several methods for screening potential police officers and sheriffs' deputies, including criminal background checks and investigations, driving record checks, medical and psychological examinations, personal interviews, drug tests, physical agility tests, written examinations, credit history investigations, polygraph tests, and personality inventories. These vary in different agencies and are depicted in Figures 6.5 and 6.6. Criminal background checks are the common ones for each, and personality inventories are the less utilized method.

Tables 6.14 and 6.15 show the educational requirements for police and deputy recruits. For most police departments and sheriff's offices, only a high school diploma is required for employment. The departments, both police and sheriffs' offices that serve a population of 500,000–999,999, are more likely to require a four-year college degree than departments serving a larger or smaller population.

The training requirements for police and deputy recruits are shown in Figures 6.7 and 6.8, which contrast the years 2000 and 2003. Departments that serve larger areas tend to require more training hours, and police departments require more training than sheriffs' offices.

Police academies provide training for a number of positions in the criminal justice field. Figure 6.9 provides a breakdown of these positions. Officers in municipal departments are the positions most engaged by the academies.

Figures 6.10 and 6.11 and Table 6.16 show the types of training provided at police academies. In-service training is the most widely used and the identification of community problems, reflecting the influence of community policing and problem-oriented policing models.

Police officers receive training in racially based policing. Figure 6.12 shows the method of instruction of this subject to the police. The most common approach to providing this training is through academic, or classroom, training rather than practical skills or field training.

Types of basic instruction involving terrorism and response to terrorist incidents are shown in Figure 6.13. The most common type of instruction in this area involves response tactics to weapons of mass destruction.

The types of facilities utilized by the training academies are shown in Table 6.17. Facilities that promote practical training are utilized much more often than other methods, such as mail correspondence courses.

Most of the funding for police academies is provided by state governments; however, other sources are used and are included in Figure 6.14.

A breakdown of police recruits by race and gender is provided in Figure 6.15. White males are the largest category; however, the numbers are close with other races and both genders.

Salaries for police officers and sheriffs' deputies are shown in Tables 6.18 and 6.19. Although the figures vary by the size of the populations served, salaries for both groups are relatively consistent.

The various duties of police officers and sheriffs' deputies are shown in Tables 6.20–6.33. These duties involve a variety of activities such as patrol duties, court-related functions, detention duties, special public safety functions, traffic-related duties, and special operations activities. Sheriff's offices are more likely than police to be involved with serving civil processes and criminal warrants, courtroom protection, inmate transport, and the operation of local jails; police departments are more likely to be involved with temporary lockup facilities, animal control, school crossing services, crime prevention education, and civil defense duties.

Community policing is an important component in both police departments and sheriffs' offices. Tables 6.34 and 6.35 show how mission statements of both groups reflect the community policing philosophy. Tables 6.36 and 6.37 depict how community-policing methods are actually utilized in both types of agencies. Municipal departments tend to contain the community-oriented philosophy and to use more activities; however, community-policing efforts are obviously important to both groups.

Figures 6.16 and 6.17 show the percentage of officers in both municipal departments and sheriff's offices that use full-time community policing officers. It is evident that the municipal police departments use more full-time officers.

Tables 6.38 and 6.39 show how different types of nonlethal weapons are used in police departments and sheriffs' offices. Pepper spray, collapsible batons, soft projectiles, and electrical devices are commonly used in both types of agencies.

Figures 6.18 and 6.19 show the use of video cameras in police vehicles, as used by both police departments and sheriffs' offices in 2000 and 2003. In both types of agencies, video cameras increased in use over the three-year period.

Other special technological advancements are shown in the Tables 6.40 and 6.41. Mug shots, fingerprints, tire deflation spikes, infrared imagers, and suspect composite drawings are the most common in both types of agencies.

How the police handle citizen complaints is a vital role in police work and directly affects police–community relations. Figure 6.20 gives information about numbers of complaints against different agencies, with the municipal police receiving the largest number. Tables 6.42, 6.43, 6.44, and 6.45 represent the dispositions of citizen complaints broken down by types of agencies.

The job of a police officer carries the inherent risk of being killed in the line of duty. The number of police killed on the job has dropped, however, since the early 1970s, as Figure 6.21 shows.

The additional information from government data, taken from the U.S. Department of Justice, Bureau of Justice Statistics, *Law Enforcement Officers Killed, 2006,* regarding the conditions involving the officers' deaths, follows.

Between 1995 and 2004, of the 636 officers killed:

- 26 percent were in arrest situations
- 18 percent were in ambush situations
- 16 percent were on disturbance calls
- 16 percent were making traffic pursuits or stops
- 13 were investigating suspicious persons or circumstances
- 10 percent were in other situations

Of the 696 assailants identified in the killing of law enforcement officers from 1995 to 2004:

- More than half had a prior conviction
- Two-fifths were on probation or parole at the time

Regarding the weapons used in the deaths of police, handguns were the most prevalent type, as shown in Figure 6.22.

TABLE 6.1
As of September 2004, Federal Agencies Employed about 106,000 Full-Time Personnel Authorized to Make Arrests and Carry Firearms

Function	Number of full-time federal officers*
Criminal investigation/enforcement	40,408
Police response and patrol	22,278
Inspections	17,280
Corrections/detention	16,530
Court operations	5,158
Security/protection	4,524
Other	176
Total	**106,354**

*Nonmilitary federal officers authorized to carry firearms and make arrests; excludes officers in foreign countries.
Source: U.S. Department of Justice, Bureau of Justice Statistics, *Federal Law Enforcement Statistics.*

TABLE 6.2
State and Local Law Enforcement Agencies and Employees
Based on June 2000 Figures

		Full-time employees					
		Total		Sworn personnel		Responding to calls	
State	Number of agencies	Number	Per 100,000 residents	Number	Per 100,000 residents	Number	Per 100,000 residents
Alabama	424	16,062	361	10,655	240	7,287	164
Alaska	95	2,151	343	1,348	215	1,031	164
Arizona	135	20,595	401	11,533	225	6,889	134
Arkansas	356	9,207	344	6,157	230	4,066	152
California	517	115,906	342	73,662	217	40,349	119
Colorado	248	15,237	354	10,309	240	5,815	135
Connecticut	125	10,277	302	8,327	245	5,143	151
Delaware	43	2,257	288	1,774	226	1,151	147
District of Columbia	3	4,914	859	3,96	693	2,041	357
Florida	383	68,165	427	39,452	247	24,264	152

continues

TABLE 6.2 Continued

State	Number of agencies	Total		Sworn personnel		Responding to calls	
		Number	Per 100,000 residents	Number	Per 100,000 residents	Number	Per 100,000 residents
Georgia	561	31,282	382	21,173	259	12,393	151
Hawaii	7	3,731	308	2,914	241	1,722	142
Idaho	122	4,522	349	2,749	212	1,732	134
Illinois	886	52,769	425	39,847	321	23,728	191
Indiana	495	17,969	296	11,900	196	7,249	119
Iowa	400	7,600	260	5,333	182	3,769	129
Kansas	353	10,343	385	6,563	244	4,265	159
Kentucky	382	9,589	237	7,144	177	4,800	119
Louisiana	343	23,573	527	18,548	415	7,639	171
Maine	139	3,638	285	2,367	186	1,721	135
Maryland	146	20,272	383	15,221	287	9,024	170
Massachusetts	351	23,593	372	18,082	285	11,784	186
Michigan	565	29,654	298	21,673	218	13,456	135
Minnesota	460	12,677	258	8,606	175	5,748	117
Mississippi	333	10,163	357	6,562	231	4,415	155
Missouri	586	20,459	366	13,630	244	8,949	156
Montana	126	2,958	328	1,760	195	1,344	149
Nebraska	237	4,776	279	3,486	204	2,296	134
Nevada	62	7,918	396	5,252	263	2,959	148
New Hampshire	195	3,268	264	2,542	206	1,736	140
New Jersey	551	37,387	444	29,062	345	16,343	194
New Mexico	135	6,324	348	4,456	245	2,792	153
New York	517	94,863	500	72,853	384	45,462	240
North Carolina	491	26,101	324	18,903	235	11,070	138
North Dakota	129	1,755	273	1,293	201	944	147
Ohio	845	36,863	325	25,082	221	15,689	138

continues

TABLE 6.2   Continued

		Full-time employees					
		Total		Sworn personnel		Responding to calls	
State	Number of agencies	Number	Per 100,000 residents	Number	Per 100,000 residents	Number	Per 100,000 residents
Oklahoma	449	11,376	330	7,622	221	5,129	149
Oregon	178	10,683	312	6,496	190	3,573	104
Pennsylvania	1,166	33,427	272	26,373	215	17,648	144
Rhode Island	51	3,390	323	2,688	256	1,636	156
South Carolina	258	13,046	325	9,741	243	5,973	149
South Dakota	170	2,468	327	1,708	226	1,201	159
Tennessee	367	22,148	389	14,494	255	9,296	163
Texas	1,800	80,535	386	51,478	247	28,831	138
Utah	129	6,346	284	4,179	187	2,545	114
Vermont	65	1,459	240	1,034	170	796	131
Virginia	327	25,842	365	20,254	286	9,900	140
Washington	256	15,513	263	9,910	168	6,367	108
West Virginia	229	4,148	229	3,150	174	2,387	132
Wisconsin	512	18,010	336	13,237	247	8,290	155
Wyoming	81	2,287	463	1,477	299	989	200
Total	**17,784**	**1,019,496**	**362**	**708,022**	**252**	**425,427**	**151**

Source: U.S. Department of Justice, Bureau of Justice Statistics, *Census of State and Local Law Enforcement Agencies,* 2000.

TABLE 6.3
The Types of Agencies That Employ Police Personnel
(Sworn and Nonsworn Employees)

Number of employees	State and local law enforcement employees					
	Full-time			Part-time		
	Total	Sworn	Nonsworn	Total	Sworn	Nonsworn
Total	1,019,496	708,022	311,474	99,731	42,803	56,928
Local police	565,915	440,920	124,995	62,110	27,323	34,787
Sheriff	293,823	164,711	129,112	22,737	10,300	12,437
Primary state	87,028	56,348	30,680	817	95	722
Special jurisdiction	69,650	43,413	26,237	13,583	4,667	8,916
Texas constable	3,080	2,630	450	484	418	66
Percentage of employees						
Total	100	69.4	31.6	100	42.1	57.8
Local police	100	77.9	22.1	100	44.0	56.0
Sheriff	100	56.1	43.9	100	45.3	54.7
Primary state	100	64.7	35.3	100	11.6	88.4
Special jurisdiction	100	62.3	37.7	100	34.4	65.6
Texas constable	100	85.4	14.6	100	86.4	13.6

Source: U.S. Department of Justice, Bureau of Justice Statistics, *Census of State and Local Law Enforcement Agencies, 2000.*

FIGURE 6.1
Full-Time Employment by Local Police Departments, 1987–2003

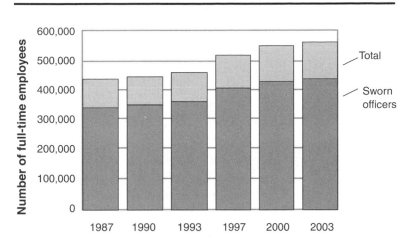

Source: U.S. Department of Justice, Bureau of Justice Statistics, *Local Police Departments, 2003.*

FIGURE 6.2
Full-Time Employment by Sheriffs' Offices, 1987–2003

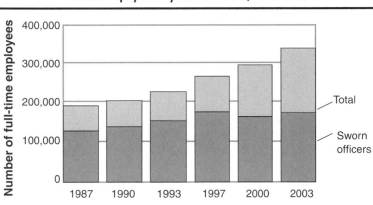

Source: U.S. Department of Justice, Bureau of Justice Statistics, *Sheriffs' Offices, 2003.*

TABLE 6.4
Local Police Departments and Full-Time Personnel,
by Number of Sworn Personnel, 2003

Number of sworn personnel*	Agencies		Full-time sworn personnel		Full-time civilian personnel	
	Number	Percentage	Number	Percentage	Number	Percentage
1,000 or more	50	0.4	153,903	34.1	45,737	35.5
500–999	39	0.3	27,370	6.1	9,183	7.1
250–499	105	0.8	36,330	8.0	11,581	9.0
100–249	400	3.2	57,767	12.8	17,877	13.9
50–99	845	6.7	56,367	12.5	16,643	12.9
25–49	1,661	13.1	53,287	11.8	13,958	10.8
10–24	3,798	30.0	46,218	10.2	10,985	8.5
5–9	3,272	25.9	15,717	3.5	2,451	1.9
2–4	1,924	15.2	4,237	0.9	561	0.4
1	561	4.4	540	0.1	41	—
Total	**12,656**	**100**	**451,737**	**100**	**129,013**	**100**

*Includes both full-time and part-time employees.

Source: U.S. Department of Justice, Bureau of Justice Statistics, *Local Police Departments, 2003.*

TABLE 6.5
Sheriffs' Offices and Full-Time Personnel, by Number of Sworn Personnel, 2003

Number of sworn personnel*	Agencies		Full-time sworn personnel		Full-time civilian personnel	
	Number	Percentage	Number	Percentage	Number	Percentage
1,000 or more	13	0.4	32,734	18.8	25,432	16.3
500–999	24	0.8	16,822	9.7	13,400	8.6
250–499	87	1.9	30,483	17.5	27,473	17.6
100–249	230	7.5	33,438	19.2	26,831	17.2
50–99	363	11.8	23,385	13.4	26,043	16.7
25–49	656	21.4	20,656	11.9	20,052	12.9
10–24	955	31.2	12,894	7.4	13,068	8.4
5–9	490	16.0	3,102	1.8	3,267	2.1
2–4	233	7.3	717	0.4	446	0.3
1	19	0.6	19	–	10	–
Total	**87**	**1.9**	**30,483**	**17.5**	**27,473**	**17.6**

*Includes both full-time and part-time employees.

– = Less than 0.05%

Source: U.S. Department of Justice, Bureau of Justice Statistics, *Sheriffs' Offices, 2003.*

TABLE 6.6
The 50 Largest Local Police Departments by Total Number of
Full-Time Sworn Personnel, Number of Full-Time Sworn Personnel
per 100,000 Residents, and Percentage of Full-Time Sworn Personnel
Regularly Assigned to Respond to Calls for Service, 2003

Jurisdiction	Full-time sworn personnel		
	Total number	Number per 10,000 residents[a]	Percentage responding to calls[b]
New York (NY)	35,973	45	57
Chicago (IL)	13,469	47	72
Los Angeles (CA)	9,307	24	51
Philadelphia (PA)	6,853	46	59
Houston (TX)	5,350	27	70
Detroit (MI)	3,837	42	26

continues

TABLE 6.6   Continued

Jurisdiction	Full-time sworn personnel		
	Total number	Number per 10,000 residents[a]	Percentage responding to calls[b]
Washington (DC)	3,632	65	44
Baltimore (MD)	3,258	52	61
Miami–Dade Co. (FL)	3,178	14	73
Dallas (TX)	2,948	24	63
Suffolk Co. (NY)	2,808	19	46
Phoenix (AZ)	2,763	20	36
Las Vegas–Clark Co. (NV)	2,640	17	49
Nassau Co. (NY)	2,497	19	54
San Francisco (CA)	2,216	30	49
Boston (MA)	2,109	36	66
San Diego (CA)	2,103	17	48
San Antonio (TX)	2,056	17	67
Milwaukee (WI)	1,989	34	68
Memphis (TN)	1,939	30	52
Honolulu (HI)	1,916	21	59
Cleveland (OH)	1,846	40	43
Columbus (OH)	1,797	25	57
Baltimore Co. (MD)	1,788	23	68
Jacksonville–Duval Co. (FL)	1,624	21	61
New Orleans (LA)	1,622	35	75
St. Louis (MO)	1,507	45	62
Charlotte–Mecklenberg Co. (NC)	1,499	22	45
Atlanta (GA)	1,462	35	76
Denver (CO)	1,429	26	42
San Jose (CA)	1,408	16	55
Newark (NJ)	1,332	48	55
Prince George's Co. (MD)	1,328	16	40
Fairfax Co. (VA)	1,317	13	69
Nashville (TN)	1,312	24	53

continues

TABLE 6.6   Continued

Jurisdiction	Total number	Number per 10,000 residents[a]	Percentage responding to calls[b]
		Full-time sworn personnel	
Kansas City (MO)	1,299	29	61
Fort Worth (TX)	1,249	21	44
Seattle (WA)	1,238	22	53
Austin (TX)	1,198	18	46
Louisville (KY)	1,195	17	78
Indianapolis (IN)	1,170	15	49
El Paso (TX)	1,137	20	56
Montgomery Co. (MD)	1,089	12	69
Cincinnati (OH)	1,047	33	48
Miami (FL)	1,038	28	53
Pittsburg (PA)	1,030	32	48
Oklahoma City (OK)	1,007	19	67
Portland (OR)	1,005	19	44
Tampa (FL)	962	30	65
Tucson (AZ)	960	19	52

Note: Sworn employees are those with general arrest powers. Officers not assigned to respond to calls for service typically were assigned to other areas of duty related to administration, investigations, technical support, jail operations, or court operations.

[a]In some cases populations were adjusted to more accurately reflect the population for which an agency provided law enforcement services.

[b]Includes all full-time sworn personnel with general arrest powers who were uniformed officers with regularly assigned duties that included responding to calls for service.

Source: U.S. Department of Justice, Bureau of Justice Statistics, *Local Police Departments, 2003.*

TABLE 6.7
Twenty-Five Largest Sheriffs' Offices, by Number and Function of
Full-Time Sworn Personnel, 2003

County or equivalent	Full-time sworn personnel	Percentage of officers by area of duty				
		Patrol	Investi-gative	Jail operations	Court Security	Process serving
Los Angeles Co. (CA)	8,622	42	6	25	15	1
Cook Co. (IL)[a]	5,555	10	1	61	27	2
Clark Co. (NV)[b]	2,640	48	18	25	0	–
Harris Co. (TX)	2,517	30	6	27	5	1
Orange Co. (CA)	1,755	29	7	40	12	1
Jacksonville-Duval Co. (FL)[b]	1,624	61	12	0	5	1
Broward Co. (FL)	1,605	84	13	0	2	1
Riverside Co. (CA)	1,542	69	9	13	9	0
San Bernardino Co. (CA)	1,541	32	12	22	11	0
Sacramento Co. (CA)	1,525	36	11	26	6	–
San Diego Co. (CA)	1,320	35	22	4	14	3
Orange Co. (FL)	1,294	62	15	0	10	4
Palm Beach Co. (FL)	1,177	65	9	0	9	3
Hillsborough Co. (FL)	1,126	65	13	0	–	2
Alameda Co. (CA)[c]	974	15	2	48	16	1
Wayne Co. (MI)	893	11	3	45	6	1
East Baton Rouge Parish (LA)	875	14	9	36	3	5
Pinellas Co. (FL)	868	48	16	0	16	3
Oakland Co. (MI)[a,c]	840	41	8	48	3	1
San Francisco Co. (CA)	824	0	1	67	9	2
Erie Co. (NY)	813	18	4	62	16	1

continues

TABLE 6.7   Continued

County or equivalent	Full-time sworn personnel	Percentage of officers by area of duty				
		Patrol	Investi-gative	Jail operations	Court Security	Process serving
Ventura Co. (CA)	760	30	12	15	10	1
Jefferson Parish (LA)	747	42	27	26	0	1
Contra Costa Co. (CA)	707	37	6	36	9	1
King Co. (WA)	705	38	22	0	4	2

Note: Sworn employees are those with general arrest powers.

— = Less than 0.05%

[a]Employment data are based on the 2004 Census of State and Local Law Enforcement Agencies.

[b]The Las Vegas Metropolitan Police Department, the result of a merger of the Clark County Sheriff's Office and the Las Vegas Police Department in 1973, serves as the local police department for the City of Las Vegas. The Jacksonville Sheriff's Office serves as the local police department for the City of Jacksonville, which is consolidated with Duval County. These two agencies, although headed by sheriffs, are classified as local police departments in LEMAS for data analysis purposes.

[c]Duty area percentages are based on the 2000 LEMAS survey.

Source: U.S. Department of Justice, Bureau of Justice Statistics, *Sheriffs' Offices, 2003.*

TABLE 6.8
Use of Sworn Reserve or Auxiliary Officers in Local Police Departments,
by Size of Population Served, 2003

Population served	Full-time sworn			Part-time sworn		
	Percentage of agencies using	Total number	Average number*	Percentage of agencies using	Total number	Average number*
All sizes	7	5,376	6	35	26,625	6
1,000,000 or more	0	0	0	44	947	131
500,000–999,999	5	69	34	35	739	55
250,000–499,999	17	454	63	37	472	30
100,000–249,999	7	114	9	43	1,137	15
50,000–99,999	4	225	13	42	2,101	12
25,000–49,999	5	206	6	33	2,590	10
10,000–24,999	5	467	5	28	3,845	7
2,500–9,999	7	1,953	6	34	7,648	6
Under 2,500	8	1,888	5	37	7,146	4

Note: Detail may not add to total because of rounding.

*Excludes agencies not using sworn reserve or auxiliary officers.

Source: U.S. Department of Justice, Bureau of Justice Statistics, *Local Police Departments, 2003*.

TABLE 6.9
Use of Sworn Reserve or Auxiliary Officers in Sheriffs' Offices,
by Size of Population Served, 2003

Population served	Full-time sworn			Part-time sworn		
	Percentage of agencies using	Total number	Average number*	Percentage of agencies using	Total number	Average number*
All sizes	13	5,209	13	44	20,844	16
1,000,000 or more	27	335	43	58	2,601	157
500,000–999,999	14	560	63	40	1,639	62
250,000–499,999	15	366	20	51	1,834	30
100,000–249,999	12	659	18	50	3,353	21
50,000–99,999	21	1,138	15	51	3,523	19
25,000–49,999	15	1,196	12	49	4,375	13
10,000–24,999	12	674	7	43	2,734	8
2,500–9,999	8	281	6	30	785	4
Under 2,500	27	335	43	58	2,601	157

Note: Detail may not add to total because of rounding.

*Excludes agencies not using sworn reserve or auxiliary officers.

Source: U.S. Department of Justice, Bureau of Justice Statistics, *Sheriffs' Offices, 2003.*

TABLE 6.10
Use of Nonsworn Reserve or Auxiliary Officers in Local Police Departments,
by Size of Population Served, 2003

Population served	Full-time nonsworn			Part-time nonsworn		
	Percentage of agencies using	Total number	Average number*	Percentage of agencies using	Total number	Average number*
All sizes	1	585	6	11	13,589	10
1,000,000 or more	0	0	0	19	4,677	1,507
500,000–999,999	0	0	0	13	637	123
250,000–499,999	2	1	1	7	51	16
100,000–249,999	2	22	5	9	273	18
50,000–99,999	2	69	9	12	814	16
25,000–49,999	–	29	13	14	1,300	12
10,000–24,999	2	280	9	15	2,625	9
2,500–9,999	1	103	4	10	1,841	5
Under 2,500	–	81	4	9	1,372	3

Note: Detail may not add to total because of rounding.

*Excludes agencies not using sworn reserve or auxiliary officers.

— = Less than 0.05%

Source: U.S. Department of Justice, Bureau of Justice Statistics, *Local Police Departments, 2003*.

TABLE 6.11
Use of Nonsworn Reserve or Auxiliary Officers in Sheriffs' Offices,
by Size of Population Served, 2003

Population served	Full-time nonsworn			Part-time nonsworn		
	Percentage of agencies using	Total number	Average number*	Percentage of agencies using	Total number	Average number*
All sizes	2	1,058	14	13	10,683	26
1,000,000 or more	4	1	1	39	4,700	425
500,000–999,999	2	111	100	14	627	71
250,000–499,999	2	75	34	11	114	9
100,000–249,999	5	356	25	25	2,326	30
50,000–99,999	2	147	21	14	692	14
25,000–49,999	1	199	21	15	1,133	11
10,000–24,999	2	97	5	10	470	6
2,500–9,999	3	73	4	9	620	11
Under 2,500	4	1	1	39	4,700	425

Note: Detail may not add to total because of rounding.

*Excludes agencies not using sworn reserve or auxiliary officers.

Source: U.S. Department of Justice, Bureau of Justice Statistics, *Sheriffs'; Offices, 2003.*

TABLE 6.12

Gender and Race of Full-Time Sworn Personnel in Local Police Departments, by Size of Population Served, 2003

Population served	Percentage of full-time sworn employees who were														
	Total			White			Black/African American			Hispanic/Latino			Other*		
	Total	Male	Female	Total	Male	Female	Total	Male	Female	Total	Male	Female	Total	Male	Female
1,000,000 or more	100	82.7	17.3	61.1	53.2	7.9	16.7	11.3	5.4	19.3	15.7	3.6%	2.8	2.6	0.2
500,000–999,999	100	84.4	15.6	61.9	54.1	7.8	24.4	18.0	6.4	7.8	6.8	1.0	6.0	5.4	0.6
250,000–499,999	100	85.4	14.6	66.6	57.7	8.9	19.4	15.3	4.1	11.3	10.0	1.3	2.7	2.4	0.3
100,000–249,999	100	89.0	11.0	76.0	68.2	7.8	11.9	9.8	2.1	9.1	8.2	0.9	3.0	2.8	0.2
50,000–99,999	100	91.2	8.8	83.3	76.6	6.7	7.4	6.3	1.1	7.0	6.2	0.8	2.3	2.2	0.1
25,000–49,999	100	91.8	8.2	87.5	80.8	6.7	5.8	4.9	0.9	5.5	5.0	0.5	1.2	1.0	0.2
10,000–24,999	100	93.3	6.8	90.4	84.6	5.8	4.4	4.0	0.4	3.0	2.8	0.2	2.1	1.9	0.2
2,500–9,999	100	93.8	6.2	89.8	84.5	5.3	4.2	3.7	0.5	3.4	3.2	0.2	2.6	2.3	0.3
Under 2,500	100	94.3	5.7	88.5	83.8	4.7	5.7	5.1	0.6	3.4	3.2	0.2	2.5	2.2	0.3
All sizes	100	88.7	11.3	76.4	69.4	7.0	11.7	9.0	2.7	9.1	7.8	1.3	2.8	2.5	0.3

Note: Detail may not add to total because of rounding.

*Includes Asians, Native Hawaiians or other Pacific Islanders, American Indians, Alaska Natives, and any other race.

Source: U.S. Department of Justice, Bureau of Justice Statistics, *Local Police Departments, 2003.*

TABLE 6.13

Gender and Race of Full-Time Sworn Personnel in Sheriffs' Offices, by Size of Population Served, 2003

Population served	Total			White			Black/African American			Hispanic/Latino			Other*		
	Total	Male	Female	Total	Male	Female	Total	Male	Female	Total	Male	Female	Total	Male	Female
1,000,000 or more	100	85.2	14.8	69.0	59.6	9.4	11.8	9.0	2.7	15.8	13.5	2.3	3.5	3.1	0.4
500,000–999,999	100	84.9	15.1	73.9	64.3	9.7	14.2	10.1	4.1	9.2	8.1	1.1	2.7	2.4	0.3
250,000–499,999	100	86.0	14.0	82.8	72.8	9.9	10.5	7.5	3.1	5.4	4.7	0.8	1.3	1.1	0.2
100,000–249,999	100	87.2	12.8	85.8	76.2	9.6	9.7	7.0	2.7	3.2	2.7	0.4	1.3	1.2	0.1
50,000–99,999	100	87.7	12.3	91.3	80.7	10.6	6.0	4.6	1.4	1.8	1.6	0.1	0.9	0.8	0.1
25,000–49,999	100	90.9	9.1	89.6	82.2	7.4	6.2	5.0	1.2	3.3	2.9	0.4	0.9	0.8	0.1
10,000–24,999	100	90.6	9.4	86.2	79.2	7.0	10.9	8.7	2.2	1.9	1.7	0.2	1.0	1.0	–
Under 10,000	100	95.0	5.0	93.9	89.1	4.8	2.9	2.8	0.1	2.4	2.3	0.1	0.9	0.9	0.0
All sizes	100	87.1	12.9	81.2	72.0	9.2	10.0	7.5	2.6	6.9	6.0	0.9	1.9	1.7	0.2

Percentage of full-time sworn employees who were

Note: Detail may not add to total because of rounding.

*Includes Asians, Native Hawaiians or other Pacific Islanders, American Indians, Alaska Natives, and any other race.

— = Less than 0.05%

Source: U.S. Department of Justice, Bureau of Justice Statistics, *Sheriffs' Offices, 2003.*

FIGURE 6.3
Female and Minority Local Police Officers, 1987–2003

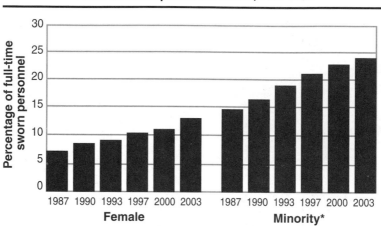

*Includes blacks or African Americans, Hispanics or Latinos, Asians, Native Hawaiians or other Pacific Islanders, American Indians, Alaska Natives, and any other racial or ethnic minority.

Source: U.S. Department of Justice, Bureau of Justice Statistics, *Local Police Departments, 2003.*

FIGURE 6.4
Female and Minority Personnel in Sheriffs' Offices, 1987–2003

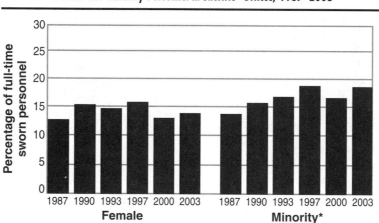

*Includes blacks or African Americans, Hispanics or Latinos, Asians, Native Hawaiians or other Pacific Islanders, American Indians, Alaska Natives, and any other racial or ethnic minority.

Source: U.S. Department of Justice, Bureau of Justice Statistics, *Sheriffs' Offices, 2003.*

FIGURE 6.5
Local Police Officers Employed by Departments
Using Various Recruit Screening Methods, 2003

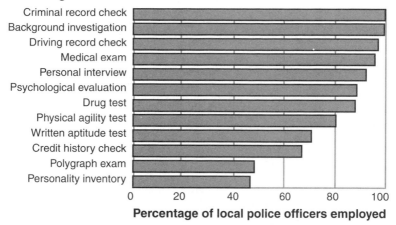

Source: U.S. Department of Justice, Bureau of Justice Statistics, *Local Police Departments, 2003.*

FIGURE 6.6
Sworn Personnel Employed by Sheriffs' Offices
Using Various Recruit Screening Methods, 2003

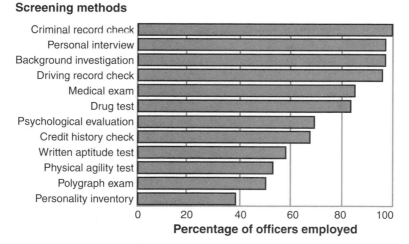

Source: U.S. Department of Justice, Bureau of Justice Statistics, *Sheriffs' Offices, 2003.*

TABLE 6.14

Minimum Educational Requirements for New Officers in Local Police Departments, by Size of Population Service, 2003

Population served	Total with requirement	Percentage of agencies requiring a minimum of			
		High school diploma	Some college*	2-year college degree	4-year college degree
1,000,000 or more	98	72	18	7	1
500,000–999,999	99	72	13	9	5
250,000–499,999	99	84	8	4	3
100,000–249,999	98	81	13	3	2
50,000–99,999	100	76	17	6	1
25,000–49,999	99	77	10	11	1
10,000–24,999	99	82	7	9	1
2,500–9,999	99	83	7	9	—
Under 2,500	97	82	6	9	0
All sizes	98	81	8	9	1

Note: Detail may not add to total because of rounding.

*Non-degree requirements.

— = Less than 0.5%

Source: U.S. Department of Justice, Bureau of Justice Statistics, *Local Police Departments, 2003.*

TABLE 6.15

Minimum Educational Requirements for New Officers in Sheriffs' Offices, by Size of Population Service, 2003

Population served	Total with requirement	Percentage of agencies requiring a minimum of			
		High school diploma	Some college*	2-year college degree	4-year college degree
1,000,000 or more	100	85	4	12	0
500,000–999,999	98	74	7	10	7
250,000–499,999	99	91	4	3	2
100,000–249,999	98	88	10	1	0
50,000–99,999	100	86	12	2	0
25,000–49,999	99	89	4	6	0
10,000–24,999	98	89	2	7	0
Under 10,000	98	93	0	5	0
All sizes	99	89	4	5	—

Note: Detail may not add to total because of rounding.

*Non-degree requirements.

— = Less than 0.5%

Source: U.S. Department of Justice, Bureau of Justice Statistics, *Sherriff's Offices, 2003.*

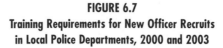

FIGURE 6.7
Training Requirements for New Officer Recruits
in Local Police Departments, 2000 and 2003

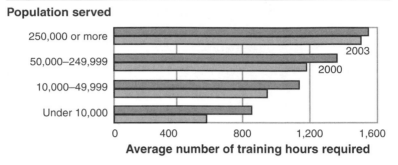

Source: U.S. Department of Justice, Bureau of Justice Statistics, *Local Police,* 2003.

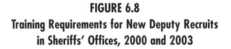

FIGURE 6.8
Training Requirements for New Deputy Recruits
in Sheriffs' Offices, 2000 and 2003

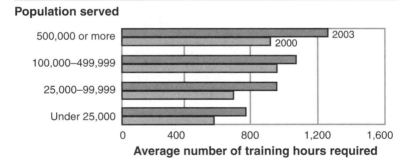

Source: U.S. Department of Justice, Bureau of Justice Statistics, *Sheriffs' Offices, 2003.*

FIGURE 6.9
Positions for which Academies Provided Training and/or Certification, 2002

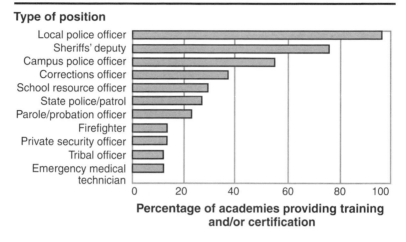

Source: Department of Justice, Bureau of Justice Statistics, *State and Local Law Enforcement Training Academies, 2002.*

FIGURE 6.10
Types of Training Provided by Academies,
in Addition to Basic Recruit Training, 2002

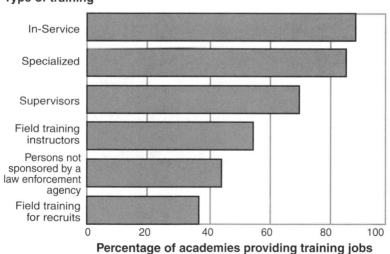

Source: Department of Justice, Bureau of Justice Statistics, *State and Local Law Enforcement Training Academies, 2002.*

FIGURE 6.11

Academies Providing In-Service Training on Community Policing Topics, 2002

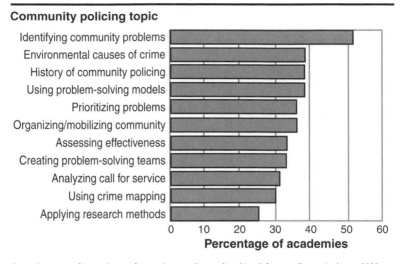

Community policing topic

Identifying community problems
Environmental causes of crime
History of community policing
Using problem-solving models
Prioritizing problems
Organizing/mobilizing community
Assessing effectiveness
Creating problem-solving teams
Analyzing call for service
Using crime mapping
Applying research methods

Percentage of academies

Source: Department of Justice, Bureau of Justice Statistics, *State and Local Law Enforcement Training Academies, 2002.*

TABLE 6.16
Academies Providing Basic Instruction on Various Topics and
Number of Hours of Instruction Required, 2002

Training topic	Percentage of academies providing training in topic area	Median number of hours of instruction required
Firearms skills	99	60
Basic first-aid/CPR	99	24
Emergency vehicle operations	99	36
Self-defense	99	44
Criminal law	98	40
Domestic violence	98	12
Ethics and integrity	98	8
Investigations	98	45
Patrol procedures/techniques	98	40
Juvenile law and procedures	98	8
Constitutional law	96	11
Cultural diversity	95	8
Health and fitness	95	50
Officer civil/criminal liability	93	6
Human relations	92	11
Use of non-lethal weapons	91	12
Community policing	90	8
Stress prevention/management	86	6
Hate crimes/bias crimes	85	4
Mediation skills/conflict management	83	8
Domestic preparedness	78	8
Problem solving (for example, SARA, CAPRA)	64	6
Computers/information systems	59	8
Basic foreign language (such as, survival Spanish)	35	16

Note: SARA stands for scanning, analysis, response, assessment; CAPRA stands for clients, acquiring and analyzing information, partnerships, response, assessment.

Source: Department of Justice, Bureau of Justice Statistics, *State and Local Law Enforcement Training Academies, 2002.*

FIGURE 6.12

Training Related to Racially-Biased Policing, by Methods of Instruction, 2002

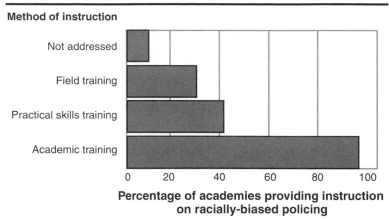

Source: Department of Justice, Bureau of Justice Statistics, *State and local Law Enforcement Training Academies, 2002.*

FIGURE 6.13

**Basic Instruction Related to Terrorism and
Responding to Terrorist Incidents, 2002**

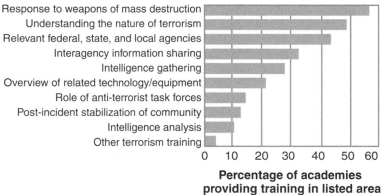

Source: Department of Justice, Bureau of Justice Statistics, *State and Local Law Enforcement Training Academies, 2002.*

TABLE 6.17
Law Enforcement Training Academy Facilities, 2002

		Percentage that have access		
	Total	**Part of academy facility**	**Not part of academy facility**	**No access**
Outdoor firearms range	96	47	49	4
Vehicle operation range	95	41	54	5
Weight room	93	60	33	7
Defensive tactics room	92	68	23	8
Desktop computers	89	61	28	11
Library	88	48	40	12
Gymnasium	87	44	43	14
Scenario training facility	79	43	36	21
Firearms training simulator	77	58	19	23
Media lab/video production facility	71	34	38	29
Obstacle course	68	42	26	32
Mock courtroom	66	14	52	34
Laptop computers	65	45	20	35
Internet/online classes	53	25	27	48
Mobile data terminals/computers	50	18	31	51
Swimming pool	44	7	37	56
Video conferencing classes	43	14	29	57
Subscription to satellite downlink Information service*	37	18	20	63
Indoor firearms range	35	17	18	65
Dormitory/residential facilities	31	18	12	69
Driving simulator	22	13	9	78
Mail correspondence courses	16	4	13	84

*For example, LETN.

Source: Department of Justice, Bureau of Justice Statistics, *State and Local Law Enforcement Training Academies,* *2002.*

FIGURE 6.14
Sources of Training Funds or Equipment, 2002

Source of funds, training and/or equipment, 2002

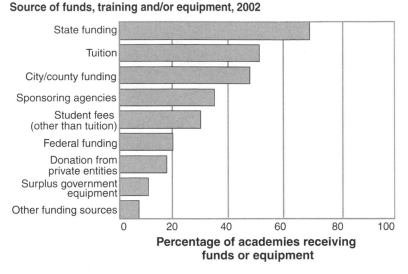

Source: U.S. Department of Justice, Bureau of Justice Statistics, *State and Local Law Enforcement Training Academies, 2002.*

FIGURE 6.15
Recruits Completing Training, by Race and Gender, 2002

Recruits completing training, by race and gender, 2002

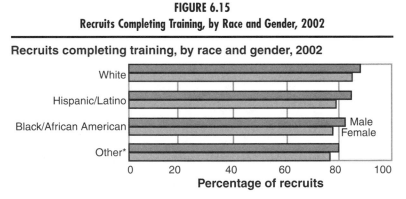

*Includes American Indian/Alaska Native, Asian, Hawaiian or Pacific Islander, and any other race.

Source: Department of Justice, Bureau of Justice Statistics, *State and Local Law Enforcement Training Academies, 2002.*

TABLE 6.18
Average Base Annual Salary for Selected Positions in Local Police Departments, by Size of Population Served, 2003

| | Average base annual salary, 2003 (U.S. dollars) | | | | | |
| | Entry-level officer | | Sergeant or equivalent | | Chief | |
Population served	Minimum	Maximum	Minimum	Maximum	Minimum	Maximum
1,000,000 or more	37,700	57,800	60,200	73,500	113,000	157,100
500,000–999,999	36,600	54,900	58,000	69,600	109,700	143,200
250,000–499,999	38,300	53,500	54,600	66,900	94,400	129,200
100,000–249,999	39,600	54,000	56,000	68,000	95,000	123,100
50,000–99,999	37,400	51,200	54,500	65,300	85,500	106,900
25,000–49,999	35,900	48,600	53,400	62,400	77,700	94,500
10,000–24,999	33,000	45,000	47,400	55,200	65,900	77,800
2,500–9,999	29,000	36,200	37,400	43,600	48,900	56,200
Under 2,500	23,400	26,800	27,100	30,800	32,700	36,500
All sizes	28,200	35,300	36,600	42,400	48,800	56,900

Note: Salary figures have been rounded to the nearest $100. Computation of average salary excludes departments with no full-time employee in that position.

Source: U.S. Department of Justice, Bureau of Justice Statistics, *Local Police Departments, 2003.*

TABLE 6.19
**Average Base Annual Salary for Selected Positions in Sheriffs' Offices,
by Size of Population Served, 2003**

| Population served | Average base annual salary, 2003 (U.S. dollars) | | | | | |
| | Entry-level deputy | | Sergeant or equivalent | | Chief | |
	Minimum	Maximum	Minimum	Maximum	Minimum	Maximum
1,000,000 or more	38,800	54,500	56,200	70,000	119,300	135,100
500,000– 999,999	35,000	51,200	51,000	62,900	96,700	111,000
250,000– 499,999	32,000	44,400	43,700	55,500	84,200	96,700
100,000– 249,999	30,000	39,800	39,600	50,200	71,600	81,200
50,000– 99,999	28,400	36,100	35,100	43,700	62,000	68,500
25,000– 49,999	25,800	30,700	31,400	36,000	53,500	57,800
10,000– 24,999	24,900	29,400	30,200	34,200	49,300	52,800
Under 10,000	23,300	26,200	28,000	30,900	37,000	40,000

Note: Salary figures have been rounded to the nearest $100. Computation of average salary excludes sheriff's offices with no full-time employee in that position.

Source: U.S. Department of Justice, Bureau of Justice Statistics, *Sheriffs' Offices, 2003.*

TABLE 6.20
Types of Routine Patrol Other Than Automobile Used
by Local Police Departments, by Size of Population Served

Population served	Percentage of agencies using each type of patrol on a routine basis				
	Foot	Bicycle	Motorcycle	Marine	Horse
1,000,000 or more	75	100	81	63	63
500,000–999,999	79	95	100	41	63
250,000–499,999	76	83	93	32	59
100,000–249,999	57	83	89	14	18
50,000–99,999	54	64	63	14	7
25,000–49,999	47	60	49	8	2
10,000–24,999	53	58	21	5	2
2,500–9,999	61	43	8	3	—
Under 2,500	61	18	3	2	—
All sizes	59	38	14	4	2

— = Less than 0.05

Source: U.S. Department of Justice, Bureau of Justice Statistics, *Local Police Departments, 2003.*

TABLE 6.21
Types of Routine Patrol Other Than Automobile Used by Sheriffs' Offices,
by Size of Population Served

Population served	Percentage of agencies using each type of patrol on a routine basis				
	Foot	Marine	Motorcycle	Foot	Horse
1,000,000 or more	56	56	72	64	32
500,000–999,999	34	41	54	40	20
250,000–499,999	27	45	36	33	15
100,000–249,999	21	36	23	21	14
50,000–99,999	24	34	16	16	6
25,000–49,999	21	18	7	6	1
10,000–24,999	25	15	6	4	3
Under 10,000	29	9	2	3	2
All sizes	25	21	11	10	5

Source: U.S. Department of Justice, Bureau of Justice Statistics, *Sheriffs' Offices, 2003.*

TABLE 6.22
Court-Related Functions of Local Police Departments,
by Size of Population Served, 2003

Population served	Percentage of agencies					
	Executing arrest warrants	Enforcing protection orders	Providing court security	Serving civil process	Enforcing child support orders	Serving eviction notices
1,000,000 or more	81	69	25	13	25	13
500,000– 999,999	79	65	13	13	13	5
250,000– 499,999	81	71	10	5	10	0
100,000– 249,999	82	71	15	9	11	3
50,000– 99,999	91	81	27	8	12	4
25,000– 49,999	95	87	29	13	11	2
10,000– 24,999	92	85	27	11	12	3
2,500– 9,999	93	87	28	14	15	8
Under 2,500	89	81	27	26	20	16
All sizes	91	84	27	18	16	10

Source: U.S. Department of Justice, Bureau of Justice Statistics, *Local Police Departments, 2003.*

TABLE 6.23
Court-Related Functions of Sheriffs' Offices,
by Size of Population Served, 2003

Population served	Percentage of agencies					
	Serving civil processes	Enforcing arrest warrants	Enforcing protection orders	Providing court security	Servicing eviction notices	Enforcing child support orders
1,000,000 or more	85	92	92	96	73	65
500,000– 999,999	93	93	95	93	87	76
250,000– 499,999	95	97	93	92	85	80
100,000– 249,999	97	97	93	93	87	83
50,000– 99,999	99	98	98	92	96	77
25,000– 49,999	99	99	97	94	92	74
10,000– 24,999	98	98	96	98	95	82
Under 10,000	97	96	96	93	87	64
All sizes	98	97	96	94	91	76

Source: U.S. Department of Justice, Bureau of Justice Statistics, Sheriffs' Offices, 2003.

TABLE 6.24
Detention Functions of Local Police Departments,
by Size of Population Served, 2003

	Percentage of agencies		
Population served	Providing inmate transport	Operating a temporary holding cell*	Operating one or more jails
1,000,000 or more	50	69	19
500,000–999,999	25	54	5
250,000–499,999	44	46	15
100,000–249,999	40	44	23
50,000–99,999	46	46	19
25,000–49,999	54	47	15
10,000–24,999	41	40	13
2,500–9,999	33	26	9
Under 2,500	24	10	6
All sizes	32	24	9

*Not for overnight detention.

Source: U.S. Department of Justice, Bureau of Justice Statistics, *Local Police Departments, 2003.*

TABLE 6.25
Detention Functions of Sheriffs' Offices, by Size of Population Served, 2003

	Percentage of agencies		
Population Served	Providing inmate transport	Operating a temporary holding cell*	Operating one or more jails
1,000,000 or more	89	69	85
500,000–999,999	97	60	71
250,000–499,999	91	53	65
100,000–249,999	86	34	79
50,000–99,999	90	21	82
25,000–49,999	95	35	82
10,000–24,999	88	29	77
Under 10,000	84	23	65
All sizes	89	31	76

*Not for overnight detention.

Source: U.S. Department of Justice, Bureau of Justice Statistics, *Sheriffs' Offices, 2003.*

TABLE 6.26
Temporary Holding (Lockup) Facilities Operated by Local Police Departments,
by Size of Population Served, 2003

| | Agencies operating temporary holding (lockup) facilities* | | | |
| | Adult | | Juvenile | |
Population served	Percentage with lockup	Median total capacity	Percentage with lockup	Median total capacity
1,000,000 or more	31	79	19	40
500,000–999,999	25	67	25	12
250,000–499,999	32	58	12	5
100,000–249,999	43	32	28	4
50,000–99,999	51	12	34	3
25,000–49,999	52	8	33	2
10,000–24,999	48	5	29	2
2,500–9,999	26	4	12	2
Under 2,500	8	4	3	1
All sizes	25	4	13	2

Note: Median capacity is based on total for all lockups, and excludes departments not operating a facility.

*For overnight detention and physically separate from a jail.

Source: U.S. Department of Justice, Bureau of Justice Statistics, *Local Police Departments, 2003.*

TABLE 6.27
Temporary Holding (Lockup) Facilities Operated by Sheriffs' Offices,
by Size of Population Served, 2003

Population served	Agencies operating temporary holding (lockup) facilities*			
	Adult		Juvenile	
	Percentage with lockup	Median total capacity	Percentage with lockup	Median total capacity
1,000,000 or more	31	175	15	7
500,000– 999,999	19	196	3	23
250,000– 499,999	23	27	13	10
100,000– 249,999	17	24	8	4
50,000– 99,999	12	30	1	15
25,000– 49,999	22	12	8	4
10,000–4,999	26	20	8	2
Under 10,000	26	10	2	1
All sizes	23	16	6	4

Note: Median capacity is based on total for all lockups, and excludes sheriffs' offices not operating a facility.

*For overnight detention and physically separate from a jail.

Source: U.S. Department of Justice, Bureau of Justice Statistics, *Sheriffs' Offices, 2003.*

TABLE 6.28
Special Public Safety Functions of Local Police Departments,
by Size of Population Service, 2003

Population served	Percentage of agencies responsible for					
	Crime prevention education	Animal control	School crossing services	Emergency medical services	Civil defense	Fire services
1,000,000 or more	94	25	50	19	31	0
500,000–999,999	87	25	59	8	17	3
250,000–499,999	90	32	46	7	17	5
100,000–249,999	94	35	56	9	18	2
50,000–99,999	95	49	54	13	16	3
25,000–49,999	95	57	51	19	18	4
10,000–24,999	92	61	49	21	21	7
2,500–9,999	79	68	47	27	18	8
Under 2,500	58	70	33	30	20	14
All sizes	74	65	42	26	19	10

Source: U.S. Department of Justice, Bureau of Justice Statistics, *Local Police Departments, 2003.*

TABLE 6.29
Special Public Safety Functions of Sheriffs' Offices,
by Size of Population Service, 2003

Population served	Percentage of agencies responsible for					
	Crime prevention education	Animal control	School crossing services	Emergency medical defense	Civil defense	Fire services
1,000,000 or more	92	19	19	12	23	4
500,000– 999,999	69	17	14	7	17	3
250,000– 499,999	66	14	19	10	16	6
100,000– 249,999	77	34	26	9	22	5
50,000– 99,999	79	30	15	9	11	2
25,000– 49,999	77	30	15	10	14	5
10,000– 24,999	70	42	14	13	19	8
Under 10,000	69	46	14	29	34	28
All sizes	73	36	16	15	20	10

Source: U.S. Department of Justice, Bureau of Justice Statistics, *Sheriffs' Offices, 2003.*

TABLE 6.30
Traffic and Vehicle-Related Functions of Local Police Departments,
by Size and Population Served, 2003

Population served	Percentage of agencies responsible for				
	Traffic law enforcement	Accident investigation	Traffic direction and control	Parking enforcement	Commercial vehicle enforcement
1,000,000 or more	100	100	88	88	81
500,000–999,999	100	100	97	71	57
250,000–499,999	100	100	95	73	61
100,000–249,999	100	99	94	81	56
50,000–99,999	100	99	90	88	51
25,000–49,999	100	99	91	93	52
10,000–24,999	100	99	95	92	45
2,500–9,999	100	98	90	89	39
Under 2,500	100	94	86	81	32
All sizes	100	97	89	86	38

Source: U.S. Department of Justice, Bureau of Justice Statistics, *Local Police Departments, 2003.*

TABLE 6.31
Traffic and Vehicle-Related Functions of Sheriffs' Offices,
by Size and Population Served, 2003

Population served	Percentage of agencies responsible for				
	Traffic law enforcement	Accident investigation	Traffic direction and control	Parking enforcement	Commercial vehicle enforcement
1,000,000 or more	89	81	81	77	65
500,000– 999,999	80	66	75	58	36
250,000– 499,999	73	61	65	41	26
100,000– 249,999	84	62	65	36	18
50,000–99,999	88	67	66	38	23
25,000–49,999	92	74	72	30	14
10,000–24,999	92	77	76	33	19
Under 10,000	94	82	72	38	14
All sizes	90	74	71	36	18

Source: U.S. Department of Justice, Bureau of Justice Statistics, *Sheriffs' Offices, 2003.*

TABLE 6.32
Special Operations Functions of Local Police Departments,
by Size of Population Served, 2003

Population served	Percentage of agencies responsible for			
	Tactical operations (SWAT)	Search and rescue	Underwater recovery	Bomb/ explosives disposal
1,000,000 or more	100	63	56	88
500,000–999,999	97	49	44	87
250,000–499,999	100	29	27	76
100,000–249,999	93	26	17	42
50,000–99,999	86	19	16	18
25,000–49,999	68	20	8	6
10,000–24,999	43	19	6	3
2,500–9,999	20	20	2	1
Under 2,500	8	22	2	—
All sizes	25	21	4	3

— = Less than 0.5%

Source: U.S. Department of Justice, Bureau of Justice Statistics, *Local Police Departments, 2003.*

TABLE 6.33
Special Operations Functions of Sheriffs' Offices,
by Size of Population Served, 2003

Population served	Percentage of agencies responsible for			
	Search and rescue	Tactical operations (SWAT)	Underwater recovery	Bomb/ explosives disposal
1,000,000 or more	69	77	65	58
500,000–999,999	63	85	46	46
250,000–499,999	54	72	52	55
100,000–249,999	51	72	44	19
50,000–99,999	53	80	47	16
25,000–49,999	52	47	26	4
10,000–24,999	60	27	21	4
Under 10,000	57	13	6	4
All sizes	56	43	27	10

Source: U.S. Department of Justice, Bureau of Justice Statistics, *Sheriffs' Offices, 2003.*

TABLE 6.34
Local Police Departments with a Mission Statement That
Includes Community Policing, by Size of Population Served, 2003

Population served	Percentage of agencies with a mission statement		
	Total	With a community policing component	No community policing component
1,000,000 or more	100	88	13
500,000–999,999	100	61	39
250,000–499,999	98	83	15
100,000–249,999	99	87	12
50,000–99,999	97	76	21
25,000–49,999	95	76	19
10,000–24,999	87	65	23
2,500–9,999	71	47	24
Under 2,500	50	32	18
All sizes	67	47	20

Source: U.S. Department of Justice, Bureau of Justice Statistics, *Local Police Departments, 2003.*

TABLE 6.35
Sheriffs' Offices with a Mission Statement That Includes Community Policing,
by Size of Population Served, 2003

| Population served | Percentage of agencies with a mission statement | | |
	Total	With a community policing component	No community policing component
1,000,000 or more	92	69	23
500,000–999,999	93	56	38
250,000–499,999	94	52	42
100,000–249,999	93	45	48
50,000–99,999	75	35	39
25,000–49,999	64	31	34
10,000–24,999	57	19	39
Under 10,000	44	17	27
All sizes	64	28	36

Source: U.S. Department of Justice, Bureau of Justice Statistics, *Sheriffs' Offices, 2003.*

TABLE 6.36
Community Policing Activities of Local Police Departments,
by Percentage of Population Served, 2003

Population served	Activities in year ending June 30, 2003				
	Problem-solving partnerships or written agreements	Partnered with citizen groups to elicit feedback	Upgraded technology for analysis of community problems	Trained citizens in community policing	Conducted citizen police academy
1,000,000 or more	88	94	69	75	81
500,000– 999,999	92	81	70	65	78
250,000– 499,999	95	85	73	71	78
100,000– 249,999	91	86	67	65	78
50,000– 99,999	86	73	54	51	65
25,000– 49,999	82	67	44	38	54
10,000– 24,999	70	54	29	28	32
2,500– 9,999	59	33	22	13	12
Under 2,500	50	23	10	10	2
All sizes	60	37	21	18	17

Source: U.S. Department of Justice, Bureau of Justice Statistics, *Local Police Departments, 2003.*

TABLE 6.37
Community Policing Activities of Sheriffs' Offices,
by Percentage of Population Served, 2003

Population served	Activities in year ending June 30, 2003				
	Problem-solving partnerships or written agreements	Partnered with citizen groups to elicit feedback	Trained citizens in community policing	Upgraded technology for analysis of community problems	Conducted citizen police academy
1,000,000 or more	81	65	58	46	62
500,000–999,999	78	62	41	45	45
250,000–499,999	79	41	30	44	38
100,000–249,999	74	55	33	23	36
50,000–99,999	64	48	32	23	20
25,000–49,999	60	41	19	13	7
10,000–24,999	58	29	12	15	4
Under 10,000	44	20	6	10	2
All sizes	59	36	19	17	12

Source: U.S. Department of Justice, Bureau of Justice Statistics, *Sheriffs' Offices, 2003.*

FIGURE 6.16
Percentage of Local Police Departments Using Full-Time
Community-Policing Officers, 1997, 2000, 2003

Population served

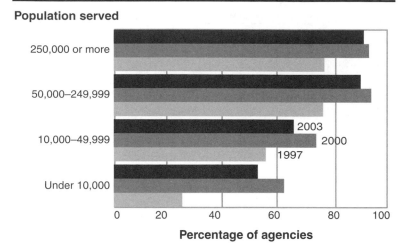

Source: U.S. Department of Justice, Bureau of Justice Statistics, *Local Police Departments, 2003.*

FIGURE 6.17
Percentage of Sheriffs' Offices Using Full-Time
Community-Policing Officers, 1997, 2000, 2003

Population served

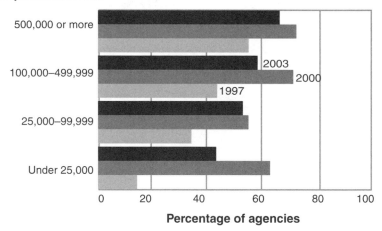

Source: U.S. Department of Justice, Bureau of Justice Statistics, *Sheriffs' Offices, 2003.*

TABLE 6.38

Types of Nonlethal Weapons Authorized for Personal Use by Sworn Personnel in Local Police Departments, by Percentage of Population Served, 2003

	Chemical agents (personal use)				Batons				Soft projectile	Electrical devices	Other weapons/actions			
Population served	Any type in survey	Pepper spray	Tear gas	CS	Any type in survey	Collapsible	Traditional	PR-24			Holds/neck restraints*	Rubber bullet	Black jack	High-intensity light
1,000,000 or more	94	94	19	19	100	88	56	44	69	75	31	25	6	0
500,000–999,999	97	97	19	22	100	89	60	38	48	43	16	16	3	0
250,000–499,999	98	95	24	22	100	83	54	44	59	56	39	22	7	2
100,000–249,999	99	99	22	24	99	93	56	44	66	50	36	22	2	2
50,000–99,999	99	97	25	27	99	92	45	39	72	46	30	22	3	2
25,000–49,999	100	100	24	21	99	93	44	39	57	39	12	19	3	1
10,000–24,999	99	98	22	17	97	91	47	45	42	31	12	10	3	—
2,500–9,999	98	98	13	14	94	88	47	41	28	21	9	6	4	0
Under 2,500	99	98	14	12	93	86	52	42	13	15	13	6	6	1
All sizes	99	98	16	14	95	88	49	42	28	23	13	8	5	1

Percentage of agencies authorizing

*Includes handheld direct contact devices (such as stun gun) and handheld standoff devices (such as taser); — = Less than <0.5%;

Source: U.S. Department of Justice, Bureau of Justice Statistics, *Local Police Departments, 2003.*

TABLE 6.39

Types of Nonlethal Weapons Authorized for Personal Use by Sworn Personnel in Sheriffs' Offices, by Percentage of Population Served, 2003

Population served	Chemical agents (personal use)				Percentage of agencies authorizing									
	Any type in survey	Pepper spray	Tear gas	CS	Batons				Soft projectile	Electrical devices	Other weapons/actions			
					Any type in survey	Collapsible	Traditional	PR-24			Rubber bullet	Holds, neck restraints*	Black jack	High-Intensity light
1,000,000 or more	100	100	23	27	100	100	69	31	73	46	31	39	15	0
500,000–999,999	100	100	20	19	98	92	48	38	51	58	20	17	0	0
250,000–499,999	100	100	27	16	98	90	50	44	46	41	16	14	3	1
100,000–249,999	99	98	21	22	94	92	43	27	48	43	16	9	0	0
50,000–99,999	98	98	32	25	93	92	56	36	55	49	22	8	1	0
25,000–49,999	98	98	18	19	91	86	43	35	31	23	12	10	2	1
10,000–24,999	97	97	19	18	91	87	40	32	22	24	9	14	4	2
Under 10,000	90	90	17	14	88	80	41	34	17	23	6	10	7	2
All sizes	96	9	21	19	92	87	44	34	32	30	12	11	3	1

*Includes handheld direct contact devices (such as stun gun) and handheld standoff devices (such as taser).

Source: U.S. Department of Justice, Bureau of Justice Statistics, *Sheriffs' Offices, 2003*.

FIGURE 6.18
Local Police Departments Using Video Cameras in Patrol Cars, 2000 and 2003

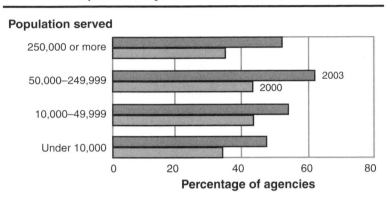

Source: U.S. Department of Justice, Bureau of Justice Statistics, *Local Police Departments, 2003.*

FIGURE 6.19
Sheriffs' Offices Using Video Cameras in Patrol Cars, 2000 and 2003

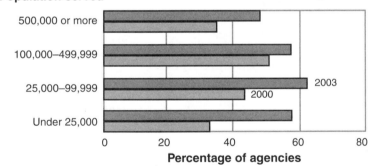

Source: U.S. Department of Justice, Bureau of Justice Statistics, *Sheriffs' Offices, 2003.*

TABLE 6.40
Special Technologies Used by Local Police Departments, by Size of Population Served, 2003

Population served	Percentage of agencies using									
	Night vision/electro-optic			Vehicle stopping/tracking			Digital imaging			
	Infrared (thermal) imagers	Image intensifiers	Laser range finders	Tire deflation spikes	Stolen vehicle tracking	Electrical/ engine disruption	Mug shots	Finger prints	Suspect composites	Facial recognition
1,000,000 or more	69	25	44	50	69	6	88	81	44	19
500,000– 999,999	76	30	24	54	68	8	87	67	59	5
250,000– 499,999	54	17	17	66	56	7	88	85	59	10
100,000– 249,999	53	25	26	60	42	5	85	81	62	6
50,000–99,999	55	19	31	57	31	—	83	71	55	9
25,000–49,999	43	18	21	61	21	1	80	55	55	9
10,000–24,999	34	16	12	43	10	1	73	29	37	7
2,500–9,999	20	10	7	33	4	0	55	22	17	3
Under 2,500	13	5	1	16	1	—	24	18	6	2
All sizes	23	10	8	31	7	—	48	26	20	4

— = Less than <0.5%

Source: U.S. Department of Justice, Bureau of Justice Statistics, *Local Police Departments, 2003.*

TABLE 6.41
Special Technologies Used by Sheriffs' Offices, by Size of Population Served, 2003

Population served	Night vision/electro-optic			Vehicle stopping/tracking			Digital imaging			
	Infrared (thermal) imagers	Image intensifiers	Laser range finders	Tire deflation spikes	Stolen vehicle tracking	Electrical/engine disruption	Mug shots	Finger prints	Suspect composites	Facial recognition
1,000,000 or more	57	27	35	65	62	12	96	89	58	27
500,000–999,999	46	20	27	56	25	0	88	90	48	8
250,000–499,999	43	18	23	58	24	0	90	79	49	9
100,000–249,999	48	18	16	66	10	2	84	82	48	9
50,000–99,999	53	16	19	66	5	1	90	67	48	12
25,000–49,999	35	11	12	52	4	0	77	49	24	6
10,000–24,999	30	9	8	40	3	0	72	36	14	5
Under 10,000	21	14	4	29	1	0	55	23	6	2
All sizes	35	13	11	48	5	1	74	4	25	6

Source: U.S. Department of Justice, Bureau of Justice Statistics, *Sheriffs' Offices, 2003.*

FIGURE 6.20

Citizen Complaints about Police Use of Force per 100
Full-Time Sworn Officers, by Type of Agency, 2002

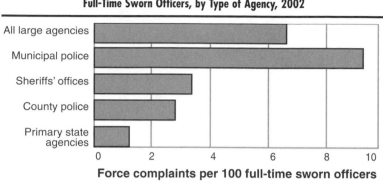

Source: U.S. Department of Justice, Bureau of Justice Statistics, *Citizen Complaints about Police Use of Force, 2002.*

TABLE 6.42

Complaint Dispositions in Large Law Enforcement Agencies,
by Type of Agency, 2002

	Percentage of complaint dispositions					
Type of agency	Total with disposition	Not sustained	Unfounded	Exonerated	Sustained	Other disposition
All large agencies	94	34	25	23	8	9
Local agencies	94	35	26	23	8	9
Municipal police	94	37	25	21	8	9
Sheriffs' offices	95	20	30	32	12	6
County police	93	25	17	35	6	17
Primary state agencies	95	16	19	52	9	4

Source: U.S. Department of Justice, Bureau of Justice Statistics, *Citizen Complaints about Police Use of Force, 2006.*

TABLE 6.43
Complaint Dispositions in Large Law Enforcement Agencies,
by Percentage of Full-Time Sworn Officers, 2002

Full-time sworn	Complaint dispositions					
	Total with disposition	Not sustained	Unfounded	Exonerated	Sustained	Other disposition
1,000 or more	93	42	23	19	6	10
500–999	96	21	26	28	14	12
250–499	95	19	33	29	12	6
100–249	97	22	31	34	10	3
Total	94	3	25	23	8	9

Source: U.S. Department of Justice, Bureau of Justice Statistics, *Citizen Complaints about Police Use of Force, 2006.*

TABLE 6.44

Citizen Complaints About Police Use of Force in Large Municipal Departments, by Selected Agency Administrative Characteristics, 2002

	Force complaints received			
	Per agency	Per 100 full-time sworn	Per 100 full-time sworn responding to calls for service	Per 10,000 population
Civilian complaint review board (CCRB)				
Jurisdictions with CCRB	158	11.9	19.6	3.70
Jurisdictions without CCRB	18	6.6	10.6	1.35
Internal affairs capacity				
Specialized unit	54	9.8	16.0	2.51
No specialized unit	5	3.7	5.5	0.68
Personnel monitoring system				
Jurisdictions with system	69	9.0	14.6	2.33
Jurisdictions without system	33	10.1	16.5	2.45
Policy requiring external investigation				
Jurisdictions with policy	67	10.0	16.3	2.80
Jurisdictions without policy	21	8.0	13.0	1.55
Right to administrative appeal				
Citizen may appeal	29	8.8	14.3	1.96
Citizen may not appeal	54	9.7	15.8	2.56
Collective bargaining				
Authorized for officers	53	9.9	16.4	2.58
Not authorized for officers	23	7.3	11.3	1.60
Total	**45**	**9.5**	**15.4**	**2.38**

Source: U.S. Department of Justice, Bureau of Justice Statistics, *Citizen Complaints about Police Use of Force, 2006.*

TABLE 6.45
Complaint Dispositions in Large Municipal Police Departments,
by Selected Agency Administrative Characteristics, 2002

	Total with dispo-sition	Complaint dispositions				
		Not sustained	Un-founded	Exon-erated	Sus-tained	Other dispo-sition
Civilian complaint review board (CCRB)						
Jurisdictions with CCRB	93	42	23	18	6	10
Jurisdictions without CCRB	95	25	31	26	11	7
Internal affairs capacity						
Specialized unit	94	37	25	20	8	9
No specialized unit	99	16	28	47	9	1
Personnel monitoring system						
Jurisdictions with system	95	30	28	23	8	11
Jurisdictions without system	93	44	22	18	8	8
Policy requiring external investigation						
Jurisdictions with policy	93	39	25	20	7	9
Jurisdictions without policy	97	28	27	24	12	9
Right to administrative appeal						
Citizen may appeal	97	33	21	24	14	8
Citizen may not appeal	93	38	27	20	6	10
Collective bargaining						
Authorized for officers	94	39	25	20	7	10
Not authorized for officers	95	24	30	26	15	6
Total	**94**	**37**	**25**	**21**	**8**	**9**

Source: U.S. Department of Justice, Bureau of Justice Statistics, *Citizen Complaints about Police Use of Force, 2006.*

FIGURE 6.21
Law Enforcement Officers Killed in the Line of Duty, 1973–2004

Number killed

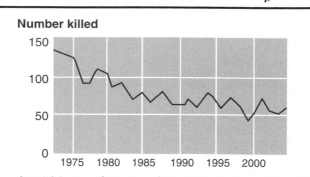

Source: U.S. Department of Justice, Bureau of Justice Statistics, *Law Enforcement Officers Killed, 2006.*

FIGURE 6.22
Law Enforcement Officers Killed in the Line of Duty by Weapon Type, 1973–2004

Number killed

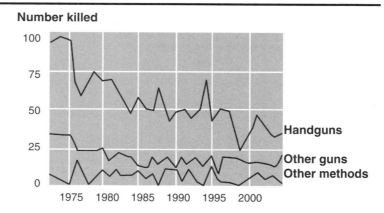

Source: U.S. Department of Justice, Bureau of Justice Statistics, *Law Enforcement Officers Killed, 2006.*

7

Directory of Organizations

There are numerous agencies and organizations in policing. The following list offers a few of these, along with contact information and a brief description of their purpose, missions, stated goals, and emphases. Some of these are privately run organizations, whereas others have governmental or business affiliations. Some are labor organizations or components to larger parent groups. All of them make up the vast number of organizations associated with policing in the United States. (The completeness of contact information may vary depending on its availability.)

Academy of Behavioral Profiling (ABP)
336 Lincoln Street
P.O. Box 6406
Sitka, AK 99835
Email: bturvey@profiling.org
Internet: http://www.profiling.org

A professional association whose function is to promote evidence-based techniques in criminal profiling to the application of legal system processes, the ABP is an international organization with over one hundred members around the globe. The use of scientific psychological methods in the solving and prediction of criminal activity is a key focus of the association. The ABP has a journal called *The Journal of Behavioral Profiling* that is published quarterly and sponsors an annual conference. In addition, the organization has a recommended reading link on its website for works on behavioral profiling.

Academy of Criminal Justice Sciences (ACJS)
P.O. Box 960
Greenbelt, MD 20768-0960
Phone: (800) 757-ACJS (2257)
Fax: (301) 446-2819
Email: ExecDir@acjs.org
Internet: http://www.acjs.org

An international society created in 1963, the ACJS has as its mission the fostering of professional and academic activity in the criminal justice field. Members of ACJS include criminal justice practitioners, scholars, and students from a variety of different areas. The provision of criminal justice education, research, and policy analysis is a key component of the organization's purpose. The ACJS has an annual meeting and publishes two journals: *Justice Quarterly* and *Journal of Criminal Justice Education.* Both journals are offered online as well as in hard copy format. The organization also produces a newsletter called *ACJS Today,* which is published four times per year and has a circulation of nearly 2,000. In addition, the ACJS has a certification process for academic institutions that has evolved from a peer review procedure to certification of institutions that meet the standards set out by the organization. The organization's web page also includes an employment bulletin for job openings in the criminal justice field.

Airborne Law Enforcement Association (ALEA)
411 Aviation Way
Suite 200
Frederick, MD 21701
Phone: (301) 631-2406
Fax: (301) 631-2466
Email: singley@alea.org
Internet: http://www.alea.org

With a membership of over 3,500 members, the ALEA has as its mission the support, promotion, and advancement of the safe and effective use of aircraft in the field of policing throughout the nation and abroad. The agency provides training through seminars, promotes networking opportunities, and presents valuable information on advancements in the field through product expositions.

American Academy of Forensic Sciences (AAFS)
410 N. 21st Street
Colorado Springs, CO 80904
Phone: (719) 636-1100
Fax: (719) 636-1993
Email: awarren@aafs.org
Internet: http://www.aafs.org

Organized in 1948, the AAFS is a nonprofit professional society devoted to improving the criminal justice system by applying science to the processes of law. Its membership of nearly 6,000 consists of physicians, lawyers, dentists, criminalists, physical anthropologists, and people of other occupations from all fifty states in the United States, as well as from fifty-five countries around the globe. The organization has a journal, the *Journal of Forensic Sciences,* an annual meeting, and newsletters, and it hosts seminars and meetings to address concerns in the field of forensic science. Billing itself as the "world's most prestigious forensic science organization," the AAFS has ten organizational sections in different subfields that provide opportunities for professional advancement, networking, awards, and other forms of recommendation, and some publish newsletters to keep section members updated on activities and developments in their field.

American Association of State Troopers, Inc. (AAST)
1949 Raymond Diehl Road
Tallahassee, FL
Phone: (800) 765-5456
Fax: (850) 385-8697
Email: scott@statetroopers.org
Internet: http://www.statetroopers.org

The AAST is a fraternal association of retired and active duty state troopers and state law enforcement officers. The group's stated goals are the promotion of esprit de corps among the officers and their families, professional development through training programs, acquisition of financial support for scholarship programs for dependants, and participation in campaigns for safety and consumer education.

American Board of Criminalistics (ABC)
No address, phone number, or fax is provided on the website.
Internet: http://www.criminalistics.com

The ABC is comprised of regional and national forensic science professionals that oversee certification to the forensic science community. Members are able to attain three levels of certification: diplomate, fellow, and technical specialist. Individuals with affiliate status are those who pass the general knowledge examination and become eligible for certification after two years. The ABC's newsletter is called the *Certification News*.

American College of Forensic Examiners Institute (ACFEI)
2750 East Sunshine Street
Springfield. MO 65804
Phone: (800) 423-9737
Fax: (417) 881-4702
Internet: http://www.acfei.com

The ACFEI is an independent professional society dedicated to advancing the field of forensics examination and consultation, and it purports to be the largest organization of its kind in the nation. The organization has a certification process for consultants, medical investigators, forensic accountants, and forensic nurses, and it offers fellow and diplomate credentials. The ACFEI hosts lectures, seminars, conferences, and continuing education programs, and it has an official journal known as *The Forensic Examiner.*

American Criminal Justice Association
(Lambda Alpha Epsilon)
P.O. Box 601047
Sacramento, CA 95860-1047
Phone: (916) 484-6553
Fax: (916) 488-2227
Email: acjalea@aol.com
Internet: http://www.acjalea.org

The ACJA was formed in 1937 in Hayward, California, after a series of summer law enforcement training sessions were provided for a selected group of police officers. Realizing a need for a fraternity of graduates and instructors in criminal justice, Lambda Alpha Epsilon (LAE) was formed and held its first convention in 1938 in Lodi, California. In the first meeting, honorary memberships were provided to the key luminaries in the field: J. Edgar Hoover, August Vollmer, and Earl Warren. The fraternal organization rapidly expanded from its base in California to a national scope in the 1950s, and several states in the United States adopted

LAE fraternities. Presently there are over 145 chapters of the American Criminal Justice Association/Lambda Alpha Epsilon, comprised of over 4,500 members.

American Deputy Sheriff's Association (ADSA)
3001 Armand Street
Suite B
Monroe, LA 71201
Phone: (800) 937-7940
Fax: (318) 398-9980
Internet: http://www.deputysheriff.org

The ADSA is a nonprofit organization whose purpose is to provide support, advocacy, and enhanced communication to the nation's county law enforcement agencies. The association has several benefits to its members, including member and nonmember line-of-duty death benefits, alternative pricing programs for body armor, communications and technical equipment, training utilizing a mobile training unit, assistance to communities, a scholarship program, and a newsletter called *The Enforcement,* among others.

American Jail Association (AJA)
1135 Professional Court
Hagerstown, MD 21740-5853
Phone: (301) 790-3930
Email: gwyn@aja.org
Internet: http://www.corrections.com/aja

The AJA is a nonprofit association that seeks to provide support for personnel who work in the nation's jails. It is a certifying agency for the certified jail manager designation and provides national and regional training to people in the field. It also boasts an award-winning magazine called *American Jails.* This organization claims to be the only national association dedicated solely to the concerns of those who operate the jails in the United States.

American Polygraph Association
P.O. Box 8037
Chattanooga, TN 37414-0037
Phone: (800) APA-8037 or (423) 892-3992
Fax: (423) 894-5435
Email: manager@polygraph.org
Internet: http://www.polygraph.org

The APA reports that it is the primary association of polygraph professionals in the world. The organization boasts over 3,200 members, comprised of practitioners from law enforcement, government, and private industry. The association establishes professional standards for the field, promotes technological advancements, supports instrumentation and research, and provides advanced techniques and continuing education programs. The APA provides standards of professional conduct and accreditation to educational programs. The organization's website provides much information on the profession that is useful to practitioners and the lay public.

American Police Veterans
P.O. Box 2623
Attleborough Falls, MA 02763
Email: Info@Policevets.Org
Internet: http://www.policevets.net

American Police Veterans is a "community of former law enforcement officers" dedicated to finding resources to benefit police veterans, promoting partnerships with like-minded individuals and groups, and providing networking opportunities for its members. Its principal mission is to create a support group for retired and disabled former police officers through peer encouragement and support, advocacy, and fellowship. Efforts with the community are encouraged to achieve the aims of the organization. The organization has a journal called *Beyond the Shield*, and its website lists several resources for retired police officers, including legislative updates.

American Society of Criminology (ASC)
1314 Kinnear Road
Suite 212
Columbus, OH 43212-1156
Phone: (614) 292-9207
Fax: (614) 292-6767
Email: asc@osu.edu
Internet: http://www.asc41.com

An international association, the ASC represents criminologists around the globe. The primary focus of the organization is the promotion of scholarly, scientific, and professional advancement of criminology (the scientific body of knowledge concerned with the causes of, prevention of, control of, and response to criminal behavior). The ASC promotes a multidisciplinary approach to understanding crime, and the membership is comprised of criminal justice (and other social science) faculty, practitioners, and students with an involvement in the profession. The association has five specialized divisions: corrections and sentencing, critical criminology, women and crime, international criminology, and people of color and crime. The organization has an annual meeting and publishes the journals *Criminology* and *Criminology & Public Policy* and the newsletter, *The Criminologist.*

Americans for Effective Law Enforcement (AELE)
841 W. Touly Avenue
Park Ridge, IL 60068-3351
Phone: (847) 685-0700
Fax: (847) 685-9700
Email: info@aele.org
Internet: http://www.aele.org

Created in 1966, this nonprofit organization provides research-driven education and legal information through training seminars via electronic media as well as classroom instruction. Its motto is "building integrity and confidence through research and education," and many national, state, and local organizations and individuals join AELE briefs, which are reported to reflect the views of police administrators throughout the nation. In addition, the organization publishes a number of legal publications such as the *Law Enforcement Liability Reporter, Jail and Prisoner Law Bulletin,* and *Fire and Police Personnel Reporter.* AELE also issues position papers regarding national criminal justice issues.

American Society of Canine Trainers (ASCT)
20726 Syndenham Farm Lane
Remington, VA 22736
Phone: (540) 937-3871
Email: asctpresident@aol.com
Internet: http://www.asct-nationalk9.com

This association is dedicated to the professional development of "elite" canine handlers in law enforcement. The ASCT offers research supported training, certification, and college academic degrees in the police specialty of canine handling. The training not only provides canine handlers with technical training but also classroom instruction in issues of criminal law involving canine units.

Associated Humane Services, Inc./Vested Interest Fund
124 Evergreen Avenue
Newark, New Jersey 07114
Phone: (973) 824-7080
Email: www.ahcares.org
Internet: http://www.vestadog.com

This animal advocacy organization has a program called Vest-a-Dog that seeks to provide police dogs with protective vests. The program has been in operation since 1999 when the organizer heard the story of a police dog that was killed in the line of duty. Donations for the program are sought by the organization.

Association of Certified Fraud Specialists, Inc. (ACFS)
P.O. Box 348777
Sacramento, CA 95834-8777
Phone: (866) 439-2327
Fax (916) 419-6318
Internet: http://www.acfsnet.org

The ACFS is a nonprofit educational organization comprised of certified fraud investigators of different disciplines who seek to better the profession through training, accreditation, and fostering best practices in the field. They have an association called the Order of the Shield that seeks to protect the public from white-collar crimes.

Association for Crime Scene Reconstruction (ACSR)
P.O. Box 51376
6332 South Cedar Place
Broken Arrow, OK 74011
Internet: http://www.acsr.org

The ASCR is an association whose members are police investigators, forensic scientists, and scholars from around the world. Formed in 1991, this organization has 555 members and seeks to promote professionalism in the field of crime scene reconstruction through training conferences, networking opportunities, promoting research, cooperation and collaboration among members, and consultation opportunities. The association also has a newsletter called *The Scene* on its website.

Association of Firearm and Tool Mark Examiners (AFTE)
No address, telephone, or fax information provided on website.
Email: Lsugarman@fss.orange.ca.us
Internet: http://www.afte.org

Formed in 1969 in recognition of the potential of the new field of criminalistics, the AFTE seeks to improve the professionalism of the specific field of firearm and tool mark examination. The organization offers certification to qualified members in the examination and evidence of firearms, tool marks, and gunshot residue.

Association of Public Safety Communications Officials (APCO)
351 N. Williamson Boulevard
Daytona Beach, FL 32114-1112
Phone: (888) 272-6911
Fax: (386) 322-2501
Email: apco@apcointl.org
Internet: http://www.apcointl.org

APCO is an association of communications professionals that has as its mission the provision of professional leadership, influence on governmental and industrial communications decisions, the promotion of professional development, and advocacy for technological advancements in the communications field. The organization facilitates meetings and conferences in the field of public safety communications.

Borderpol
80 Fieldrow Avenue
Ottawa, ON, Canada
K1C 7G6
Phone: (416) 352-6501
Internet: http://www.borderpol.org

This organization is the only international association that seeks to provide a feasible institutional framework for enforcing the world's border control initiatives. It supports the management of the border control agencies of the various countries in the spirit of the Universal Declaration of Human Rights. The organization hosts a World Border Security Symposium as well as regional meetings.

Boy Scout's Crime Prevention Program
P.O. Box 152079
Irving, TX 75015-2079
Phone: (972) 580-2241
Internet: http://www.usscouts.org

The Boy Scouts of America, with support from the National Crime Prevention Council, began a program in 1996 to teach crime prevention to the scouts. By using an initiative that promotes parent–child communication skills, that collaborates with law enforcement organizations from federal, state, and local levels, and that coordinates with grassroots groups, the program allows the boy scouts to earn a merit badge for their efforts in planning and executing a home or community crime prevention project, usually guided by a police officer.

Clandestine Laboratory Investigators Association (CLIA)
P.O. Box 22074
Honolulu, HA 96823
Fax: (808) 356-1524
Email: clialabs.com
Internet: http://www.clialabs.com.

CLIA is a nonprofit organization whose mission is to provide support, training, legislative advocacy, and expert testimony to police agencies, prosecutors, and emergency service providers. Its mission is to provide professional training to police regarding the dangers of clandestine drug laboratory investigation such as explosions, fires, and respiratory hazards. It has an annual conference that provides information on this dangerous aspect of police work.

Commission of the Accreditation of Law Enforcement Agencies (CALEA)
10302 Eaton Place
Suite 100
Fairfax, VA 22030

Phone: (800) 368-3757
Fax: (703) 591-2206
Email: calea@calea.org
Internet: http://www.calea.org

CALEA is a nonprofit corporation that provides accreditation for police agencies through the cooperation of other associations such as the International Association of Chiefs of Police (IACP), the National Sheriff's Association, the National Organization of Black Law Enforcement Officers (NOBLE), and the Police Executive Research Forum (PERF). Using a successful model of administration, CALEA provides police administrators from the various police agencies involved in the accreditation process with a plan for providing effective law enforcement services in their departments. CALEA requires involved agencies to prepare an organizational plan with sound standard operating procedures and a preparedness plan in case of natural or human-made disasters. The reported benefits of a CALEA accreditation is a strengthening of departments' accountability and reputation and a corresponding improvement with the communities they serve. It can also limit liability and risk vulnerability to the many different complaints made of police agencies. In addition to national accreditation, the organization provides training, maintains a profession website, and produces a newsletter called *CALEA Today* for its members.

Community Policing Consortium
1726 Main Street N.W.
Suite 801
Washington, D.C. 20036

The Community Policing Consortium is an association administered and funded by the Office of Community Oriented Policing Services (COPS), a division of the U.S. Department of Justice. It consists of a partnership of five police associations: the International Association of Chiefs of Police (IACP), the National Organization of Black Law Enforcement Executives (NOBLE), the National Sheriff's Association (NSA), Police Executive Research Forum (PERF), and the Police Foundation. All of these play an integral role in developing social science research in the area of community policing as well as training and technical assistance in this area.

Concerns of Police Survivors, Inc. (COPS)
P.O. Box 3199
3096 S. State Highway 5
Camdenton, MO 65020
Phone: (573) 346-4911
Fax: (573) 346-1414
Email: cops@nationalcops.org
Internet: http://www.nationalcops.org

This nonprofit association provides support and resources for survivors of officers killed in the line of duty. It also provides survivor victimization education and training to law enforcement agencies and to the public. COPS, formed in 1984, has seen a large increase in membership since its inception and provides scholarships, counseling programs, a summer camp, retreats, an annual Survivors' Conference, and other assistance resources.

Crime Stoppers International
P.O. Box 614
Arlington, TX 76004-0614
Phone: (800) 850-7574
Email: rpage@kmts.org
Internet: http://www.c-s-i.org

Crime Stoppers International is a partnership of the community, the media, and the police that uses citizens sending tips on crimes involving homicides, sexual assaults, drug trafficking, robberies, and many others. Started in Albuquerque, New Mexico, in 1976, Crime Stoppers now has programs in approximately 1,200 communities in the United States and several other countries. The organization is a not-for-profit, and citizens who provide tips that help solve crimes are often rewarded. According to the organization's web page, around 600,000 arrests have been made based on citizens reporting crimes through the program and nearly $7 billion in recovered property and drugs has been seized.

Disabled Public Safety Employee's Association (DPSEA)
Email: dpsea_prez@yahoo.com
Internet: http://www.dpsea.org

This organization represents sworn police officers, corrections officials, and other public agents who are disabled, and it offers emotional support, guidance, and fellowship. The members of the organization are all disabled public servants who wish to make life better for their "fallen brothers and sisters."

Drug Abuse Resistance Education (DARE)
DARE America
P.O. Box 512090
Los Angeles, CA 90051-0090
Phone: (800) 223-DARE
Fax: (310) 215-0180
Internet: http://www.dare-america.com

The DARE (Drug Abuse Resistance Education) program is a school program that endeavors to keep kids from using illicit drugs. The program began in 1983 in Los Angeles and has grown to being implemented in approximately 75 percent of schools nationwide and is now used in over forty-three countries around the world. The educational program is led by police officers who reach children from kindergarten through high school. The model offers a supplement to the community policing philosophy and now has international recognition, supported by the U.S. Department of Justice. The organization's website has numerous resources for educators, policy makers, and others interested in promoting drug resistance education.

Family Badge
P.O. Box 5396
Galveston, TX 77554
Phone: (888) 788-8967
Internet: http://www.familybadge.org

The Family Badge is a national support network for law enforcement officers and their families. Comprised of peace officers from various jurisdictions, the organization disseminates information on member activities, legislative issues, grants and programs, scholarships, and benefits for disabled officers or the families of those killed in the line of duty. The organization also operates a police news site on the Internet.

Federal Law Enforcement Officers Association (FLEOA)
P.O. Box 326
Lewisberry, PA 17339
Phone: (717) 938-2300

Fax: (717) 932-2262
Email: fleoa@fleoa.org
Internet: http://www.fleoa.org

The FLEOA claims over 20,000 members, constituting the largest membership of federal law enforcement officers in a nonpartisan, voluntary, professional association. Its members come from over fifty federal agencies and are all active duty agents. The goal of the organization, which was formed in 1977, is to provide members with a legislative voice in many areas including wages, disability, and retirees' carry authority.

Fight Crime: Invest in Kids
1212 New York Avenue NW
Suite 300
Washington, DC 20005
Phone: (202) 776-0027
Internet: http://www.fightcrime.com

This organization is a national, nonprofit, anticrime collective consisting of over 3,000 police chiefs, sheriffs, state attorneys, other law enforcement officials, and survivors of violent crime. Crime prevention is key component of this organization and Fight Crime: Invest in Kids facilitates educational and after-school programs, child abuse initiatives, and interventions for at-risk youth. The organization promotes these programs but does not provide funding or direct supervision of them.

Hellenic American Police Association (HAPA)
P.O. Box 59401
Chicago, IL 60659-0401
Internet: http://www.members.aol.com/chicagohapa.org

Founded in 1993, this organization is a nonprofit association representing police officers of Hellenic origin. The majority of the membership is located in Illinois, but there are members in other states as well. The purpose of the organization is to unite officers of Hellenic ancestry to promote their heritage. Membership is open to officers with such a heritage or by adoption.

High Tech Crime Consortium
1506 North Stevens Street
Tacoma, WA 98406-3826

Phone: (253) 752-2427
Fax: (253) 752-2430
Email: President@HighTechCrimeCops.org
Internet: http://www.hightechcrimecops.org

The motto for this organization is "using high-tech tools to fight high-tech crime." The consortium seeks to educate and train police agencies in the detection, investigation, and analysis of high-tech crime. The organization incorporates a pool of experts in intelligence analysis, investigation supervision, computer forensics, crime analysis, crime research, and computer technology to assist agencies in these areas.

Hispanic American Police Command Officers Association (HAPCOA)

HAPCOA National
6450 N.W. Loop 410, PMB 1546
San Antonio, TX 78238
Phone: (210) 431-7349
Fax: (210) 434-8744
Email: info@hapcoa.org
Internet: http://www.hapcoa.org

Formed in 1973, HAPCOA reports that it is the oldest association of Hispanic American law enforcement command officers. It also claims to be the largest, having members and chapters in many police agencies throughout the United States and Puerto Rico. The organization is comprised of police administrators from municipal, county, state, and federal police agencies. Its purpose is to advance the selection, promotion, and retention of Hispanic Americans in law enforcement and to address the concerns and needs of their communities, especially in regard to police–community relations. One of the initiatives of the organization is a partnership with the National Highway Transportation Administration to provide public safety materials in Spanish. The association has a national training conference and a newsletter.

International Association for the Study of Organized Crime (IASOC)

IASOC Executive Director
Department of Criminal Justice, Indiana University
302 Sycamore Hall
Bloomington, IN 47405

Phone: (812) 855-0889
Fax: (812) 855-5522
Email: iasoc_office@yahoo.com
Internet: http://www.iasoc.net

The IASOC is a professional association founded in 1984 and comprised of criminologists, criminal justice researches, practitioners, educators, and students. Its purpose is to promote increased awareness and research about organized crime and its manifestations. The organization has an annual meeting, held in conjunction with the American Society of Criminology in which information about organized crime is disseminated to participants. As a benefit of membership the peer-reviewed journal, *Trends in Organized Crime,* is published quarterly. The organization's web page also provides a link to websites whose focus is organized crime.

International Association of Campus Law Enforcement Administrators (IACLEA)
342 North Main Street
West Hartford, CT 06117-2507
Phone: (860) 586-7517
Fax: (860) 586-7550
Email: info@iaclea.org
Internet: http://www.iaclea.org

The IACLEA is an organization representing more than a thousand colleges and universities in twenty countries whose purpose is to provide educational resources, advocacy, and opportunities for professional development for campus police personnel. Formed in 1958 on the campus of Arizona State University, this organization's membership is over 1,600 and consists of campus public safety staff members, criminal justice faculty, and municipal chiefs of police. The organization has an annual meeting and a bimonthly journal called *Campus Law Enforcement Journal,* with a readership of more than 1,700. In addition, the IACLEA has an accreditation program for college and university law enforcement, public safety, and security departments. This program, started in 1995, promotes greater consistency and higher standards for campus departments who receive the accreditations.

International Association of Chiefs of Police (IACP)
515 North Washington Street
Alexandria, VA 22314

Phone: (703) 836-6767; (800) THE IACP
Fax: (703) 836-4543
Email: information@theiacp.org
Internet: http://www.theiacp.org

The IACP is a not-for-profit international organization of police chiefs whose aims are to advance both the art and science of police work, to provide improvements in administrative, technical, and operational procedures, to promote collegiality; increase professionalism through improved training and recruitment methods; and to promote high professional and ethical standards. Begun in 1863, the organization was the impetus behind many important law enforcement projects, including the Uniform Crime Records (UCR) system and the FBI's Identification Division, among others. The slogan "Global Leadership in Policing" reflects its international scope. The organization's web page has numerous resources and a link to several publications produced by the organization such as the *Police Chief* magazine.

International Association of Directors of Law Enforcement Standards and Training (IADLEST)
2521 Country Club Way
Albion, MI 49224
Phone: (517) 857-3828
Fax: (517) 857-3826
Email: PJudge@worldnet.att.net
Internet: http://www.iadlest.org

Serving as the national forum of Peace Officer Standards and Training (POST) agencies, the IADLEST is an international association of managers and executives involved in police training and certification. Its mission is to facilitate research in the field in order to produce and disseminate vital information, ideas, and advancements to law enforcement agencies throughout the United States. The association has several projects underway including a driver training reference guide, an organizational sourcebook, a reciprocity handbook that consolidates employment issues for police officers in all fifty states, terrorism response training for police officers, among others.

International Association of Law Enforcement Intelligence Analysts (IALEIA)
IALEIA, Inc.

P.O. Box 13857
Richmond, VA 23225
Fax: (804) 565-2059
Internet: http://www.ialeia.org

Founded in 1981, this organization has as its primary function the advancement of professional standards in law enforcement intelligence analysis operating at the local, state or provincial, national, and international levels. The IALEIA promotes the profession of law enforcement intelligence and competence by encouraging research and training standards; acts in an advisory capacity to governments; provides and shares technological advancements in the field; and generally improves the profession. Started in the United States, this organization presently has members in many countries and facilitates training to law enforcement agencies.

International Association of Law Enforcement Planners (IALEP)
P.O. Box 11437
Torrance, CA 90510-1437
Phone: (310) 225-5148
Email: ialep@ialep.org
Internet: http://www.ialep.org

Representing nearly a thousand police professionals in fifteen nations around the globe, the IALEP is an association for people working in planning and research for criminal justice agencies. Formed in 1991 from a merger of the Association of Police Planning and Research Officers (APPRO) and the National Association of Police Planners (NAPP), the organization has many useful features for its members, including a list serve that provides rapid access of answers to pertinent questions, a quality newsletter (*The Exchange*), and a certification program for people who seek the Professional and Advanced Certification designation.

International Association of Undercover Officers (IAUO)
Phone: (800) 876-5943
Fax: (800) 876-5912
Email: Charlie@undercover.org
Internet: http://www.undercover.org

The promotion of safety and professionalism among its membership of undercover police officers is the aim of the IAUO. It desires to promote communication and cooperation among its international memberships and maintains a confidential database that provides information on techniques, trends, information on criminal establishments, promising products to aid undercover workers, and potential funding sources. The association IAUO provides start-up assistance to newly forming units as well as for the management of established ones.

International Association of Women Police (IAWP)
1417 Derby County Crescent
Oakville, ON, Canada
L6M 318
Email: amy.ramsay@jus.gov.on.ca
Internet: http://www.iawp.org

The IAWP's stated mission is to provide unity and support for female peace officers and to elevate the status of women officers on an international level. To accomplish this mission, the association supports efforts to increase professional development and training, mentoring initiatives, networking opportunities, peer assistance, and recognition for the contributions of female police officers.

International Center for Criminal Law Reform and Criminal Justice Policy
1822 East Mall
Vancouver, BC, Canada
V6T 121
Phone: (604) 822-9875
Fax: (604) 822-9317
Email: icclr@law.ubc.ca
Internet: http://www.icclr.law.ubc.ca

This not-for-profit center based in Vancouver, Canada, was founded in 1991 and is a component of the United Nations Crime Prevention and Criminal Justice Program. Its mission is to promote a better quality of justice through the use of democratic principles to reform criminal law and criminal justice policy and practice; it aims to do this by utilizing humane principles that promote respect and dignity. The center's primary function is providing expert consultation and information, promoting research projects, and getting involved in policy formulation and legislation in a host of areas of the criminal justice system.

International Crime Scene Investigators Association (ISCIA)
PMB 385
15774 S. LaGrange Road
Orland Park, IL 60462
Phone: (708) 460-8082
Internet: http://www.iscia.org

The ISCIA is an international association created to assist police in the processing of crime scenes. The organization desires to promote crime scene processing as a unique subfield in forensic law enforcement. The ISCIA is totally web-based and communicates information in the field to members via its website. It intends to keep these communications clear and simple for the correct and rapid dissemination of the information.

International Criminal Police Organization (Interpol)
General Secretariat
200, quai Charles de gaulle
69006 Lyon, France
Fax: (33) 4 72 44 71 63
Internet: http://www.interpol.int

Interpol is the largest international police organization in the world with 186 member nations. It was created in 1923 with the purpose of facilitating cross-border cooperation among policing agencies. It seeks to facilitate issues of transnational criminality with all countries, even those with whom there are no diplomatic relations. Interpol's three core functions consist of the security of global police communication services, the operationalization of crime databases, and the operationalization of police support services.

International Footprint Association (IFU)
P.O. Box 1652
Walnut, CA 91788-1652
Phone: (877) 432-3668
Email: footprint@footprinter.org
Internet: http://www.footprinter.org

Originally consisting of members from the law enforcement fields, the IFU now has approximately 4,000 members of people from all occupational backgrounds who support law enforcement activities. Its slogan is "Bigger and Better Footprints." Its symbol—Robinson Crusoe discovering Friday's footprints in the island sand, beginning a relationship of mutual concern and co-operation—is a reference to the cooperation needed between the police and those they serve. The organization is involved with charities, scholarships, and Boys and Girls Clubs.

International High Technology Crime Investigation Association (HTCIA)

HTCIA, Inc.
4021 Woodcreek Oaks Boulevard
Suite 156 #209
Roseville, CA 95747
Phone: (916) 408-1751
Fax: (916) 408-7543
Email: exec_secty@htcia.org
Internet: http://www.htcia.org

The HTCIA is an organization whose function is to encourage increased knowledge and information among its members about the methods, processes, and techniques vital to the investigation of crime as well as security issues. The association has regional chapters and facilitates training in the use of technology in criminal investigation. The HTCIA has a website with a forensic tool kit link that allows the viewer to access other websites with a focus on issues of technology and forensic science.

International Organization of Asian Crime Investigators and Specialists (IOACIS)

P.O. Box 612
North Scituate, MA 02060-0612
Email: ioacisdirector@ioacis.com
Internet: http://www.ioacis.com

With the motto "leading change in the twenty-first century through communication, cooperation, and collaboration," this organization seeks to provide support to members through an exchange of professional ideas and good will in the United States and abroad. It also seeks to foster global communication through educational training, outreach, and networking opportunities, and to reward and develop the contributions of Asian criminal investigators and specialists.

International Police Association (IPA) (United States Section)
100 Chase Avenue
Yonkers, NY 10703
Email: info@ipa-usa.edu
Internet: http://www.ipa-usa.org

The IPA is an international organization whose motto is "Service through Friendship." Its membership consists of active duty and retired peace officers, and its primary focus is extending friendship and comradeship among offices in member nations. The association was formed in 1950 by a police sergeant from England, Arthur Troup. The United States Section was created in 1962 in Toledo, Ohio. Travel abroad to meet members is a focal point of the organization, and an exchange vacation is coordinated through the IPA. There is also an International Children's Exchange Program that gives the children of the members an opportunity to spend time with a host family in another country.

International Police Executive Symposium (IPES)
No mailing address on website.
Phone: (318) 274-2526
Fax: (318) 274-3101
Email: dilipkd@aol.com
Internet: http://www.ipes.info

This organization, founded in 1994 by criminal justice scholar Dilip Das is a not-for-profit educational corporation. Its purpose is to bring together police researchers and practitioners from different cultures for the sharing of ideas to facilitate the betterment of the police profession. Its primary initiative consists of a four-day annual meeting held in different countries throughout the world to discuss specific topics in policing. Scholars, high-level governmental ministers, police administrators, and many other involved persons from sixty countries attend the annual meetings and present academic papers on the theme from their own country's perspective. A core belief of the IPES is that policing is one of the fundamental means of promoting quality of life and justice in all nations.

International Police Mountain Bike Association (IPMBA)
583 Frederick Road
Suite 5B

Baltimore, MD 21228
Phone: (410) 744-2400
Fax: (410) 744-5504
Email: info@ipmba.org
Internet: http://www.ipmba.org

This organization is a nonprofit educational that provides training, educational services, resources, and networking opportunities for police bicyclists. There are over 3,000 members of this association in over forty-three states and four countries. There is an organization newsletter and an annual conference, and they sponsor a police cyclist course for police bikers around the nation.

International Society of Crime Prevention Practitioners (ISCPP)
P.O. Box 476
Simpsonville, SC 29681
Phone: (864) 884-8466
Internet: http://www.iscpp.org

Calling itself the "crime prevention people," this organization serves its members through the dissemination of information related to crime prevention. Membership in the ISCPP allows members to receive the organizational newsletter, *The Practitioner*, which is also available online, to attend the society's annual symposium, and to receive crime prevention–related training.

International Union of Police Association (IUPA)
1549 Ringling Boulevard
Suite 600
Sarasota, FL 34236
Phone: (941) 487-2560
Fax: (941) 487-2570
Email: iupa@iupa.org
Internet: http://www.iupa.org

With the motto "speaking with one voice, moving with one purpose," the IUPA is the only AFL-CIO–affiliated police union. It reports that its connection with the AFL-CIO provides its membership, comprised of both active and retired law enforcement officers, with greater strength in legislative matters directed toward greater police protection and support, and meeting the specific needs of law enforcement personnel with regard to wages, staffing, and equipment.

Law Enforcement Legal Defense Fund
1611 North Kent Street
Suite 901
Arlington, VA 22209
Internet: http://www.leldf.org

This organization's mission is to provide legal assistance to police personnel who take action in the line of duty deemed necessary to enforce the law. It performs this mission by providing financial support, legal advocacy, and public service education on various aspects of the policing profession and the criminal justice system.

Metropolitan Alliance of Police (MAP)
684 Boughton Road
Suite 204
Bolingbrook, IL 60440
Phone: (630) 759-4925
Fax: (630) 759-1902
Email: mapunion@msn.org
Internet: http://www.mapunion.org

MAP is a labor organization of peace officers and others involved with law enforcement in any municipal, county, or state agency. Its goal is to use collective bargaining and legal strategies to settle grievances and administrative actions, improve occupational conditions, promote positive relationships between members and line personnel and management, and increase educational and occupational knowledge in police work.

Multijurisdictional Counterdrug Task Force Training (MCTFT)
P.O. Box 13489
St. Petersburg, FL 33733
Phone: (800) 243-5550
Fax: (800) 346-4412
Email: information@mctft.com
Internet: http://www.mctft.com

The MCTFT provides training of various aspects of counter–drug law enforcement. It is federally funded though the Department of Defense, the Florida National Guard, and St. Petersburg College. It operates at St. Petersburg College's Southeastern Public Safety Training Institute state-of-the-art training academy.

National Asian Peace Officers Association (NAPOA)
P.O. Box 50973
Washington, D.C. 20091-0973
Phone: (202) 431-2175
Email: info@napoaonline.org
Internet: http://www.napoaonline.org

The NAPOA's goal is to promote the interests of Asian-American law enforcement officers. Through advocacy for equal opportunity in the selection, training, and promotion of Asians in police work as well as ensuring the rights of its members. The organization, founded in San Francisco in 1980, seeks to foster relationships with its counterparts in other nations.

National Association of Police Organizations (NAPO)
750 First Street, N.E.
Suite 90
Washington, D.C. 20002
Phone: (202) 842-4420
Fax: (202) 842-4396
Email: info@napo.org
Internet: http://www.napo.org

NAPO is a collection of association and unions in the United States that are related to law enforcement. The organization was founded in 1978 and has as its mission advocacy for police officers through legislation and legal means, educational provision, and political activism. NAPO represents over 2,000 unions and associations, 236,000 active peace officers, 11,000 retired officers, and over 100,000 citizens concerned with various aspects of policing.

National Association of Property Recovery Investigators, Inc. (NAPRI)
5715 Will Clayton #1503
Humble, TX 77338
Phone: (386) 479-5329
Fax: (309) 422-2112

Email: info@napri.org
Internet: http://www.napri.org

This organization reports to be the premier association of property crime investigation in North America. It supports the efforts of criminal investigators and provides resources, training, publications, and intelligence exchanges on all matters involving thefts, larcenies, burglaries, cyber theft, counterfeiting, and other types of property crimes. The association has a national conference, and membership is free for property crime investigators.

National Association of Town Watch (NATW)
P.O. Box 303
Wynnewood, PA 19096
Phone: (610) 649-7055
Email: info@natw.org
Internet: http://www.nationaltownwatch.org

A national, nonprofit association, the NATW has as its primary mission the development and promotion of crime and drug prevention programs that operate with the assistance of various policing agencies. A collaborative effort is made between the police agencies and other groups such as neighborhood and community groups, regional crime prevention programs, civic groups, and community businesses to prevent criminal activity and make communities safer. The association supports a program called National Night Out: America's Night Out Against Crime, which is held each August and draws support from community and police agencies to control the crime problem. The organization has a newsletter called *New Spirit* and updates members on crime and drug news. The group also sponsors an award for member areas with high levels of achievement.

National Association of Women in Law Enforcement Executive (NAWLEE)
3 Dunham Street
Carver, MA 02330
Phone: (781) 789-9500
Fax: (508) 866-8707
Email: info@nawlee.com
Internet: http://www.nawlee.com

NAWLEE is a nonprofit organization devoted to addressing the specific issues of women administrators in law enforcement fields. The association was developed to promote the ideals of female police executives, to provide professionalism through training—especially in the areas of leadership, management, and police administrations—and to create an environment of information exchange with regard to effective law enforcement procedures. The organization also has mentoring programs for mid-level and new senior-level female administrators and a newsletter called the *NAWLEE News.*

National Center for Missing and Exploited Children
Charles B. Wang International Children's Building
699 Prince Street
Alexandria, VA 22314-3175
Phone: (703) 274-3900
Fax: (703) 274-2200
Internet: http://www.missingkids.com

The mission of this nonprofit organization is to prevent the abduction and sexual exploitation of children, to assist in finding missing children, and to assist the victims of child abuse and their families and caregivers. It has an extensive clearinghouse of information on the subject, a cyber tip line to report the Internet exploitation of children, technical assistance to police, and other public service agencies. It also offers training and public service education, provides exchange and networking with child service agencies, assists with federal initiatives, and distributes photographs of missing children worldwide.

National Coalition of Italian American Law Enforcement Associations
92 Sheffield Avenue
Babylon, New York 11704
Internet: http://www.ncoialea.com

This organization is an ethnic collective of police officers whose stated mission is the provision of national membership to preserve the heritage of law enforcement officers of Italian ancestry. The coalition aims to be a voice for the concerns of Italian-American police officers in the nation's capital and in the rest of the county. On the association website, it is "emphatically stated" that ethic policies promoted by the coalition will not affect municipal negotiations.

National Conference of Law Enforcement Emerald Societies, Inc. (NCLEES)
8 Zaleski
Sayreville, NJ 08872-1858
Internet: http://www.nclees.org

The NCLEES is a registered nonprofit organization that represents police officers from Irish and Gaelic descent. Founded in 1995, this group has many chapters throughout the nation and several objectives, including the promotion of fraternity among the members, the preservation of the Irish culture, the recognition of the contributions of Irish-American police officers, the dissemination of information among members of the organization, the promotion of a strong and unified voice in policy matters, and collaboration with civic groups and public safety organizations. The association has an annual meeting and produces a newsletter called *An Leargas.*

National Drug Enforcement Officers Association (NDEOA)
FBI Academy
Quantico, VA 22134-1475
Phone: (202) 298-9653
Internet: http://www.ndeoa.org

An arm of the National Drug Enforcement Administration, this organization for officers with drug enforcement duties has as its purpose the cooperation, education, and information exchange among police agencies involved in the enforcement of drug laws.

National Institute of Ethics
100 Maple Cove
Long Beach, MS 39560
Phone: (800) 273-2559
Fax: (228) 864-0125
Email: ethicsinstitute@cableone.net
Internet: http://www.ethicsinstitute.com

This nonprofit organization, according to its website, is the largest provider of ethics training in the nation. It also provides certification in the area of ethics to police officers at different lev-

els of government. It conducts customized seminars to requesting police agencies that focus on the specific needs and concerns
of these agencies.

National Internal Affairs Investigators Association (NIAIA)
P.O. Box 28571
Raleigh, NC 27611-8511
Phone: (919) 861-3125
Fax: (919) 733-0126
Email: ia@niaia.org
Internet: http://www.niaia.org

Formed in 1985, this organization was founded by a group of police internal affairs officers who desired to form a professional organization to develop and establish standards of performance
and ethics for internal affairs officers. It exists to perform these
functions as well as to provide training, discussion, and exchange,
as well as a forum to better the field of internal investigation in
police organizations.

National Latino Peace Officers Association (NLPOA)
P.O. Box 1717
Las Vegas, NV 89125
Phone: (702) 355-8704
Fax: (702) 388-6082
Internet: http://www.nlpoa.org

Founded in 1974 in California to improve the representation of
Latino law enforcement officers, the NLPOA purports to be the
largest organization of Latino police and other criminal justice
practitioners in the United States. The membership is comprised of
police chiefs, sheriffs and deputies, police officers, probation and
parole officers, and federal agents at all levels of government. The
association is a nonprofit organization whose primary mission is
to remove prejudice and discrimination in the field of law enforcement, to lower the incidence of juvenile crime, and to alleviate
police–citizen conflict in predominantly Latino communities.

National Law Enforcement and Corrections Technology Center (NLECTC)
Address: 2277 Research Boulevard, M/S 8J
Rockville, MD 20850
Phone: (800) 248-2742

Fax: (301) 519-5149
Email: asknlectc@nlectc.org
Internet: http://www.nlectc.org

This center is an organizational component of the National Institute of Justice's Office of Science and Technology and provides support services, research findings, and technical assistance to police departments across the nation for them to function more effectively with the increasing demands for knowledge of technology in the criminal justice system. The system has regional centers that support this mission.

National Narcotic Detector Dog Association (NNDDA)
379 CR 105
Carthage, TX 75633
Phone: (888) 289-0070
Email: thennddda@yahoo.com
Internet: http://www.nndda.org

This nonprofit organization, founded in 1978, provides certification to police scent detector dogs in a variety of areas, including police service dog certification, narcotics certification, cadaver search certification, and explosive detection certification. It hosts a national training conference as well as regional conferences.

National Organization of Black Law Enforcement Executives (NOBLE)
Hubart T. Bell Jr. Office Complex
Alexandria, VA 22312-1442
Phone: (703) 658-1529
Fax: (703) 658-9479
Internet: http://www.noblenatl.org

The NOBLE mission is to make sure that the justice system is fair and equitable for those who provide administration in the law enforcement field. Founded in 1976 when sixty African-American police executives in Washington, D.C., met during a symposium and decided an organization was needed to address concerns such as the high rates of black urban crime, socioeconomic conditions related to race, fairness in the criminal justice system, the relationships between the police and the communities they serve, equality for minority officers, and the unique challenges of African-American police administrators. It has an electronic newsletter called *NOBLE News Online.*

National Police Bloodhound Association (NPBA)
67120 Ovante Road
Cathedral City, CA 92234
Internet: http://www.npba.com

This organization is a nonprofit association dedicated to the professional advancement of training bloodhounds for police duty. The association provides training to police bloodhounds and their trainers in seminars.

National Police Defense Foundation (NPDF)
21 Kilmer Drive
Building 2, Suite F
Morganville, NJ 07751
Phone: (888) SAFE-COP
Fax: (732) 446-3360
Email: NPDF1@optionline.com
Internet: http://www.npdf.org

This association is a nonprofit foundation comprising over 80,000 members and supporters in the United States and twelve countries abroad. Membership is available to active and retired police personnel, and the organization has recently adopted a civilian component through associate and honorary membership. The NPDF is an advocacy organization to "protect and serve" the interest of federal agents, chiefs of police, state police officers correctional officers, and police personnel from municipal, county, state, and federal levels of law enforcement.

National Sheriff's Association (NSA)
1450 Duke Street
Alexandria, VA 22314-3490
Phone: (703) 836-7827
Internet: http://www.sheriffs.org

The NSA is a nonprofit organization for sheriffs' departments and other law enforcement officials in its sixty-fifth year of operation. Its primary purpose is to elevate the level of professionalism of criminal justice practitioners. The organization hosts numerous training and professional assistance programs to assist sheriffs and deputies and others in law enforcement occupations to better serve the needs of their jurisdictions. Its web page has a large number of resources for county law enforcement personnel, including the *Sheriff* magazine and a clearinghouse of information called the Ultimate Guide for Sheriffs.

National Tactical Officers Association (NTOA)
P.O. Box 797
Doylestown, PA 18901
Phone: (800) 279-9127
Fax: (215) 230-7552
Internet: http://www.ntoa.org

Established in Los Angeles in 1983, the NTOA is a primary training organization for special weapons and tactical (SWAT) units, patrol units, crisis negotiation programs, and other agencies that deal with critical incidents situations. In addition to its training functions, the association coordinates a week-long training seminar and operates a national policing library, offering research support and two journals: *The Tactical Edge* and *The Crisis Negotiator.*

National Troopers Coalition (NTC)
Phone: (800) 232-1392
Email: chairman@ntctroopers.com
Internet: http://www.ntctroopers.com

An organization that purports to be the only coalition representing solely the interests of state troopers and other state highway officials, NTC is a nonprofit organization formed in 1977. This is a 30,000-member organization that advocates for employees of state policing agencies.

Park Law Enforcement Association (PLEA)
Email: webmaster@parkranger.com
Internet: http://www.parkranger.com

PLEA is an affiliate of the National Recreation and Park Association and has as its mission the improvement of safety and security issues in federal, state, and local parks and recreation areas. Formed in 1984, PLEA is comprised of a variety of park law enforcement personnel and provides education and other informational services regarding park enforcement and park safety to park visitors and to other police officials. In addition, it strives for better communication between recreational and park enforcement and other policing agencies.

Police Executive Research Forum (PERF)
1120 Connecticut Avenue, N.W.
Suite 930
Washington, DC 20036
Phone: (202) 466-7820
Fax: (202) 466-7826
Internet: http://www.policeforum.org

PERF is a national organization comprised of progressive police administrators from the largest urban police departments in the United States. Begun in 1977, the forum is concerned with the improvement of the police profession by advancing research and public policy debates on matters of policing. PERF desires to take a leadership role in discussions on crime and broader issues of fear of crime and the fair and humane treatment of all citizens. Two current initiatives are (1) a response to citizen concern over traffic stop fairness and racial profiling and (2) collaboration between police and religious leaders to explore antiviolence measures in urban communities.

Police Foundation
1201 Connecticut Avenue, NW
Washington, DC 20036-2636
Phone: (202) 833-1460
Fax: (202) 659-9142
Email: pfinfo@policefoundation.org
Internet: http://www.policefoundation.org

The purpose of the Police Foundation is to promote innovations and improvements in law enforcement. Founded in 1970, it is an independent, not-for-profit organization that conducts research on many areas of policing, including law enforcement policies and procedures and police behavior. It also seeks to disseminate appropriate empirically based information to local agencies. The Police Foundation has an academic series of works called Ideas in American Policing and sponsors regular lectures on a variety of policing issues.

Reserve Police Officers Association (RPOA)
105 Fullerton Avenue
Yonkers, NY 10704
Phone: (800) 326-9416
Fax: (212) 555-1234
Internet: http://www.reservepolice.org

The RPOA represents law enforcement officials who are volunteer police or part-time citizen peace officers. Reserve officers go by a variety of other names, such as auxiliary, special part-time, supernumerary, or seasonal officers, and they are generally recognized as being differentiated from "regular" or "career" officers who provide police services as a primary source of income and who receive insurance and pension benefits. The association seeks to foster public awareness of reserve officers and their function to policing, provide financial assistance to disabled reservists or their families to those who died in the line of duty, support agencies through the donation of equipment, provide training, serve as a clearinghouse of information or reserve duties, and promote the sharing of ideas in the profession. The organization's website includes an interesting history of the use of reserve police officers.

Society of Certified Criminal Analysts (SCCA)
201 E. Washington Street
Suite 940
Phoenix, AZ 85004
Phone: (602) 776-5498
Fax: (602) 776-5519
Email: Edward.Feingold@atf.gov
Internet: http://www.certifiedanalysts.net

Formed in 1989 to augment the International Law Enforcement Intelligence Analysts (IALEIA), the SCCA became the certification arm of the parent organization in 1996 and reaffirmed this role in 2003. Its purpose is to promote high standards and increasing professionalism by certifying intelligence analysts, of which there are over two hundred in the world in ten nations: Argentina, Australia, Austria, Belgium, Canada, France, the Netherlands, South Africa, the United Kingdom, and the United States.

Society of Police and Criminal Psychology (SPCP)
Department of Criminal Justice
Texas State University

San Marcos, TX 78666
Email: msurrett@spfdcol.edu
Internet: http://psychweb.cisat.jmu.edu/spcp/

SPCP bills itself as an eclectic association that supports the scientific study of crime and the practical application of that knowledge to problems existing in the criminal justice system, the organization's members' study of crime and its causation, criminal victimization, and influences from criminal justice organizations. The association has an annual meeting and offers a diplomate in police psychology designation. In addition, the SPCP has two journals: *The Journal of Police* and *Criminal Psychology.*

Southern Poverty Law Center
400 Washington Avenue
Montgomery, AL 36104
Phone: (334) 956-8200
Email: Internet: http://www.splcenter.org

Founded as a small civil rights firm in 1971 by two Montgomery attorneys to protect racial minorities from inadequate treatment in the justice system, the Southern Poverty Law Center has grown into an internationally known nonprofit organization that promotes tolerance and battles hate activity. Headquartered appropriately in the home of the civil rights movement, the center initially represented clients in racially based legal cases that few other local attorneys would accept. In the 1980s, the center moved from protecting individual rights to investigating and reporting the activities of hate organizations and has achieved several legal victories in this area, including prominent Supreme Court decisions. The center's Intelligence Project provides information to police agencies, the media, and the public on the activities of extremist organizations and publishes a quarterly magazine called *The Intelligence Report* that provides updated information on these groups. The center also produces and maintains an educational program called Teaching Tolerance and a community-based program (Tolerance.org). In addition, the center provides training and support to police agencies, schools, and community groups in the area of civil rights issues.

United States Border Patrol Supervisor's Association (BPSA)
539 Telegraph Canyon Road PMB. #656
Chula Vista, CA 91910-6497
Email: Internet: http://www.bpsups.org

This nonprofit professional association seeks to advance the profession of border patrol through leadership directives, professional standards, and excellence. It offers training and networking with other law enforcement agencies and provides legal defense funding to its members in Arizona and California but plans to offer this service to members nationally. The BPSA is an association member with the National Association of Police Organizations (NAPO), Federal Manager's Association (FMA), Peace Officers Research Association of California (PORAC), and the Combined Law Enforcement Associations of Texas (CLEAT).

United States Canine Police Association (USPCA)
P.O. Box 80
Springboro, OH 45066
Phone: (800) 531-1614
Email: Internet: http://www.uspcak9.com

The USPCA is a nonprofit organization that purports to be the largest and oldest organization of canine law enforcement handlers. It offers training in the areas of patrol, tracking, and detection of different types on contraband, including drugs, explosives, accelerants, as well as animals and cadavers. It offers certification in a number of areas including patrol, tracking, detection, and certification of trainers and judges.

Volunteers in Police Service (VIPS)
International Association of Chiefs of Police
515 N. Washington Street
Alexandria, VA 22314
Phone: (800) THE IACP
Internet: http://www.policevolunteers.org

This is one of the five Citizen Corps partnership programs operated through the USA Freedom Corps program, started by President George W. Bush in 2002. The VIPS program is administered by the International Association of Chiefs of Police (IACP) in conjunction with the White House Office of the USA Freedom Corps and the Bureau of Justice Assistance, Office of Justice Programs, U.S. Department of Justice. The program provides support and resources to agencies that wish to learn about the use of volunteers in their agencies, start a volunteer program in their departments, increase the number of volunteer officers, and assist citizens involved in volunteer police programs in their communities. The primary resource is the organization web page, which provides information and assistance to police agencies either that have or that have requested volunteer personnel. It has an informative newsletter called *VIPS in Focus.*

Women in Federal Law Enforcement (WIFLE)
2200 Wilson Boulevard
Suite 102 PMB-204
Arlington, VA 22201
Phone: (703) 548-9211 / (866) 399-4353
Fax: (410) 451-7373
Email: WIFLE@Comcast.net
Internet: http://www.wifle.org

WIFLE was formed in 1999 from an Interagency Committee on Women in Federal Law Enforcement that was established in 1977 to bring more women into the criminal justice field and retain them. The organization's mission is to promote equality with regard to women in law enforcement; it seeks to assist police agencies in recruiting and retaining female officers, emphasizes police management practices, promotes a positive image of the police, and sponsors research projects in issues regarding gender in policing. The organization's website provides a number of resources for practitioners and scholars and has an electronic news link called *WIFLE-Enews.*

Federal Government Agencies Related to Policing

The following list represents a partial listing of the federal agencies associated with policing and their websites. The list is certainly not all-inclusive, but the websites provide useful information to people wanting to know more about federal police agencies.

Bureau of Alcohol Tobacco and Firearms (ATF)
http://www.atf.gov

Bureau of Diplomatic Security Rewards for Justice
http://www.rewardsforjustice.net/index.htm

Bureau of Indian Affairs
http://www.doi.gov/bureau-indian-affairs.html

Bureau of Justice Assistance (BJA)
http://www.ojp.usdoj.gov/BJA

Bureau of Justice Statistics (BJS)
http://www.ojp.usdoj.gov/bjs

Central Intelligence Agency (CIA)
http://www.cia.gov

Community Oriented Policing Services (COPS)
http://www.cops.usdog.gov

Customs Service
http://www.customs.ustreas.gov/

Defense Security Service
http://www.dss.mil

Department of Homeland Security (DHS)
http://www.dhs.gov/dhspublic/

Directory of Federal Agencies
http://www.fedworld.gov

Drug Enforcement Administration (DEA)
http://www.usdoj.gov/dea/

Federal Bureau of Investigation (FBI)
http://www.fbi.gov/

Federal Bureau of Prisons (FBP)
http://www.bop.gov/

Federal Protective Service (FPS)
http://www.ice.gov/graphics/fps/index.htm

Federal Trade Commission (FTC)
http://www.ftc.gov/

Internal Revenue Service (IRS)–Compliance and Enforcement
http://www.irs.gov/compliance/enforcement/

National Crime Reference Service (NCRS)
http://www.ncjrs.org

National Drug Intelligence Center (NDIC)
http://www.usdoj.gov/ndic

National Highway Traffic Safety Administration (NHTSA)
http://www.nhtsa.dot.gov/

National Institute of Justice (NIJ)
http://www.ojp.usodj.gov/hjj

National Park Service (NPS)
http://www.nps.gov/morningreport/

National Security Agency (NSA)
http://www.nsa.gov/

Office of Legislative Affairs (OLA)
http://www.usdoj.gov/ola

Office of Police Corps and Law Enforcement Education (OPCLEE)
http://www.ojp.usdoj.gov/opclee

Postal Inspection Service
http://www.usps.gov/websites/depart/inspect/

U.S. Department of Housing and Urban Development (HUD) Office of Inspector General
http://www.hud.gov/offices/oig/

U.S. Department of Justice (USDOJ)
http://www.usdoj.gov

U.S. Fish and Wildlife Service (FWS)
http://www.fws.gov/

U.S. Marshalls Service
http://www.usdoj.gov/marshals

U.S. Park Police (USPP)
http://www.nps.gov/uspp/

U.S. Secret Service
http://www.treas.gov/usss/index.shtml

U.S. Securities and Exchange Commission
http://www.sec.gov/

State Departments of Public Safety

The following is a list of state departments of public safety for the fifty states and their websites. For a complete overview of these agencies, the reader is directed to an inclusive directory found at http://www.statetroopersdirectory.com. The states vary in their use of state police. Some have clearly defined roles involving highway patrol, capital security, protection of the governor, training, criminal investigation, or some combination of these. All of the states have state policing systems that give certain agencies statewide jurisdiction of crime control, and these are administered in some fashion by the state departments of public safety.

Alabama
http://www.dps.state.al.us/

Alaska
http://www.dps.state.ak.us/

Arizona
http://www.dps.state.az.us/default.asp

Arkansas
http://www.dps.state.az.us/default.asp

California
http://www.chp.ca.gov/index.html

Colorado
http://csp.state.co.us/

Connecticut
http://www.ct.gov/dps/site/default.asp

Delaware
http://www.state.de.us/dsp/

Florida
http://www.fhp.state.fl.us/

Georgia
http://www.fhp.state.fl.us/

Hawaii
http://www.hawaii.gov/psd/psd_home.php

Idaho
http://www.isp.state.id.us/

Illinois
http://www.isp.state.il.us/

Indiana
http://www.ai.org/isp/index.html

Iowa
http://www.dps.state.ia.us/ISP/index.shtml

Kansas
http://www.kansashighwaypatrol.org/

Kentucky
http://www.kentuckystatepolice.org/

Louisiana
http://www.lsp.org/index.html

Maine
http://www.maine.gov/dps/msp/index.shtml

Maryland
http://www.mdsp.org/

Massachusetts
http://www.mass.gov/?pageID=eopsagencylanding&L=3&L0=
Home&L1=Public+Safety+Agencies&L2=Massachusetts+State+
Police&sid=Eeops

Michigan
http://www.michigan.gov/msp

Minnesota
http://www.dps.state.mn.us/patrol/index.htm

Mississippi
http://www.dps.state.ms.us/dps/dps.nsf/main?OpenForm

Missouri
http://www.mshp.dps.missouri.gov/MSHPWeb/Root/index
.html

Montana
http://www.doj.mt.gov/enforcement/highwaypatrol.asp

Nebraska
http://www.nsp.state.ne.us/

Nevada
http://nhp.nv.gov/

New Hampshire
http://www.nh.gov/safety/divisions/nhsp/

New Jersey
http://www.state.nj.us/lps/njsp/index.html

New Mexico
http://www.nmsp.com/

New York
http://www.troopers.state.ny.us/

North Carolina
http://www.nccrimecontrol.org/Index2.cfm?a=000003,000014

North Dakota
http://www.nd.gov/ndhp/

Ohio
http://statepatrol.ohio.gov/

Oklahoma
http://www.dps.state.ok.us/ohp/

Oregon
http://egov.oregon.gov/OSP/

Pennsylvania
http://www.psp.state.pa.us/psp/site/default.asp

Rhode Island
http://www.risp.state.ri.us/

South Carolina
http://www.schp.org/

South Dakota
http://hp.state.sd.us/greeting.htm

Tennessee
http://www.state.tn.us/safety/

Texas
http://www.txdps.state.tx.us/

Utah
http://highwaypatrol.utah.gov/

Vermont
http://www.dps.state.vt.us/vtsp/

Virginia
http://www.vsp.state.va.us/

Washington
http://www.wsp.wa.gov/

West Virginia
http://www.wsp.wa.gov/

Wisconsin
http://www.dot.state.wi.us/statepatrol/

Wyoming
http://dot.state.wy.us/Default.jsp?sCode=whp

8

Resources

This chapter contains a list of print resources including books, journal articles, and core periodicals that deal with issues in policing. It also includes nonprint resources such as video/DVD documentaries, and police-related Internet sites. Also included is a list of legal cases that affect the daily functioning of the police.

Print Resources

Books

The following books have all made an important contribution to the field of policing and law enforcement. The list is certainly not all-inclusive but provides a mix of scholarly texts (both classics and more recent volumes) and popular works that shed light on the field.

Alex, Nicholas. 1969. *Black in Blue: A Study of the Negro Policeman.* New York: Appleton-Century-Crofts.

This work is an ethnographic study of African American police officers in an urban American police department. The study, conducted in 1964 and 1965, describes the special problems experienced by black police officers in that period. Case studies provide a backdrop for the analysis of racial prejudice and discrimination that took place at the time. Although the sample size was quite small, the analysis was in-depth and helped usher in more discussion on race and police work.

Bittner, Egon. 1990. *Aspects of Police Work.* Boston: Northeastern University Press.

This work provides a scholarly analysis of the police by a police scholar who spent years performing ethnographic and quantitative studies of the police and consulting with agencies on law enforcement issues. In this work he explores in detail the functions of the police, examines the role of the urban police, and looks at specialty functions such as police work with the mentally ill and juveniles. He also describes the role of research and proposes a theory of policing.

Bordua, David J., ed. 1967. *The Police: Six Sociological Essays.* Hoboken, NJ: John Wiley and Sons.

This collection of six essays on the police offers contributions from such key police experts as Albert J. Reiss Jr., Jerome Skolnick, and James Q. Wilson, with the essays addressing such important issues in law enforcement as crime and riots, gangs, police morale, police recruitment, and organizational issues. Although written decades ago, it deserves a new review in light of current policing models and philosophies.

Cannon, Lou. 1999. *Official Negligence: How Rodney King and the Riots Changed Los Angeles and the LAPD.* Boulder, CO: Westview Press.

This work, written by a political reporter, chronicles the 1991 Rodney King beating by four officers of the Los Angeles Police Department and the resulting explosion of violence that occurred with the 1992 acquittal of the officers. The book uses a historical framework for the incident including the "legacy of Dragnet"— the LAPD's aggressive tactics under Chief William Parker and others. It takes an in-depth look at the intersection of race, class, politics, and policing strategies in American's second-largest city. At 706 pages, it is a comprehensive social analysis of the Rodney King story that goes much deeper than this one incident.

Carte, Gene E., and Elaine M. Carte. 1975. *Police Reform in the United States: The Era of August Vollmer, 1905–1932.* Berkeley: University of California Press.

This is an interesting and complete biography of August Vollmer, America's premier police reformer whose ideas transformed police philosophy in the early twentieth century. It also provides a vivid description of the beginning of police professionalism in the country and the cultural milieu in which the reforms were implemented.

Critchley, T. A. 1967. *A History of Police in England and Wales.* Montclair, NJ: Patterson Smith.

The definitive work on early policing in England and Wales, Critchley's book should be required reading for those interested in the earliest forms of law enforcement. This oft cited reference provides a strong historical foundation for the analysis of contemporary police systems throughout the world.

Delattre, Edwin J. 2002. *Character and Cops: Ethics in Policing,* 4th ed. Washington, DC: AEI Press.

This fourth edition of a popular book on police ethics is written by a professor of philosophy and education, and it uses a philosophical perspective to discuss many issues of police work such as the changing police mission, discretion, corruption, and brutality. An entire chapter is devoted to the O. J. Simpson case, reinforcing the importance of this case to the field. This edition includes a chapter on ethics and the future of policing including the growing role of terrorism in policing.

Denziger, Steven R., ed. 1996. *The Real War on Crime: The Report of the National Criminal Justice Commission.* New York: HarperCollins.

This report provides the findings of a group of citizens concerned with crime rates and the response to crime in the United States. Concerned that there had been no presidential commission established to deal with the issue of crime since 1969, the group, calling itself the National Criminal Justice Commission, set out to determine some of the problems with the system in the hope of providing some suggestions for improvement. The recommendations for the police sector included greater community involvement ("neighborhood-oriented policing" and external review boards), better training and incentives for prevention-oriented officers, and recruitment of officers based on racial and ethnic similarities to the communities they serve.

Domanick, Joe. 1994. *To Protect and to Serve: The LAPD's Century of War in the City of Dreams.* New York: Pocket Books.

The author, a journalist, provides an account of the LAPD. It is a candid work drawing on key historical events in the force's history. The book includes commentaries on race relations and other social factors that shaped and molded the city's police. Predictably, William Parker is featured prominently, as is the Rodney King beating.

Douglas, John, and Mark Olshaker. 1995. *Mind Hunter: Inside the FBI's Serial Crime Unit.* New York: Scribner's.

This is an autobiography of John Douglas, one of the FBI's earliest criminal profilers. In addition to its autobiographical section, the book provides information on psychological profiling through Douglas's recollection of a series of cases in which he used profiling to determine the identity of offenders.

Fletcher, Connie. 1990. *What Cops Know: Cops Talk About What They Do, How They Do it, and What It Does to Them.* New York: Villard Books.

This is a popular book using interviews with police officers to explain that police officers have a special "knowledge" of human behavior not possessed by most people. This knowledge comes from the fact that the officers' experiences allow them greater insight into certain aspects of the human condition not normally encountered by others. Though not an academic work, the book is a compilation of very candid responses from the officers and gives an interesting look "behind the shades."

Friedman, Lawrence. 1993. *Crime and Punishment in American History.* New York: Basic Books.

A detailed historical account of crime and the system of correction throughout the stages of American history, this work is comprehensive and provides a cultural context for the control of crime in America. The book covers policing, the courts, and corrections in three stages: the colonial period, the period from the Revolutionary War to the end of the nineteenth century, and the twentieth century.

Goldstein, Herman. 1977. *Policing a Free Society.* Cambridge, MA: Ballinger.

In this landmark work, Goldstein attempts to explore the core problems of police in American society such as corruption, ineffective training, and poor police–community relations; he also offers his views on how effective police administration can negate many of these problems. Goldstein recommends higher standards from police managers, more effective recruitment and training of line staff, increasing minority applicants, more educational opportunities for officers, and many other progressive reforms.

Heidensohn, France. 1992. *Women in Control? The Role of Women in Law Enforcement.* Oxford: Clarendon Press.

An analysis of the role of women in police work, this volume provides a sociohistorical assessment of the social control measures that have traditionally been used in society and of the role of women in these measures. It provides an examination of the entrance of women into policing in the United States and Britain and is an excellent comparative study of the law enforcement systems in these two countries.

Hibbert, Christopher. 2003. *The Roots of Evil: A Social History of Crime and Punishment.* Phoenix Mill, UK: Sutton Publishing.

A British work originally published in 1963, this appropriately subtitled social history of crime and punishment provides a good deal of information on the history of policing throughout the world. The section on policing in the "New World" covers the period of the G-men and gangsters in the early twentieth century.

Jenkins, Herbert. 1970. *Keeping the Peace: A Police Chief Looks at His Job.* New York: Harper and Row.

This work is an autobiography of Jenkins, who served as police chief of the Atlanta, Georgia, Police Department in the 1930s and 1940s. The book is a historical account of law enforcement and especially of race relations in the city. Jenkins was a progressive reformer and when the President's Commission on Law Enforcement and Administration of Justice released its report recommending the hiring of more black police officers, Atlanta already had a higher percentage of minority officers than most major cities.

Jones, Mark. 2005. *Criminal Justice Pioneers in U.S. History.* Boston: Pearson.

An informative work on some of the key figures in criminal justice, the book is divided into the primary theorists in the field, pioneers in policing, key legal scholars and practitioners, and prominent names in the criminal justice system. Its section on policing has the largest bibliography of all the sections in the book and is recommended reading for those with an interest in the contributions of the major pioneers.

Kappeler, Victor E., Richard D. Sluder, and Geoffrey P. Alpert. 1998. *Forces of Deviance: Understanding the Dark Side of Policing,* 2nd ed. Long Grove, IL: Waveland Press.

A scholarly work often used in college classrooms, *Forces of Deviance* is an examination of the police throughout American history from the colonial era to the present. Concise but detailed, this is an informative introduction to police deviance and should be read by people interested in understanding the darker history of policing in America.

Kelling, George, Tony Pate, Duane Dieckman, and Charles E. Brown. 1974. *The Kansas City Preventive Patrol Experiment: A Technical Report.* Washington, DC: Police Foundation.

This detailed, data-filled report describes the groundbreaking study in Kansas City conducted during 1972 and 1973 regarding the effects of three different patrol levels. The study found that the patrol practices did not have a statistically significant effect on criminal behavior, law enforcement service delivery, or citizens' feelings of safety and protection. This book provides the data from the study, replete with statistical analyses in numerous charts, graphs, and tables. Not a recommended read for nonacademics, this report provided information on police patrol that has affected police organizations throughout the country.

Kelling, George L., and Catherine M. Coles. 1997. *Fixing Broken Windows: Restoring Order and Reducing Crime in Our Communities.* New York: Touchstone.

One of the most influential books on policing published during the late twentieth century, this revolutionary text begins with a quote by none other than Robert Peel that "the police are the public and the public are the police" and with a foreword by another police visionary, James Q. Wilson. In this work, Kelling and Coles provide the framework for the broken windows theory of community disorganization as well as the prevention-oriented broken windows policing model that was introduced earlier by Kelling and Wilson in an article in the *Atlantic*. Using contemporary data from a variety of sources, the work sets out a model of policing that provides a nice fit with community-oriented models that are continuing to gain in popularity in departments across the nation. The book and its theoretical perspective have been challenged by several authors, opening up a beneficial dialogue on policing that continues to the present.

Kerik, Bernard B. 2001. *The Lost Son: A Life in Pursuit of Justice.* New York: Regan Books.

This book is a chronicle of the experiences of Kerik, the fortieth police commissioner of New York City, during whose tenure the September 11, 2001 attacks of the World Trade Center took place. This work is especially interesting in that it is an autobiography of America's top cop who describes his rise to that position and at the same time juxtaposes his unrelenting desire to find justice on a personal level. Kerik is driven by the fact that he was abandoned by his mother, who was herself the victim of murder in a case that was never solved. The book is also noteworthy in that it provides insight into the events of September 11, 2001 from a law enforcement perspective.

Klockars, Carl B. 1985. *The Idea of Police.* Beverly Hills, CA: Sage Publications.

This work, the third volume of the Law and Criminal Justice Series by Sage, is a sociological study of the police profession. Explored in this book are adequate definitions for the police, the reasons we have police, the patrol and detective roles of the police, the issue of selective enforcement, and measures of good policing. In a chapter entitled "Varieties of Avocational Policing," Klockars (in the vein of *Wilson's Varieties of Police Behavior*) differentiates between types of policing in which citizens fulfill some of the functions of the police as an avocation, in part-time, amateur, often unpaid positions.

Leiner, Stephen. 1984. *Black Police, White Society.* New York: New York University Press.

A sociologist and former New York Police Department police officer describes the working world of African-American officers through a series of interviews, observations, and personal experience. Leiner attempts to provide an update of the classic work *Black in Blue,* which explored the problem of black police officers in the 1960s.

Martin, Susan Ehrlich. 1980. *Breaking and Entering: Police-women on Patrol.* Berkeley: University of California Press.

A groundbreaking study of gender in policing, the work was a Ph.D. dissertation in which the author completed a study on women who "broke into" the traditionally male dominated occupational field of police patrol. In the mid-1970s, Martin was a police reserve officer in Washington, D.C., who completed a field study examining the different worlds of the male and female officers. The study was a seminal work in the beginning field of scholarly feminist criminology.

Middleton, Michael L. 2000. *Cop: A True Story.* New York: MJF Books.

This is a collection of true stories written by a police officer of the Los Angeles Police Department for over twenty-one years. The work, a popular book written for laypersons, gives the reader a feeling of being a police officer in an urban area. Dealing with the harsh realities of gangs, drug-related crimes, and grisly violence and deaths; the book also looks at the more heroic side of police work. He also describes the effects of racism and sexism in the police force and makes a candid exploration of police misconduct.

Miller, William R. 1977. *Cops and Bobbies: Police Authority in New York and London, 1830–1870.* Chicago: University of Chicago Press.

This work provides a historical account of the police practices of five decades of the mid-nineteenth century in both New York and London. The book compares and contrasts the "cops" of the New York Municipal Police with the "bobbies" of the London Metropolitan Police. The time frame covers what many police scholars consider to be the advent of the "new police" in both cities.

Monkkonen, Eric H. 1981. *Police in Urban America, 1860–1920.* Cambridge: Cambridge University Press.

Police historian Monkkonen's often cited history of the urban police in the United States includes chapters on the development of the urban police, arrest rates, and the changing role of the police from being a welfare agent to a crime fighter.

New York Knapp Commission. 1973. *Knapp Commission Report on Police Corruption.* New York: George Braziller.

This report, issued in 1972 and published in book form a year later, was submitted to the mayor of New York City by Whitman Knapp, chairman of the Commission to Investigate Alleged Police Corruption that was established two years earlier. The report detailed the "widespread corruption" in the New York Police Department made famous by the allegations of plainclothes officer Frank Serpico. The report called for an immediate "rooting out" of police corruption by agency commanders, reorganization of internal inspections, and a host of other recommendations.

Niederhoffer, Arthur. 1967. *Behind the Shield: The Police in Urban Society.* New York: Doubleday.

A classic in the study of police misconduct, this book examines the existence of an authoritarian police personality, in which a strict and unyielding police personality is formed through intense socialization in the occupation. Other areas of police socialization, such as prevalent cynicism, are examined.

Niederhoffer, Arthur, and Elaine Niederhoffer. 1978. *The Police Family: From Station House to Ranch House.* Lanham, MD: Lexington Books.

This is one of the earliest works to focus on the families of police officers, which are labeled by the authors the blue circle. It includes police concerns such as occupational stress as it affects the family, relationship problems, and issues involving the children of police.

Philbin, Tom. 1996. *Copspeak: The Lingo of Law Enforcement and Crime.* Hoboken, NJ: John Wiley and Sons.

Billing itself "part dictionary, part encyclopedia, part etymological tract, and hopefully all entertaining," this is a small reference book to terms used by the police and the "perps." This introduction to police argot is beneficial to anyone studying the police or considering a career in policing.

President's Commission on Law Enforcement and Administration of Justice. 1967. *The Challenge of Crime in a Free Society.* Washington, DC: U.S. Government Printing Office.

This report is the culmination of data gathering and recommendations on the three arms of the criminal justice system by a large staff of commissioners, members, staff, and advisors on the issue of crime in America during a specially disconcerting period in American policing—the 1960s. The fourth chapter of the book provides a discussion of the functions of the police sector of the criminal justice system. The work analyzes the state of the police and makes a number of recommendations, including increased positive involvement with the community, the efficient use of police personnel, the advocacy from legal council, specialized police duties, a bureaucratic structure, policies for police integrity, a team policing approach, among many others. A truly groundbreaking report, the work helped bring about a series of progressive changes in American policing.

Reiss, Albert J., Jr. 1971. *The Police and the Public.* New Haven, CT: Yale University Press.

This is a landmark study of police officers and their relationships with the communities they serve. Starting as an observational study by Reiss and graduate students doing ride-alongs with police patrol officers in the mid-1960s, the efforts were discovered by the National Crime Commission who sought to better understand police–community relations, which were strained at the time. Field studies were conducted in Boston, Chicago, and Washington, D.C.

Reynolds, Elaine A. 1988. *Before the Bobbies: The Night Watch and Police Reform in Metropolitan London, 1720–1830.* Stanford, CA: Stanford University Press.

This account of policing in early London is derived from the author's doctoral dissertation and posits that pre-1829 policing in London was probably not as unprofessional as is often thought. Reynolds traces the earliest form of professional policing to 1735 in the West End parishes. Reynolds also argues that the London officials did not resist the idea of policing itself: The sticking point was the idea of *centralized* policing. The author spent much time reviewing official London documents to come to her conclusions and developed an interesting thesis: There was more continuity between the pre-Peelian era and the era of professional policing than is normally explored in the literature.

Richmond. 1976. *Scenes in the Life of a Bow Street Runner*. Introduction by E. F. Bleiler. New York: Dover Publications.

Written in 1827, this work is considered to be "the first collection of detective stories in English" by an unknown writer using the pen name Richmond. The work has an introduction by E. F. Bleiler that provides an excellent description of London's famed Bow Street Runners, who are often considered the world's first detective squad.

Rousey, Dennis C. 1996. *Policing the Southern City: New Orleans 1805–1889.* Baton Rouge: Louisiana State University.

Rousey argues in this compelling work that the earliest form of policing in the United States occurred in the southern part of the country, especially in New Orleans, in the form of the slave patrols. He also describes the unique racial and cultural makeup of the city and provides contrasts to other cities in the South.

Schneider, John C. 1980. *Detroit and the Problem in Order, 1830–1880: A Geography of Crime Riot, and Policing.* Lincoln: University of Nebraska Press.

A historical account of policing in Detroit from the beginning of the police until 1880, this work examines the specific crime problem and racial strife occurring in the city and the measures taken by the police to control them.

Schulz, Dorothy Moses. 1995. *From Social Worker to Crime-fighter: Women in United States Municipal Policing.* Westport, CT: Praeger.

This is a historical account of women in policing in the United States. A chronicle of female police from the days of the police matrons to the present day, Schulz covers the periods of the women's bureaus, the Depression and World War II, and the

1950s, which she argues, opened the doors for the entrance of women into the field in the late 1960s and early 1970s.

Schulz, Dorothy Moses. 2004. *Breaking the Brass Ceiling: Women Police Chiefs and Their Paths to the Top.* Westport, CT: Praeger.

The pioneering female law enforcement administrators give their stories of breaking into the top ranks of the traditionally male-dominated field of police work. Using questionnaires, Schulz received information from the women police chiefs and sheriffs throughout the nation regarding their climb to the top of the police ladder. In addition to the surveys, the author used phone and e-mail messages and reviewed conference and publication data from the subjects.

Silverman, Charles E. 1978. *Criminal Violence, Criminal Justice.* New York: Random House.

At 540 pages, this work is a comprehensive exploration of crime and violence in America. It investigates crime and criminal violence in all areas of the criminal justice system. One chapter is wholly devoted to the police entitled, "The Wisdom of What the Police Do—and Don't Do." This chapter uses individual case studies to examine the role of the police.

Skolnick, Jerome H. 1966. *Justice Without Trial: Law Enforcement in Democratic Society.* Hoboken, NJ: John Wiley and Sons.

This landmark work started an in-depth description of the police subculture. Using the term "working personality," Skolnick described the often cited elements of the police personality: danger and authority. The additional element of social isolation is a key characteristic of this social psychological analysis. These three components create the unique behavioral traits of police officers. Skolnick also analyzes other aspects of police work such as police discretion and the code of secrecy.

Skolnick, Jerome H., and James J. Fyfe. 1993. *Above the Law: Police and the Excessive Use of Force.* New York: Free Press.

A major analysis of police misconduct through the use of excessive force, *Above the Law* is a book that is easily accessible to both police scholars and laypersons interested in policing. The common thread throughout the work is the Rodney King beating, and this theme is present from the first to the last page; this is understandable since the book was written shortly after this incredible event unfolded. The book takes a historical perspective to view the issue of police aggression and is candid in its presentation of the material. All students of policing should read this work.

Stark, Rodney. 1972. *Police Riots.* Belmont, CA: Wadsworth.

This is a seminal work on police violence written at the height of controversy surrounding police behavior and misbehavior and at the apex of the "hippie era," when many aspects of society, especially social control measures, were questioned. Stark, a sociologist who had originally planned to complete a study on a particular disturbance in 1968 ended up examining a phenomenon in which police, when engaged in efforts to control disorder, actually contribute to increased disorder by reacting violently toward the citizenry. Candid and controversial, thus work exemplified the growing chasm between the police and community during the late 1960s and early 1970s.

Stead, Philip John, ed. 1977. *Pioneers in Policing.* Montclair, NJ: Patterson Smith.

One of the finest collections of minibiography in the field of policing, this work is an edited volume with contributions on several key figures in the field, including the Fielding brothers, Robert Peel, Alphonse Bertillon, August Vollmer, O. W. Wilson, and several others. This work is a must read for those interested in the subject.

Walker, Samuel. 1977. *A Critical History of Police Reform: The Emergence of Professionalism.* Lanham, MD: Lexington Books.

This is a major contribution to the history of the American police. With the expressed motivation to explain that the American policing system is static and resistant to change, Walker begins his analysis with the mid-nineteenth century policing systems and continues through the end of the 1930s. He states that the problems that erupted in the 1960s in law enforcement were due to a policing structure that had changed little since the 1940s. Prior to that time, however, many changes had taken place as new ideas surfaced to deal with the various social changes of the time. This is an often quoted reference to many books on police history and police reform.

Wambaugh, Joseph. 1989. *The Blooding.* New York: William Morrow and Co.

Breaking from his usual police fiction, former Los Angeles Police Department officer and novelist Joseph Wambaugh wrote this book about the first case in which DNA evidence was used to convict the murderer/rapist of two teenage girls. The offenses took place in Britain three years apart, and it was because a geneticist at a nearby university was experimenting with DNA analysis that a "bloodprint" was analyzed and the offender was brought to justice.

Whitehead, Don. 1956. *The FBI Story: A Report to the People.* New York: Random House.

This book is an interesting historical and philosophical account of the Federal Bureau of Investigation, primarily under the long directorship of J. Edgar Hoover. Hoover, in fact, contributed the foreword to the work and congratulated the author for "his accurate portrayal of the record of the FBI." Many critics have dismissed the work as simply one of Hoover's methods of propaganda, and it certainly does its share of embellishment. Nevertheless, it provides a detailed history of the organization as well as a framework for the zeitgeist of Cold War–era policy. Readers with a taste for a more critical examination of the FBI should look elsewhere.

Williams, Kristian. 2004. *Our Enemies in Blue: Police and Power in America.* Brooklyn, NY: Soft Skull Press.

This work is an analysis of police power and authority from a critical perspective. It provides a historical framework for policing in regard to the abuse of power and overt social control. Controversial in its radical treatment of the subject, the book nevertheless provides a well researched, if slanted, analysis of police and community relations in America.

Wilson, James Q. 1968. *Varieties of Police Behavior: The Management of Law and Order in Eight Communities.* Cambridge, MA: Harvard University Press.

Derived from a study of patrol officers in eight American cities that took place in the mid-1960s, this is one of the most notable works on the police in the United States. The text introduces the now famous three styles of policing: the watchman, legalistic, and service styles.

Wilson, O. W. 1950. *Police Administration.* New York: McGraw-Hill.

The gold standard among early works on police management, this work by one of the era's top cops provides a series of guidelines for police administrators. The text went through several editions and covered areas such as police department organization, planning and research in policing, personnel management, police tasks, communications in law enforcement, and buildings and equipment. *Police Administration* was the standard college text and a great reference for historical analysis of policing during the days when crime fighting was a major police focus.

Journal Articles

Adler, Jeffrey S. 2006. **"'It Is His First Offense. We Might as Well Let Him Go': Homicide and Criminal Justice in Chicago, 1875–1920."** *Journal of Social History* 40 (1): 5–24.

This is a historical essay on the state of the criminal justice system in Chicago from 1875 to 1920, with an emphasis on conviction rates in the city, which were incredibly low during the period. At the time, Chicago was a center of progressive reform in criminal justice: It was the first city to create a juvenile court system and was at the vanguard of progressive policing; it instituted such measures as a homicide squad and other specialized units; it introduced the Bertillon criminal identification system (which was cutting-edge technology for the time), used fingerprint analysis, produced a psychological testing lab, and increased profession training for police officers. Chicago was, after all, a "natural laboratory" for the nation's first sociologists and criminologists who were studying the effects of rapid immigration and urbanization.

Adler notes that juries were hesitant to convict defendants in spite of the city's progressive ideals. Only four groups were likely to receive convictions: wife beaters, robbers, African Americans, and killers of police. A comparative study provides information that other cities in the United States and even other countries had low conviction rates. The inference is that, even though there were many institutional and legal changes in place during the late nineteenth to early twentieth centuries, traditional notions of justice, manliness, and honor overrode progressive reforms.

Bartels, Elizabeth C., and Eli B. Silverman. 2005. **"An Exploratory Study of the New York City Civilian Complaint Review Board Mediation Program."** *Policing* 28 (4): 619–630.

The article describes an exploratory study of citizens' and police officers' satisfaction levels of a mediation program currently operated by the New York Police Department. Sixteen police complaint mediation centers in the United States seek to find remedies for complaints against officers rather than proceeding to a formalized process. Mediation in this format involves a face-to-face meeting with the arresting officer and citizen complainant to facilitate dialog and a better understanding of the situation that brought them together. It also reviews any actions arising from the incident to assist in finding a mutually agreed-upon disposition, if possible.

The researchers used a survey to gather data from both the police officers and the civilian complainants regarding their experiences with the program. The study found higher levels of satisfaction with both police and citizens in the mediation process than with the full investigation procedure. The primary motivation for the mediation program of both parties was providing them with the chance to meet with the other person and seek resolution of the matter. The study had a very low response rate (18.2 percent), a major concern for the researchers, and used a cross-sectional survey design rather than a pre-post design. However, the authors report this study to be the first of its kind to provide a serious look at this interesting police–community oriented program, which is a fine starting point for replication studies.

Beckett, Katherine, Kris Ngrop, and Lori Pfingst. 2006. **"Race, Drugs, and Policing: Understanding Disparities in Drug Delivery Arrests."** *Criminology,* 44 (1): 105–137.

This study examined the disparities in drug arrests rates related to race in Seattle, Washington, a city with a high level of drug activity. It uses primary data from a needle exchange program operated by the city as well as ethnographic observations of people buying and selling drugs in active outdoor drug markets. In addition, interviews with police officers provided additional information on the law enforcement perception of the sellers of drugs.

The findings of this study were that black drug dealers were more likely to be involved with the sale of one drug—crack cocaine. Whites, on the other hand, were more likely to sell methamphetamine, ecstasy, powder cocaine, and heroin; however, blacks accounted for 64 percent of those arrested for these drugs.

Three factors are believed to account for these finding. First, the focus on crack dealers, which began in the 1980s, places more emphasis on observing African Americans. Second, police officers tend to pay more attention to outdoor markets, which are racially disparate. Lastly, the outdoor markets in communities of color are patrolled more aggressively than those in white communities.

Cope, Nina. 2004. **"Intelligence-led Policing or Policing-led Intelligence?"** *British Journal of Criminology* 44 (2): 188–203.

This article describes a qualitative study of a law enforcement model known as intelligence-led policing. The study takes place over a two-month period in England (the locations were not disclosed), and it follows two police forces, one an urban force and the other rural. Both have begun using the intelligence-led philosophy, which employs the use of intelligence in police work to be proactive to dealing with crime. Although the study takes place in England, its findings can be useful in America or in other countries that are considering the adoption of the model.

The study used participant observation and interviews to describe how in both police forces, the intelligence-led model is not effectively utilized because there is a general lack of understanding of, and appreciation for, the differences between crime analysts and the street-level officers. One of the key reasons for this chasm is the difference in orientation between the two groups. The officers tend to be contextual and experiential, basing their understanding of crime on their own experiences, whereas the analysts are analytical, basing their understanding on volume crime data from empirical sources.

An additional problem in this "clash of cultures" is the reluctance of the police to take advice or suggestions from civilians (most of the analysts were nonpolice personnel). Termed the "cop culture" (more often dubbed the "police subculture" in America), this concept—with its salient characteristics of a sense of mission, masculinity, isolation, cohesion, and a suspicion of nonpolice—often interferes with the intelligence-led process and sometimes causes the police to use intuition and experiences on the street, losing the potential proactive benefit of the model.

The author of the study recommends that both groups must be adequately trained in the use of the intelligence-led policing model and each must understand the other's role in the process. In this way, a mutual respect can develop and the model will have a chance as a successful approach to police work. It would be highly beneficial to see a similar study conducted in America or other nations to provide comparative information on this emerging model of policing.

Engel, Robin S., and Jennifer M. Calnon. 2004. **"Examining the Influence of Driver's Characteristics During Traffic Stops with Police: Results from a National Study."** *Justice Quarterly* 21 (1): 49–90.

This study examines the factors that influence police decision making after traffic stops. The backdrop for this study is the effect of the nation's war on drug policies, particularly the incidence of racial profiling in America—a potential effect of aggressive police strategies that often emphasizes the differential treatment of minority suspects. Data was obtained for the Police–Public Contact Survey in 1999, a national survey sponsored by the Bureau of Justice Statistics.

The findings of the study suggest that, even after legal and extralegal factors are controlled, minority males have the highest incidence of police involvement such as citations, searches, arrest, and the use of force. This is in spite of the fact that minorities are less likely to have illegal contraband in their possession. The researchers offer a call for reform in the present tactics that reinforce the legitimacy of racial profiling.

Felson, Richard B., Jeffrey M. Ackerman, and Catherine A. Gallagher. 2005. **"Police Intervention and the Repeat of Domestic Violence."** *Criminology* 43 (3): 563–588.

This study, headed by noted criminal justice scholar, Richard Felson, examines whether the reporting of incidents of domestic violence to the police and the arrest of the batterers have a deterrent effect on subsequent episodes of such violence. The researchers used a longitudinal analysis of the National Crime Victimization Study covering the years 1992–2002. The "retaliation hypothesis" was tested to see if the retaliation occurred when the victim reported violence and if the perpetrator was arrested.

The study's findings suggest that arrest after a domestic violence situation does not have a pronounced deterrent effect on future offending; there might be a small effect but it is statistically insignificant. Reporting the incident to the police, however, does have a deterrent effect, according to this research. Some potential reasons are posited for this finding: Perhaps batterers who are likely to be affected by an arrest are already deterred by police involvement; it is also possible that the punishment resulting from the domestic violence arrest is not adequately severe to have a deterrent effect.

The authors also posit some reasons that reporting appears to reduce recidivism. Perhaps a visit from the police lets abusers realize that their actions are indeed a criminal act, forcing them to change their minds about their behavior. It could cause them to realize the personal costs of continuing their aggressive behavior. The stigma of being recognized as an abusive partner is also a possibility. The authors also note that it is possible that couples involved in intimate partner abuse may seek counseling as a result of the police intervention, thereby reducing the effects.

The researchers also provide some policy suggestions based on this and earlier studies regarding the reporting of domestic violence to the police. Although it is obviously easier to change local arrest policy than reporting behavior, some changes are recommended. Informing the public about the deterrent effect of reporting domestic violence is one suggestion. Also, since some people do not report incidents of domestic violence due to the stigma of having a uniformed officer come to their residence, having a plainclothes officer respond to domestic violence calls might be a less visible way to handle such a complaint.

Maguire, Edward R., and Charles M. Katz. 2002. **"Community Policing, Loose Coupling, and Sensemaking in American Police Agencies."** *Justice Quarterly* 19 (3): 503–536.

This study examines the utility of community policing by connecting the philosophy with two major concepts borrowed from organizational theory: loose coupling and sensemaking. The authors begin the article by discussing how community policing can be seen as the bright and shining new philosophy in policing or simply as an old idea with a lot of media and organizational hype.

The researchers explain that loose coupling in organizational theory seeks to explain the interconnectedness of different elements in an organization. The concept not only provides an organizational model to understand the linkage but also a cognitive model to assist in understanding and analyzing how police departments react to and interpret structural changes and reforms.

The concept of sensemaking is a by-product of loose coupling and refers to how organizations are presented with new and often ambiguous philosophical changes and how they attempt to understand them. The perspective views the construction of reality on the part of the actors and therefore bases a social psychology framework on these interpretations.

The study uses data from a national Police Foundation survey that was conducted in March 1993 of 2,314 police departments and sheriff's offices. The agencies were asked about their level of involvement in community policing practices. The study's findings suggest that moderate coupling exists at some levels and that patrol officers and organization level activities are more positively correlated with the ideals of community policing, followed by citizen activities. Recommendations were made to reeducate communities as to their role in the community policing process to garner more involvement from citizens.

This study used a survey from 1993, which occurred prior to the passage of the 1994 Crime Act, which provided funding and other means of support to police agencies that accepted the community policing philosophy. Using more current data, produced after the 1994 Crime Act was promulgated, would provide an interesting follow-up to this study.

Ratcliffe, Jerry H. 2004. **"Crime Mapping and the Training Needs of Law Enforcement."** *European Journal of Criminal Policy and Research* 10 (1): 65–83.

This essay on crime mapping and training needs of police officers in this regard explain the development of the three areas of spatial investigation and analysis (crime mapping) currently used by the police: hotspot crime mapping, CompStat mapping, and geographic profiling. Hotspot crime mapping dates back to the "pushpin" method in police substation houses when pins were placed on maps of the city (or other geographic areas) to determine where resources were most needed; computerized crime mapping has brought this outdated method into the present.

CompStat (a shortened version of computer-assisted statistics) is the management system started by administrators in the New York City Police Department in the 1990s. Its use of crime mapping is primarily a management tool intended to force area commanders to bring crime rates down in their areas. The model has been quite popular and modified for use in other cities in the United States as well as other nations.

Geographic profiling is the spatial equivalent to the psychological profiling of offenders. It seeks to determine patterns that give clues as to where an offender lives or works, or possibly to movement patterns that could help locate victims, contraband, etc. According to the author, this field is part of the branch of criminology called environmental criminology.

A key concern of the essay's writer is that police agencies, especially those in the United States, will not use crime mapping or the broader police philosophy known as intelligence-led policing, instead focusing organizational training objectives in other areas such as tactical responses and police administration. A content analysis of the International Association of Police Chiefs' training catalog is discussed to validate this concern.

Roh, Sunghoon, and William M. Oliver. 2005. **"Effects of Community Policing upon Fear of Crime: Understanding the Causal Linkage."** *Policing: An International Journal of Police Strategies and Management* 28 (4): 670–683.

This study seeks to explain conflicting findings of earlier studies regarding the relationship between community policing initiatives and the fear of crime. Recent studies suggest that police presence produces a reduction in fear among citizens but does not have a positive impact on public satisfaction with police; other studies have suggested that citizen perception of community policing has a strong positive relationship with satisfaction with police but not on levels of fear. The present study seeks to determine if other factors, such as demographic characteristics, perception of community disorganization, and concern over community safety helped account for the relationship between community policing and fear of crime.

Reducing the level of fear of crime is one of the primary goals of community policing, along with crime prevention, the reduction of social disorder, and the improvement of the overall quality of life for citizens. The fear of crime should be diminished due to the ideals promoted by community policing for four reasons:

- Increased police presence will alleviate fear.
- Engagement with the public will increase satisfaction and reduce fear.
- Partnerships and collaboration will assist in lowering levels of fear.
- The strategies of community policing themselves will lower crime and the resulting fear of criminal activity in neighborhoods.

Three models were used to form a theoretical framework: (1) the indirect victimization model, which posits that citizens with awareness of their vulnerability characteristics (the demographic variables of age, gender, education, and race that are perceived as risk factors) are more likely to fear crime; (2) the perceived disorder model, which states that the fear of crime increases with citizen experiences of physical or social incivility; and (3) the common concern model, which explains that fear is closely correlated with citizen concerns of community decline.

The data used in this study was derived from the 1998 research project, Criminal Victimization and Perception of Community Safety in Twelve United States Cities, conducted by the Office of Community Policing and the Bureau of Justice Statistics. The findings of the study reveal that vulnerability variables are not positively correlated with community policing and the fear of crime, as described in the indirect victim model, but with the perception of incivilities and concerns of quality of neighborhood life in the perceived disorder model, respectively.

Ruf, Jamie. 2006. **"Expanding Protective Sweeps Within the Home."** *American Criminal Law Review* 43 (1): 143–163.

This legal essay on protective sweeps as employed by the police reviews the constitutional framework of the Fourth Amendment protection from illegal searches and seizures in the home. The author believes that this protection is eroding during this "era of preemptive strikes," referring to the abandonment of individual protections for the sake of investigating terrorist-related activity.

The constitutional basis for protective sweeps employed by the police is appropriately provided in this essay through a historical review of precedent cases such as *Terry v. Ohio, Ker v. California,* and *Katz v. United States* to explain the growing chasm between civil liberties and social protection in the newer cases of *Maryland v. Buie,* which established the protective sweep doctrine, and *United States v. Gould,* which indicated that the "Buie sweep" need not always happen incident to an arrest.

The author states that the home, long held as a bastion of privacy, is now being increasingly open to searches and seizures, very much in contradiction to the ideas of the framers of the Constitution who feared that government intrusion into citizens' home will damage democratic ideals.

Schaefer, Joseph A. 2005. **"Negotiating Order in the Policing of Youth Drinking."** *Policing* 28 (2): 279–300.

In this study the researcher sought to understand the use of negotiated order by police officers who use discretionary leniency in prominent crimes in their communities. Police–citizen relations in a medium Midwestern college community provided the venue for studying this concept. Though the use of a field study combined with interviews, the research project utilized interviews with general patrol officers, patrol managers, and members of a specialized alcohol enforcement unit involving questions centering on perspectives on policing, interactions with the community's younger citizens (primarily from a local state university), alcohol regulations, views on police–community relations, agency and administrative relationships and perceptions, and comparative and contrasting views of their agency and other police departments.

The police in this agency commonly dealt with alcohol violations by young offenders, because theirs is a college environment; therefore in many of their contacts with young people, alcohol was the direct or indirect reason for police intervention. The officers' primary methods for dealing with the alcohol-abusing young people involved more leniency than many other agencies. One of the key factors involved in a more lenient response by officers was the variable of citizen demeanor. The agency adopted a "firm but friendly" approach to these calls, and, although informal controls were often used, formal controls including arrest were common in situations in which:

- Students were contemptuous toward the police ("contempt of cop").
- Students were involved in vandalism, assault, violations of liquor laws in cars, possession of alcohol by an underage person, the use of fake identification, or the illegal sale of alcohol to others.
- Businesses sold alcohol to minors.

The study focuses on what has been termed the "attitude test," a determination of whether the citizen offender appropriately defers to the police. The outcomes of future studies that determine whether such a concept is valid should consider if the use of deferential displays is an adequate criterion for officer discretion.

Slansky, David Alan. 2006. **"Private Police and Democracy."** *American Criminal Law Review,* 43 (1): 89–105.

In this essay, the author provides an exploration of the privatization of police work that is missing in the current literature on policing. The emphasis of this piece is on the potential effect of private policing on the ideals of a democratic society. The author seeks to develop two points: First, police privatization is a complex issue, complicated by the facts that private police work can take on various and overlapping forms; that policing is a multifarious political philosophy with different meanings for different people; and that private policing can easily transmute from an augmentation to public policing into a structure like itself—a movement that is clearly discernible in several police organizations already.

The second major point made in this article is that two threats exist and should be evaluated more carefully by law enforcement administrators and policy makers. The first is the fact that privatization can make policing less egalitarian by forcing the poorer citizens to have the reactive public police and the richer citizens to receive the services of the more proactive private police at their disposal. This scenario also removes political pressure from the public agencies to conform to due process concerns and the basic ideals of human dignity. The second threat concerns the possibility of public police agencies adopting a business-oriented managerial logic approach to a social control agency whose primary responsibility in a democratic society is the protection of all citizens. It is recommended by the author that police administrators and policy makers carefully examine the direction of privatization to ensure that democratic values are not lost in the process.

Tyler, Tom T. 2006. **"Viewing CSI and the Threshold of Guilt: Managing Truth and Justice in Reality and Fiction."** *The Yale Law Journal* 115 (5): 1050–1085.

This essay examines the so-called CSI effect. This recently coined term describes the possibility that jurors in a criminal trial are so influenced by the forensic television show *CSI: Crime Scene Investigation,* and its spin-offs, *CSI: Miami* and *CSI: New York,* along with other forensic-oriented shows, that they are more likely to acquit defendants unless there is significant forensic science evidence to prove their guilt. Newspapers and magazines have recently claimed that such an effect exists and have used some high-profile cases to support the claim, such as the well publicized acquittal of actor Robert Blake in the murder of his wife and the acquittal of eccentric millionaire Robert Durst, who had been accused of murder and dismemberment.

The author notes that no scientific studies have found evidence of the CSI effect, and many scholars think that viewing forensic crime shows might make some jurors actually *less* likely to acquit. The reason is that many jurors feel the need to see the case have a successful closure, as they do on most TV shows; this helps to satisfy a psychological need for justice for victims of crime. The cases in CSI and other shows of this genre always have a rapid conclusion, and this might prompt jurors in real court cases to work toward the same end. In addition, when jurors are motivated by a desire to punish an offender, they can easily mentally exaggerate scientific evidence presented at trial to confirm their suspicions of guilt.

The article also presents three other possible motivations for juror reluctance to convict defendants: (1) identification and sympathy with the defendants, (2) a natural reluctance to convict that is underestimated by people with legal training, and (3) suspicion and distrust of the courts and the criminal justice system that makes it less likely for them to defer to the legal professionals' knowledge. The source of these motivations is unclear, as well as what empirical support, if any, supports the conclusions. The CSI effect is certainly an area deserving of empirically based studies to give prosecutors and police officers in criminal trials a better understanding of the social psychology of juror behavior and the role of the media.

Xie, Min, Greg Pogarsky, James P. Lynch, and David McDowall. 2006. **"Prior Police Contact and Subsequent Victim Reporting: Results for the NCVS."** *Justice Quarterly* 23 (4): 481–501.

The authors of this study seek to fill a void in the crime victimization literature. They provide a study designed to how police response to prior cases of victimization of the present victim and household members influences future reporting by the victim.

The researchers used longitudinal data from the National Crime Victimization Survey for the years 1998–2000. The study presents two major findings. The first two findings are that the prior investigation of victimization by the police affected subsequent reports but that prior arrests involving the victimization did not. The third finding is that direct reporting of the crime to the police by the victim, rather than by a third party, had an effect on subsequent reporting. The fourth finding is that victim reporting was not correlated with prior police response to a prior family member's victimization, even if the events were similar in nature and regardless of the closeness in relation to the family member.

Scholarly Journals

Criminology
Blackwell Publishing Ltd.
9600 Garsington Road
Oxford OX4 2DQ, UK
Internet: http://www.blackwellpublishing.com/journal.asp?
ref=0011–1384

Although presenting a somewhat broader scope in the criminal justice field than just policing, this journal is published on behalf of the American Society of Criminology. It is a prominent journal in the field and includes many articles about policing. The journal is peer reviewed, places emphasis on empirical research, and publishes scholarly studies on a variety of criminal justice issues.

Journal of Criminal Law and Criminology, The
JSTOR User Services
301 East Liberty, Suite 250
Ann Arbor, MI 48104-2262
Internet: http://www.jstor.org/journals/00914169.html

Describing itself as one of the nation's most widely read and cited legal-oriented journals, this journal, formerly known as the *Journal of Criminal Law, Criminology, and Police Science,* publishes criminal law research that is of benefit to practitioners in all sectors of the criminal justice field. It encourages intellectual debate in the belief that this is the best means of bettering the profession.

Police Practice and Research
Taylor and Francis Group
UK Head Office: T and F Informa Academic (Journals)
Building 4, Milton Park
Abingdon, Oxfordshire OX14 4RN, UK
Internet: http://www.tandf.co.uk/journals/titles/15614263.asp

This peer-reviewed journal focuses on new and innovative police practices from around the world. The journal seeks to connect current academic research with modern law enforcement practices. Special issues are published that explore police practices in different counties or continents.

Police Quarterly
Sage Publications
2455 Teller Road
Thousand Oaks, CA 91320
Internet: http://www.sagepub.com/journalsProdDesc.nav?
prodId=Journal201421

Published in association with the Police Executive Research Forum and the Police Section of the Academy of Criminal Justice Sciences, this journal emphasizes policy-oriented research and covers many areas of interest of policing to scholars and practitioners. The peer-reviewed journal publishes qualitative and quantitative studies, essays, book reviews, and other submissions.

Policing and Society
Taylor and Francis
4 Park Square Milton Park

Abingdon, Oxfordshire OX14 4RN, UK
Internet: http://www.tandf.co.uk/journals/titles/10439463

The focus of *Policing and Society* is social scientific investigations of three areas: police policy, legal analysis of police powers and constitutionality, and research into police administration; however, other areas of concern are considered, such as police functions, police decision making, and private policing agencies. It also takes up the issue of the political economy of policing. The journal is international in orientation and scope, and it is committed to high levels of scholarship and policy debate.

Policing: An International Journal of Police Strategies and Management
Emerald Group Publishing Limited
60–62 Toller Lane
Bradford, BD8 9BY, UK
Internet: http://www.emeraldinsight.com/info/journals/pijpsm/pijpsm.jsp

This stated mission of this journal is to provide discourse in police and law enforcement practice and administration that seeks to add professionalism to the field. This peer-reviewed journal publishes research and case studies with an international and comparative police focus.

The Police Journal
Vathek Publishing
Bridge House
Dalby, Isle of Man, IM5 3BP, UK
Internet: http://www.vathek.com/pj/index.shtml

The Police Journal offers expert advice on some of the most pressing issues in the field. Subjects such as police procedure, technology, statistical data, new ideas in police practice, and laws affecting the police are all addressed using evidence-based research.

Magazines

American Police Beat
One Battle Square, 4th Floor
Cambridge, MA 02138

This newsmagazine has many articles on relevant topics in policing, including current police news, training information, personnel information, product information, and the like. It has an online version as well. The subscription rate is $16.95 per year.

Subscription information: http://www.apbweb.com/subscribe.htm

FBI Law Enforcement Bulletin
U.S. Department of Justice
Federal Bureau of Investigation
Washington, D.C. 20535-0001

Published monthly, this FBI-sponsored magazine provides practical and current information on the policing profession. It includes ViCAP (Violent Criminal Apprehensive Program) Alerts, Bulletin Reports (an edited compilation of reports related to criminal justice), Legal Digests, Bulletin Notes (acknowledgments and recognition of police who perform notable and dangerous acts), as well as a host of speeches, practice recommendations, and commentaries. The subscription rate is $38 per year.

Subscription information: http://www.fbi.gov/publications/leb/leborder.htm

Law and Order
Hendon Publications
130 N. Waukegan Road
Suite 202
Deerfield, IL 60015-5652

Law and Order is a widely read publication and has a readership of 36,000 police administrators. It offers a number of articles pertinent to policing, including information on personnel management, training resources, community relations, technical innovations, and other issues. It has a large number of advertisers for various police products. Its website gives the reader a chance to rate and comment on many of the articles, which is true of the other Hendon publications.

Subscription information: http://www.subforms.com/lao

Police Chief
International Association of Chiefs of Police
515 N. Washington Street
Alexandria, VA 22314-2357

This, the official magazine of the IACP, has information of concern to police administrators, on personnel management, current events, legislation, products and services, among other areas. The subscription rate is $25 a year to non-IACP members.

Subscription information: http://www.policechiefmagazine.com/subscribe/

Police Fleet Manager
Hendon Publications
130 N. Waukegan Road
Suite 202
Deerfield, IL 60015-5652

This magazine, for police personnel involved with transportation, provides information on police automobiles and parts. It has a number of relevant articles, including vehicle tests, police packages for automobiles, and other items of interest.

Subscription information: http://www.subforms.com/pfm

Police Magazine
3520 Challenger Street
Torrance, CA 90503

Offering articles written by police, firearms, and legal experts, as well as special issue contributions from other law enforcement journalists, *Police Magazine* is concerned with providing police officers with information that will benefit them in the profession.

Subscription information: Send an email message to info@policemag.com.

Police Times
American Federation of Police and Concerned Citizens
6359 Horizon drive
Titusville, FL 32780

The official magazine of the AFB & CC, this magazine is published quarterly and contains information on police training, news, products and services, innovations in the field, and related subjects.

Subscription information: http://www.aphf.org/ptsubscribe.html

Tactical Response
Hendon Publications

130 N. Waukegan Road
Suite 202
Deerfield, IL 60015-5652

Specifically concerned with police special tactical units, this magazine provides articles on weaponry, tactics, personnel management, and new innovations.

Subscription information: http://www.subforms.com/tac

Nonprint Resources

Videos and DVDs

Behind the Blue Wall
Date: Unknown
Type: DVD
Length: 50 minutes
Cost: $24.95
Source: Distributed by Arts and Entertainment Networks
Internet: http://www.aetv.com

This documentary, as part of A&E Channel's Investigative Reports series, uses different incidents of police misconduct in the New York City Police Department and the friction that still exists between the police and the citizens they serve.

Best Kept Secrets in Law Enforcement
Date: 2000
Type: DVD-R
Length: 50 minutes
Cost: $159.95
Source: Distributed by Insight Media
Internet: http://www.insight-media.com

This film is a police training film that uses recreations, crime scene footage, and interviews to describe twenty-first-century police innovations, such as Taser technology and a new computer program that detects deception in facial expressions.

Best Kept Secrets in Law Enforcement
Date: 1999
Type: VHS
Length: 39 minutes each

Cost: $159.95 (for each part)
Source: Distributed by Insight Media
Internet: http://www.insight-media.com

This documentary training film describes the collaboration between police agencies, school, communities, and business in order to thwart violence in schools. The film is in two parts: The Warning Signs and Response.

Beyond the Blue: Life as a Female Police Officer
Date: 1997
Type: DVD-R, VHS
Length: 25 minutes
Cost: $129.95
Source: Distributed by Films for the Humanities and Sciences
Internet: http://www.films.com

This documentary describes the story of a woman who is a wife, mother, and member of a SWAT team. It shows the conflicts that come with the additional stressor in family life that comes with having a very high-stress occupation.

Body Detectives: Forensic Anthropology and the Body Farm
Date: 2000
Type: DVD-R, VHS
Length: 52 minutes
Cost: $129.95
Source: Films for the Humanities and Sciences
Internet: http://www.films.com

This film takes a close-up look at the University of Tennessee's open-air forensic crime lab, dubbed the body farm, where decomposing human bodies give investigators insight that will hopefully help them solve crimes. This broadcast was initially released as *Body Detectives*.

Cop World, Parts 1 and 2
Date: Unknown
Type: DVD
Length: 50 minutes
Cost: $24.95
Source: Distributed by Arts and Entertainment Networks
Internet: http://www.aetv.com

This video, part of the A&E Channel's Investigative Reports series, depicts police work around the globe—in Moscow, Rio, South Africa, and the United States. It gives a glimpse into the complicated world of comparative policing and explains how undercover sting operations and gun battles are a common component of police work in many nations, including our own.

G-Man: The Making of an FBI Agent
Date: 2001
Type: DVD-R, VHS
Length: 52 minutes
Cost: $129.95
Source: Films for the Humanities and Sciences
Internet: http://www.films.com

This film describes the intensive sixteen-week training and instruction undertaken by the select candidates accepted into the FBI academy at Quantico, Virginia. Candidates are interviewed in the film and express their feeling of the rigor of the training, which includes firearms, forensics, surveillance, and terrorism control tactics. This is a Discovery Channel production.

Inside the Interrogation Room
Date: 2003
Type: DVD-R, VHS
Length: 19 minutes
Cost: $69.95
Source: Films for the Humanities and Sciences
Internet: http://www.films.com

Showcasing the different interrogation procedures used by the police, this documentary features the Reid technique and describes both the positive and negative aspects of the method. Police scholars, lawyers, and people who have been interrogated and confessed to crimes, only later to be exonerated of guilt, provide commentary in this film.

New York City Police Academy
Date: 2000
Type: DVD-R, VHS
Length: 46 minutes
Cost: $129.95

Source: Films for the Humanities and Sciences
Internet: http://www.films.com

This documentary follows new recruits in the country's largest police agency through seven months of intensive training. The recruits are trained in a number of areas including police tactics, communication skills, firearms use, defense measures, hostage negotiation, crowd control, and courtroom testimony. This is a Discovery Channel production.

Patrolling the Border: National Security and Immigration Reform
Date: 2004
Type: DVD-R, VHS
Length: 22 minutes
Cost: $69.95
Source: Films for the Humanities and Sciences
Internet: http://www.films.com

This documentary explores the continuing controversy over controlling the nation's southern border and examines the relationship between the undocumented people who enter America, the terrorist attacks of September 11, 2001, and the nation's economy. Border patrol agents in Arizona are interviewed in the film.

Police
Date: 1997
Type: DVD
Length: 100 minutes
Cost: $29.95
Source: Distributed by Arts and Entertainment Networks
Internet: http://www.aetv.com

This is a highly informative exploration of the police in America narrated by Bill Kurtis. It intersperses current police concerns, such as community policing, with historical information about policing, including its British antecedents and the effect of Robert Peel's innovations on modern policing. Interviews with police officials highlight this investigation into law enforcement practices.

Police Pursuit
Date: Unknown
Type: DVD

Length: 50 minutes
Cost: $24.95
Source: Distributed by Arts and Entertainment Networks
Internet: http://www.aetv.com

This film describes one of the most controversial areas of police work: high-speed chases. In hot pursuit situations, many people can get injured or killed; therefore some departments have policies to abort chases unless there is an overriding reason to continue pursuit. However, if pursuits are aborted, dangerous offenders are free to continue committing crimes. This video shows the latest technological advancements in automobiles and boats.

Protect and Serve? De-policing in Urban Neighborhoods
Date: 2001
Type: DVD-R, VHS
Length: 23 minutes
Cost: $69.95
Source: Distributed by Films for the Humanities and Sciences
Internet: http://www.films.com

This video looks at how police work in some departments has been transformed from an active and engaged process into new forms of passive involvement with citizens. New police lingo, such as "selective disengagement," "tactical detachment," and "NC/NC" (code for no contact, no complaints) demonstrates this new philosophy.

Racial Profiling and Law Enforcement: America in Black and White
Date: 1998
Type: DVD-R, VHS
Length: 41 minutes
Cost: $129.95
Source: Distributed by Films for the Humanities and Sciences
Internet: http://www.films.com

This film explains the phenomenon of DWB: driving while black (or brown). The issue of racial profiling is a major one in police work and is explored in this two-part documentary narrated by ABC news anchor Ted Koppel.

Suicide and the Police Officer
Date: Unknown
Type: DVD-R, VHS
Length: 39 minutes
Cost: $149.95
Source: Films for the Humanities and Sciences
Internet: http://www.films.com

Funded by the New York City Police Foundation, this film describes the very real incidence of suicide by police officers. It also examines some underlying and related problems such as substance abuse, relationship problems, and violence. This documentary received Honorable Mention at the American Correctional Association Film Festival.

Tales of the Gun: Police Guns
Date: Unknown
Type: DVD
Length: 50 minutes
Cost: $24.95
Source: Distributed by Arts and Entertainment Networks
Internet: http://www.aetv.com

This documentary takes a look at police weapons from early times to the present. The Massachusetts State Troopers are highlighted in this film, and interviews with the officers are shown. Viewers also visit the New York Police Department Museum, which displays weapons almost two centuries old. Interviews with police handgun trainers are also included in the video.

The Life of a Black Cop
Date: 1999
Type: DVD-R, VHS
Length: 22 minutes
Cost: $89.95
Source: Distributed by Films for the Humanities and Sciences
Internet: http://www.films.com

This film, narrated by ABC news correspondent David Turecamo, describes the price that minority officers often pay when they report incidents of police brutality and racism. It tells the story of one minority officer who did just that and explains the consequences of taking such a stand.

The Thin Blue Line
Date: 1988
Type: DVD
Length: 103 minutes
Cost: Varies by distributor
Internet: Source: Metro Goldwin Meyer.

This is a reenactment documentary of a 1976 incident in which a drifter was given a ride by a teenage sociopath who had run away from home. When a police officer was killed, the drifter was charged with his murder. This award-winning documentary reportedly helped free the drifter from prison after it was broadcast.

Websites

http://www.amw.com

This is the website for the popular television series *America's Most Wanted* and keeps observers up-to-date on unsolved crimes in which the police seek the viewers' help. It has sections on fugitives, missing persons, and updates on captures.

http://www.apbweb.com

Self-billed as "the online voice of the nation's law enforcement community," this site is maintained by *American Police Beat* and offers news involving the police, a job search link, law enforcement events, a merchandise link, and other information.

http://www.copnet.org

This is a general directory of law enforcement items and information with links to events, merchandise, and a newsletter called *CopNet Chronicles*.

http://www.crime.org

This site gives much information about crime and its control. It has news updates, a web log, and a newsletter called *Grassroots News*.

http://www.officer.com

Officer.com is a comprehensive site for people involved with policing. It has an extensive up-to-date police news section, free training webcasts, product information, articles, a job list link, magazines called *Law Enforcement Technology* and *Law Enforcement Product News,* discussion forums, and links to many other criminal justice concerns.

http://www.policeone.com

This is a site with extensive information on a large number of policing issues. Calling itself the "one complete resource for law enforcement," the site includes current police news stories in a format called PoliceOne roll call, video feeds, product information, articles, columns, alerts, chat rooms, job postings, training courses, and others.

http://www.policing.com

This site, the self-reported "headquarters for community policing," is dedicated to providing information relevant to police through advice and discussion. With community policing as its focal point, the site has a free newsletter, online training capabilities, and a host of links to other police-related resources.

http://www.popcenter.org

This is the website for the Center for Problem-oriented Policing. It contains a variety of different types of information based on Goldstein's model of policing and has guides such as problem-specific guides, response guides, and problem-solving tool guides to assist police practitioners with the different problems they face. It also contains a library, a forum, conference information, and a host of technical and analytical tools related to the problem-oriented policing model.

http://www.talkjustice.com

Described on its web page as "the world's criminal justice forum," this site seeks to involve students, scholars, practitioners, crime victims, and interested citizens in ongoing discussions about issues in criminal justice. It has message boards, chat rooms, a large cybrary, and links to many other related sites.

Court Cases

Bond v. United States, 529 U.S. (2000)

On a bus bound for Little Rock, Arkansas, from California, a routine border stop occurred in Sierra Blanca, Texas. A border patrol agent squeezed a soft piece of luggage in an overhead storage compartment as he was exiting the bus and felt a "brick-like object" inside it. The agent checked the bag and found a "brick" of methamphetamine wrapped in duct tape and rolled in a pair of pants. The defendant, Bond, was indicted for conspiracy to possess and possession with the intent to distribute methamphetamine, and he was found guilty on both counts. He appealed on the grounds that the examination of the luggage violated his Fourth Amendment protection from unreasonable searches. The Court of Appeals affirmed the conviction, and the case was sent to the U.S. Supreme Court, who reversed the judgment stating that people are guaranteed rights that prohibit physically invasive inspections by police.

Brown v. Texas, 443 U.S. 47 (1979)

Two police officers in El Paso, Texas, were patrolling an area of high drug activity when they observed two people in an alley walking away from each other. When they stopped one of the subjects, Brown, they asked him for his name and what he was doing in the alley. The subject refused to identify himself and stated the officers had no right to stop him. He was arrested on a state statute for failing to follow a lawful order to disclose information to the police. He was searched, but nothing illegal was found on his person. He was charged and convicted in a municipal court. He exercised his right to have a trial de novo in county court and moved to set aside the information in the first trial for violating his First, Fourth, and Fifth Amendment rights. The county court maintained the lower court sentence and imposed a fine. The defendant appealed to the U.S. Supreme Court, who reversed the decision due to the fact that the officers in the case lacked reasonable suspicion in detaining the defendant prior to arrest.

California v. Ciraolo, 476 U.S. 207 (1986)

In Santa Clara, California, the police received a tip from an anonymous caller that Ciraolo was growing marijuana in his backyard behind a high fence. Being unable to see the items behind the fence, the police used a plane to fly over the suspect's house at about 1,000 feet where they spotted seventy-three marijuana plants. The plants were seized, and Ciraolo pleaded guilty to the cultivation of marijuana. Upon appeal to the state court of appeals, the conviction was reversed because it was found that the aerial observation by police was illegal. The case was appealed to the Supreme Court, which determined by a divided court that flying over the suspect's home was not intrusive and took place in public airspace; other people flying overhead could have easily viewed the marijuana.

Carroll v. United States, 267 U.S. 132 (1925)

In the bootleg era of the 1920s, federal agents heard that some suspects were transporting illegal alcohol from Detroit to Grand Rapids, Michigan. When stopped, George Carroll and John Kiro were driving a 1921 Oldsmobile Roadster with a rumble seat. No alcohol was visible in the front of the car, and the rumble seat was closed. When it was opened, no alcohol was visible in the rumble seat area either, but, when the back seats were checked, the upholstery seemed unusual to one of the officers, who cut the seats and found sixty-nine quarts of illegal gin and whiskey. George Carroll attempted to bribe the agents but they refused. Carroll was found guilty, but appealed to the Supreme Court because no warrant was used in the search. The Supreme Court ruled that, due to the fact that the vehicle could easily drive away prior to a warrant being obtained, the search was allowed. This ruling is often called the automobile exception to the Fourth Amendment search warrant rule. It is less formally referred to as the Carroll doctrine.

Escobedo v. Illinois, 378 U.S. 478 (1964)

The prior case of *Gideon v. Wainwright* (1963) determined that all defendants have the right to an attorney, even those who are indigent. The case of Escobedo occurred a year later, after the defendant was being questioned for a murder charge. During questioning, Escobedo was not informed of his right to remain silent or given the opportunity to speak with an attorney. One of the officers explained that Escobedo would be allowed to leave if he confessed to the crime. He confessed and was later convicted for the murder, but the case was reversed in the Supreme Court. The ruling made clear that questioning is investigatory until the focus moves to eliciting a confession from a suspect.

Illinois v. Wardlaw, 528 **U.S.** 119 (2000)

Officers in four cars were patrolling a high-crime area where a suspect was standing alone holding a small bag. The suspect, Wardlaw, noticed one of the officers and fled, being chased by police. When given a Terry (frisk) search, a handgun was found. The case found its way to the Supreme Court, where it was determined that officers have a reasonable suspicion when flight by a suspect is accompanied by other factors such as time of day, how crowded the area is, if it occurs in a high-crime area, suspicious actions by the suspect, and the like. In other words, the flight of a suspect in tandem with other conditions is required to form a basis of reasonable suspicion.

Jacobson v. United States, 503 **U.S.** 540 (1992)

In this case, the Supreme Court reviewed what has been termed "entrapment" by the police in which police actions contribute to the criminal activity. Jacobson was under observation by the United States postal inspectors as receiving pornographic materials depicting preteen sexuality. The inspectors sent a number of false advertisements for child pornography over a two-and-a-half-year period, and Jacobson eventually responded by ordering a magazine. The Court determined that the government used excessive influence on the suspect to entice him to purchase the illegal materials.

Mallory v. United States, 354 **U.S.** 449 (1957)

A nineteen-year-old man with mental deficiencies was arrested and charged with rape. Officers did not explain to Mallory his rights to remain silent, have an attorney, or appear before a magistrate. The defendant was questioned for hours, and, obtaining no confession, officers placed him on a polygraph (lie detection) test and interrogated him further before having him arraigned. Mallory was found guilty, but the Supreme Court reversed the decision due to the delay of arraigning the defendant.

Mapp v. Ohio, 367 **U.S.** 643 (1961)

Mapp was a woman suspected by police of concealing gambling paraphernalia and hiding a person who was implicated in a bombing incident. Officers approached her residence, but Mapp refused to let them enter without a search warrant. The officers returned and forcibly entered her house. When she asked for a search warrant, the officers produced a piece of paper they reported to be a warrant, which she grabbed and placed in her blouse. The officers struggled with the suspect and retrieved the paper, which was in fact not a legal search warrant. They then searched the house and found some pornographic materials. Mapp was convicted for possession of the obscene materials and the case was appealed to the Supreme Court, who determined that illegally seized materials could not be used as evidence; the decision was therefore overturned. This rule applied to both state and federal laws, and *Mapp* is a landmark case in the search and seizure issue.

Maryland v. Buie, 494 U.S. 325 (1990)

Following an armed robbery that was committed by two men in Maryland, police were looking for a man in a red running suit, as reported by an observer. When officers approached Buie's home with an arrest warrant, the suspect was returning from his basement when arrested by one officer, and another officer went to his basement in case someone else was there. In the basement, the officer found the red running suit. Buie sought to suppress the evidence found at his home, but the trial court denied the request and the defendant was found guilty of armed robbery and a weapons violation. On appeal, the conviction was affirmed by an intermediate appellate court but reversed by the state court of appeals. The United States Supreme Court heard the case and found that officers are able to conduct a "protective sweep" of an offender's home if it is reasonable to think that there is a potential for danger in it.

Miller v. United States, 357 U.S. 301 (1958)

In response to a narcotics offense, federal officers with no search warrant approached the home of the defendant. When the officers knocked on the door, officers responded in a low voice, "Police." Miller opened the door (which had a door chain attached) and asked the officers what they wanted, but, before they responded, he attempted to close the door. The officers put their hands inside the door before it closed, ripped off the chain, and entered the home, where they found and seized contraband. The case found its way to the United States Supreme Court where the Court held that the officers were acting in an unlawful manner by breaking into his home without appropriate notice; the evidence seized was therefore not admissible. This case was the beginning of a series of court cases that dealt with the knock and announce rule.

Miranda v. Arizona, 384 U.S. 436 (1966)

This landmark case involved a young man who was arrested for rape and questioned by officers who failed to advise Miranda of his rights to have an attorney present. He was found guilty and convicted, and he appealed to the state supreme court, where the sentence was confirmed. An appeal to the superior court, however, reversed the decision, stating that the defendant was not given proper notice of his constitutional rights even though he signed a sworn confession. *Miranda* established that, before an interrogation into a criminal matter can be conducted of a person in custody, four warnings must be given: (1) that the suspect has the right to remain silent during questioning; (2) that anything the suspect says during questioning may be used as evidence against him or her; (3) that the suspect has the right to speak with an attorney and have that attorney present during questioning; and (4) that, if the suspect does not have the means to obtain an attorney, one will be provided. Police often give this warning verbatim to avoid any departure from the original intent of the language. The purpose of the Miranda warning is to ensure that the constitutional rights of the accused are protected. The reading of the Miranda warnings has now become a standard part of American police practice.

New York v. Quarles, 467 U.S. 649 (1984)

This is the "public safety exception" to the use of the Miranda warning. Quarles was suspected of rape. When he was questioned by police, an empty gun shoulder holster was found on him. The officers asked for the location of the firearm without Mirandizing the suspect, who informed them of the gun's location. The case was appealed through the New York state judicial system, and the United States Supreme Court determined that, where there is a significant concern for public safety (in this case a gun whose whereabouts were unknown to police), the Miranda rights are not required. The gun and Quarles's statements in court about the weapon's location were deemed admissible, a point of contention with many jurists.

Pennsylvania v. Labron, 518 U.S. 938 (1996)

In this case, the defendant Labron was observed by police to be participating in several drug transactions from his automobile. The police, having probable cause but no search warrant, searched the vehicle and found an amount of cocaine. The search was determined to be unconstitutional by the state supreme court on the grounds that such an automobile search requires both exigent circumstances and probable cause if a search warrant is not used. A parallel case, *Pennsylvania v. Kilgore* was also overturned in the state supreme court on the same grounds. *Pennsylvania v. Labron* was appealed to the U.S. Supreme Court, where the Court found that if a vehicle is potentially mobile, it could be searched without a warrant if probable cause exists; exigent circumstances need not be present.

Rhode Island v. Innis, 446 U.S. 291 (1980)

A suspect in a robbery was identified by a victim and was subsequently arrested for the offense. After the arrest, the officers read the Miranda rights to the suspect Innis, who stated he wanted to speak with his attorney. While being transported in the patrol car, three of the officers began discussing the case and one of them explained that a school for handicapped children was located near the crime scene and that if one of the students came across the weapon used in the robbery, a shotgun, the child could easily be injured or killed. Innis interrupted the conversation and told the officers he would take them to where the shotgun was discarded, which he did. The case was appealed to the U.S. Supreme Court on the grounds that the discussion in this case amounted to an interrogation during the car ride. It was determined that the officers did not violate the suspect's constitutional rights in this case as the conversation did not constitute an interrogation.

Spano v. New York, 360 U.S. 315 (1959)

The defendant Spano was indicted for a retaliatory killing of another man. He turned himself in to authorities but refused to talk with officers on advice of his attorney. Six police interrogated Spano for a long period but obtained no confession. An officer named Bruno who was on a probationary period with the police department told Spano, whom he knew before the incident, that unless he confessed, Bruno's job was in jeopardy. Spano relented and confessed to the crime for which he received a death sentence. The case was appealed to the United States Superior, where the conviction was reversed due to the fact that, although no physical coercion was used to obtain the confession, psychological pressure and fatigue were used; therefore the confession was not made voluntarily.

Tennessee v. Gardner, 471 U.S. 1 (1985)

This case modified the fleeing felon rule that had been in effect for many years and that allowed officers to shoot a person who fled from the police after committing a felony. The court ruled that people who do not appear to pose an immediate threat to others should not have deadly force used against them. However, officers still are able to exercise the right to use deadly force if the fleeing person is thought to be dangerous to the officer or others.

Terry v. Ohio, 392 U.S. 1 (1968)

This landmark case established the ability of the police to perform a stop-and-frisk, or Terry search (named after the defendant in the case) of suspects. The Terry search is a brief pat-down of a suspect's outer garments with the purpose of finding weapons that can be used against an officer who will be questioning the suspect. In this case, two people were observed by a plainclothes officer to be "casing" a store (observing it carefully to determine the best method of breaking into the store to steal items). The two were joined by a third person, who appeared to be helping them plan the robbery. The officer intervened and commenced to perform a cursory search of their clothing. The frisk produced weapons on two of the suspects. One of them, Terry, received a sentence of two years' confinement. During the trial, the defense attorney moved to suppress the evidence but the motion was denied. On appeal to the U. S. Supreme Court for violation of Fourth Amendment rights through the performance of an unlawful search, the Court determined that the search was indeed constitutional and that the frisk was appropriate to ensure the officer's safety. In this case, the Court differentiated between an investigative stop and an arrest, and a cursory pat-down (or frisk) and a full search for evidence.

United States v. Banks, 540 U.S. 31 (2003)

In this case, the issue of the reasonable amount of time between the police knocking on a suspect's door and actually entering the residence was considered. A search warrant for the offender was being executed to enter the residence and search for cocaine. The police announced their presence and waited fifteen to twenty seconds before forcing open the door. The United States Supreme Court ruled that this was enough time before entering the residence and that providing more time gives offenders more opportunity to destroy evidence. This circumstance overrides privacy protections of individuals.

United States v. Leon, 468 U.S. 897 (1984)

This case invoked the good faith exception to the exclusionary role of searches and seizures. Information regarding two drug dealers was provided to police, who then put the suspects under surveillance. Two additional subjects, including Leon, were placed under observation and subsequently arrested. At the trial the defense argued that the officers involved did not have a valid search warrant because they acted on a tip from an unknown person. The magistrate who issued the warrant should not have done so, according to the defense, due to the lack of probable cause, regarding an unknown informant. The case was appealed and the U.S. Supreme Court found that the exclusionary rule (as developed in *Mapp*, which states that illegally obtained evidence cannot be admitted into evidence at the trial) does not apply if the officers act in good faith in the execution of the warrant. It also confirmed that the exclusionary role was meant to curtail unlawful searches by the police, not punish magistrates for their actions.

Glossary

Beat A geographic area assigned to an officer for patrol duties.

Blending operation A police operation in which an officer goes undercover, posing as a member of a criminal group (a gang, an organized criminal group, and the like) to gather intelligence.

Blue curtain A code of silence in police agencies by which officers protect other each other, even those in involved in corruption.

Blue-ribbon commissions Panels of people knowledgeable about law enforcement practices and procedures who come together to investigate police misconduct. The commissions normally have a formal name as well as an informal one that reflects the name of the lead investigator.

Bobbies The nickname for the police officers of the London Metropolitan Police, a reference to the first name of the agency's founder, Robert Peel.

Bow Street Runners Also called the Bow Street Flying Squad or Bow Street Flyers, this group, founded by Henry Fielding, was a precursor to professional police detectives.

Broken windows theory A theory that disorganization in communities (typified by the broken windows metaphor) creates situations that invite crime. Therefore, communities and police should pay attention to crimes of disorder, help clean up neighborhoods, and work toward reducing levels of fear in communities.

Civilianization The replacement of sworn police officers with private citizens for certain law enforcement occupations.

Civil service A major movement in law enforcement to eliminate or reduce the influence of powerful political figures over the police.

Clearance rate A measure of accomplishment in law enforcement whereby a suspect has been identified, investigated, and arrested, completing the cycle; it is the ratio of solved to reported crimes in a certain area.

Cold case files   Files of unsolved crimes that have been reopened for investigation after a significant period of time. Many cold cases are currently under reinvestigation due to new technological advances in investigation techniques.

Community policing   A model of policing that encourages a symbiotic relationship between the police and the community. In this model of policing, the police are more engaged with their communities and the citizens are more cognizant of their roles to assist the police.

CompStat (computer-assisted statistics)   A model of policing introduced by the New York City Police Department (NYPD) in 1994 whose function is to use intelligence, provide effective law enforcement methods, assist in the rapid response to crime, and evaluate the effectiveness of police methods.

Constable   A law enforcement position that is primarily responsible for the service of warrants and units. This position with a lengthy history, which normally occupied a status just below that of sheriff, is still in use today in the United States.

Contempt of cop   The disrespectful conduct and attitude of some citizens toward the police.

Crime mapping   The police practice of visually displaying crime trends on a geographical map to determine where and what type of police resources are most needed.

Criminalistics   The science of analyzing physical evidence that is involved with criminal activity. Examples of evidence studied by criminalists are DNA, fingerprints, firearm evidence, fibers, soil, and shoe and tire prints.

Critical incident stress debriefing   A systematic process to immediately assist officers or other emergency personnel after a critical incident, or crisis situation: for example, a shooting, a hostage event, a violent riot situation, a response to a gruesome crime scene, or any event that involves the actual threat of death or injury to the officer or others.

Deadly force   The legal right held by law enforcement officers to kill a person if necessary to protect themselves or others.

Decentralization   In law enforcement, this refers to the relocation of decision-making responsibilities to community precincts rather than police headquarters.

Decoy operations   When law enforcement officers pose as potential victims (elderly, cab drivers, and the like) where criminal victimization of these types is taking place.

Demand reduction groups   Strategies used by law enforcement agencies to reduce the demand of drugs by users (such as the DARE program and Just Say No campaign).

Differential response　A proactive police measure in which calls sent in to dispatch are screened and prioritized. Nonemergency calls, often handled by nonsworn personnel, are reported over the phone, fax, or Internet.

Directed patrol　The practice, sometimes called aggressive patrol, of patrolling an area with increased attention to certain types of offenders, crimes, or geographical areas.

Entrapment　When an officer incites a person to commit a criminal act that he or she would normally not commit.

Exclusionary rule　The rule that all evidence illegally obtained by the police is inadmissible in court.

Field training officer (FTO)　An experienced police officer responsible for field training new officers.

Fleeing-felon rule　A right formerly held by officers to use deadly force to stop a fleeing victim.

Forensic science　The use of scientific investigation procedures in matters that will be brought into the legal system.

Good cop–bad cop　An interrogation tool in which one officer responds to a suspect in a demeaning and threatening manner while another pretends to be sympathetic and comforting. The plan is to create an environment where the suspect confesses, usually to the "good cop."

HAZMAT situation　An incident that involves hazardous materials and requires special police knowledge and training.

High-speed pursuit　A chase at high speeds involving a fleeing motorist and the police.

Hot spots　Areas in cities or counties with high crime rates that are often given special attention by the police operating under a proactive model.

Internal affairs bureau　An investigative body inside a police agency that inquires into allegations of police misconduct.

Miranda rights　The rights verbalized to criminal suspects that they have the right to remain silent, that anything they say may be used against them in a court of law, that they have the right to have a lawyer present, and that they have the right to a court-appointed attorney, if they're indigent. These warnings are meant to protect against unwitting self-incrimination by suspects.

Peace officer　A status granted to certain occupations that have greater control than ordinary citizens over others: for example, the police, probation and parole officers, and correctional officers.

Plain view doctrine　A rule stating that evidence that is easily seen by officers can be seized.

Police brutality　Excessive physical force used by police officers.

Police–community relations The establishment and maintenance of mutually beneficial interactions between the police and the communities they serve.

Police corruption The abuse of authority by officers with the intent of personal gain.

Police discretion The degree of freedom by individual law enforcement officers to make arrests, investigate crimes, and make other decisions in the field.

Police interrogation The interview of a suspect by the police in relation to a criminal act. The police use a number of interview methods to determine what happened and to ascertain the suspect's level of involvement.

Police misconduct An action by a law enforcement officer that entails a violation of his or her sworn duties and responsibilities.

Police subculture The distinct social environment collectively experienced by law enforcement officers due to the unique aspects of their occupation.

Proactive policing The anticipation by police of criminal behavior before it occurs and the actions taken to prevent it.

Probable cause The reasonable belief that a suspect has committed a crime. This is the evidentiary standard required for police officers to arrest and search suspects.

Problem-oriented policing A model of policing in which officers determine problems in their jurisdictions through detailed observation and take measures to alleviate them.

Racial profiling The practice by police officers of investigating suspects primarily on the basis of race.

Reactive policing The response of police to reports of criminal behavior after a crime has been committed.

Response time The time between the commission of a crime and the arrival of the police.

Reverse sting operation When officers pose as sellers of illegal goods (such as drugs or weapons) or services (such as prostitution). *See also* Sting operation.

Routine activities theory A theoretical perspective that identifies three elements necessary for a crime: a valued object, a motivated offender, and lack of a capable guardian. When the police (or other appropriate people or things) become involved, the valued object is protected and no crime occurs.

Selective enforcement The ability of police officers to use discretion in deciding which laws to enforce.

Sheriff   The chief law enforcement official of a county. The term is a corruption of the two words from Middle English: *shire* (region or county) and *reeve* (leader).

Special weapons and tactics (SWAT) teams   Teams of officers with advanced training in high-risk situations such as the apprehension of dangerous suspects or hostage situations.

Stakeout   Surveillance of a person or an area by police officers or detectives.

Sting operation   When law enforcement officials pose as buyers of illegal goods (such as drugs or weapons) or services (as from prostitutes). *See also* Reverse sting operation.

Stop-and-frisk   A cursory search, also called a pat-down search, of a suspect conducted to ensure that the person does not have a weapon.

Suicide by cop   The death of a criminal suspect who purposefully puts him- or herself in a situation that inevitably results in the use of deadly force by police officers.

Supply reduction programs   Initiatives by law enforcement agencies to reduce the supply of drugs in an area.

Target hardening   Various methods of making it more difficult for crime to occur, such as access control, increased lighting, increased police presence, surveillance, and similar measures.

Thin blue line   The metaphor of police officers as representing the line between order and chaos in society.

Third degree   The physical abuse of a suspect under interrogation by police.

Tithing system   Also called the frankpledge system, an early form of group policing in which groups of ten families called *tithings,* were responsible for maintaining social order.

Uniform Crime Reports (UCR)   Crime data maintained and published by the Federal Bureau of Investigation.

Use of force continuum   A graduated system of force to be used by officers, according to the situation, ranging from the least needed to deadly force.

Vice   Crimes, such as those involving narcotics, prostitution, and gambling, that lack a complainant. Police departments often have a specific unit to deal with these crimes.

Watch   In the early days of policing, a group of citizens who patrolled their community; this was a prominent system during the colonial period in America. Although a very early institution, it can still be found in some forms, such as neighborhood watch programs.

Zero-tolerance policing   A model of policing that focuses on increased vigilance on crimes of disorder and on the punishment of these crimes. It is believed that vigorous enforcement of smaller crimes will drive more serious crimes from the area.

Index

About the Author

Leonard A. Steverson, Ph.D., is assistant professor of sociology at South Georgia College in Douglas, Georgia. He teaches courses in sociology and criminal justice. Prior to his teaching career, Dr. Steverson was a probation officer, correctional counselor, and director of a child and adolescent social service program. He lives in Douglas, Georgia, with his wife, Betty, and enjoys spending time with their children and grandchildren.